The Porter-Dugger Debate

A Written Discussion on The Sabbath and the Lord's Day

ISBN 1-58427-040-3

Guardian of Truth Foundation
P.O. Box 9670
Bowling Green, Kentucky 42102

PROPOSITIONS FOR DEBATE

1. *The Scriptures teach that the seventh day of the week as a Christian sabbath is enjoined upon God's people in this age of the world.*

> Affirmative: A. N. Dugger
> Negative: W. Curtis Porter

2. *The Scriptures teach that the first day of the week as a day of worship is enjoined upon God's people in this age of the world.*

> Affirmative: W. Curtis Porter
> Negative: A. N. Dugger

AGREEMENT

1. This is to be a written discussion.

2. The purpose of it is that it may be printed in book form.

3. Each disputant will write four articles to each proposition as nearly like he would deliver them orally as possible.

4. Length of each article will be 4,000 words, not varying more than 100 words shorter than that nor more than 100 words longer.

> Signed:

> W. CURTIS PORTER
> A. N. DUGGER

THE SABBATH QUESTION

PROPOSITION

The Scriptures teach that the seventh day of the week as a Christian sabbath is enjoined upon God's people in this age of the world.

DUGGER'S FIRST AFFIRMATIVE

We believe the Scriptures teach that Saturday, the seventh day of the week, is the Christian sabbath to be observed by Christians in this age, for the following reasons:

When the Lord created the heavens and the earth in six days he did not class the seventh day with the other working days which he gave to mankind, upon which to perform his labor. We read in Genesis 2:1-3, "Thus the heavens and the earth were finished, and all the hosts of them. And on the seventh day God ended his work which he had made; and he rested on the seventh day from all his work which he had made. And God blessed the seventh day and sanctified it: because that in it he had rested from all his work which God created and made."

Here we find that the seventh day was not classed with the other days. It was sanctified. That is, it was set apart for a sacred use. It was God's day then, while the other six days were given to man to use for days of toil and labor. The seventh day, which is Saturday, still belongs to God. We have no record where he has ever classed it with the other days, or placed it on common grounds with them. It was sanctified, that is, separated from them, for a sacred purpose. We have no record where it was ever placed back with the other six days, or ever given to man for a secular day of use. God told us to keep this day for him in many places throughout the Scriptures. The seventh day was never man's day to use for himself, but it has always been placed where man could keep it for God, or use it for himself. And the Lord has always tested the loyalty of mankind over the way they regarded that which was not theirs, the sabbath, which always has, and always will belong to God.

We pass now to the time when God's people were in Egypt. We find Pharaoh complaining because Moses and Aaron made the children of Israel "rest" from their burdens. We find that this word "rest" is taken from the Hebrew "sabat," or sabbatize. Israelites were here keeping the sabbath day, which caused the complaint against them.

Also when God called his people out of Egypt he tested their loyalty to him on the way they regarded his day, the sabbath. He rained the manna for forty years, but it never fell on God's day. It fell on the six days given to man, for it required considerable labor to gather it; consequently, the Lord did not rain it on the day that belonged to him.

When the people went out on the sabbath day to gather the manna the Lord rebuked them saying, "How long refuse you to keep my commandments and my laws" (Exodus 16:28). Hence the seventh day, sabbath, was in the commandments and laws the Lord had given the people before Israel had reached Mount Sinai. Abraham kept these commandments and laws; hence, Abraham kept the sabbath day for God, and did not use it for himself. It reads in Genesis 26:5 as follows, "Because that Abraham obeyed my voice and kept my charge, my commandments, my statutes and my laws."

God's people, whoever they have been, have always been known as such because of their separation from the world in fellowship with him, obeying his voice and keeping his commandments. When he wrote the ten commandments on tables of stone, with his own finger, he said: "Remember the sabbath day to keep it holy, for in six days the Lord made the heavens and the earth and rested the seventh day" (Exodus 20:8, 9). This sabbath precept was made a part of the ten commandments, and in this code of law, God said: "The seventh day is the sabbath of the Lord thy God" (Verse 9). He confirms the fact again of the proper ownership of this day. It is God's day, and we only hold it in trust, and are to keep it for God by doing his work on that day, and abstaining from our own secular labor.

The seventh day can be traced down through the Scriptures with peculiar reverence. God's people of all nationalities, whether Jew or Gentile, were duty bound to observe the sabbath, keeping it for God, in order to enjoy the blessings of heaven and possess eternal life. In Isaiah 56:6 the Lord says: "Also the sons of the stranger (Gentile), that join themselves to the Lord, to serve him, and to love the name of the Lord, to be his servants, every one that keepeth the sabbath from polluting it, and taketh hold of my covenant, even them will I bring to my holy mountain, and make them joyful in my house of prayer."

The Gentiles, therefore, in olden times were tested out by the way they handled the day that was not their own, but that of another. It belonged to God, and the Gentiles must realize that divine ownership, and keep God's day for him and for his service, and not use it for themselves.

Again we find the Lord testing Israel, and bringing rebuke upon that nation because they coveted the sabbath day, then laid hold upon it, using it for their own secular work. He speaks thus: "Thus saith the Lord, take heed to yourselves and bear no burden on the Sabbath day, nor bring it in by the gates of Jerusalem. Neither carry any burden out of your houses on the sabbath day, neither do ye any work, but hallow ye the sabbath day as I commanded your fathers. . . . . And it shall come to pass if you diligently hearken unto me, saith the Lord, to bring no burdens through the gates of this city on the sabbath day . . . . this city shall remain forever" (Jeremiah 17:21-35).

Jerusalem would never have been destroyed, neither would Israel or Judah been scattered among the nations, suffering such terrible persecutions as they have been suffering, if they had kept the sabbath as God commanded. God's punishments upon Judah and Israel are again clearly set forth in Deuteronomy 28th chapter, and the Lord tells us it was because they broke his commandments. The Gentile nations today are suffering God's judgments, for the same reasons as did Israel; viz., because they are breaking his commandments. The Lord speaks of the world in general in the following language: "The earth also is defiled under the inhabitants thereof, because they have transgressed the laws, changed the ordinance, and broken the everlasting covenant. Therefore hath the curse devoured the earth, and they that dwell therein are desolate, therefore the inhabitants of the earth are burned, and few men left" (Isaiah 24:5, 6). The Gentiles today who are boasting themselves against Israel, and at the same time committing the same offenses against God as Israel committed, will soon be victims of his wrath and judgments. God is no respecter of persons (Romans 2:11 and Ephesians 6:9), and he changes not (Malachi 3:6).

Coming now to the New Testament we are not disappointed in finding that God regards his day just as he did in the Old Testament age. He has not changed, and is no respecter of persons. We find Jesus keeping the sabbath, and making it his custom to use that day especially for God (Luke 4:14, 16). It says he went into the synagogue on the sabbath day as his custom was. Then before Jerusalem was destroyed, we find Jesus instructing his diciples to "Pray that their flight would not be on the sabbath." He was telling them about the terrible destruction awaiting Jerusalem, and he knew as the prophet Isaiah had previously said that the city awaited her doom, because of sabbath desecration (Jeremiah 17:21-35). When a hostile army overruns a country and the people have to flee, there is great discomfort if it is winter because of the cold; and if they flee on the sabbath, they must labor, carrying their burdens out of their homes on the sabbath which God forbade them doing. Hence Jesus told them to pray that their flight would not be on the sabbath. He well knew Jerusalem would not be taken, and the land overrun until long after he died on the cross. The event did not happen until 70 A.D. as all histories affirm. Therefore, Jesus proclaimed the divine importance of that day, belonging to God nearly forty years after he was crucified. As the sabbath was still holy, and remained God's day, 70 distinction today. It is still God's day, and not man's day for secular labor, but we are to keep it in trust for God, doing his work, and not our own labor on that day.

The apostle Paul labored among the Jews and went into their synagogues to preach. They were observing the seventh day of the week the same as they do at this time, and they have never ceased to cherish and honor the sabbath. When Paul went to one of their synagogues and preached to the Jews on the sabbath the Lord says: "And when the Jews were gone out of the synagogue, the Gentiles besought that these words might be preached to them the next sabbath day. . . . . And the next sabbath day came almost the whole city together to hear the word of God" (Acts 13:42, 44).

This was about 63 A.D. At a still later date when the Holy Spirit recorded the event, we were informed that the day these Jews met on was the sabbath. Therefore it was the sabbath then at least 66 years down in this gospel dispensation. The Jews were meeting on the seventh day of the week, or on Saturday as the day is now called. Hence, the Holy Spirit called Saturday the sabbath day in this age, and surely it is the sabbath. If the seventh day is not the sabbath, why did the Holy Spirit deceive us by calling it the sabbath? As it was the sabbath then it is the sabbath now.

Again we find in Acts 16:12 to 14 where Paul went out by the river side where prayer was accustomed to be made, and preached to people there. Also in Acts 17:2 we read as follows: "And Paul as his manner was went in unto them and three sabbath days reasoned with them out of the scriptures." It was Paul's manner to meet with both Jews and Gentiles, as it says here, on the sabbath day. Furthermore, in chapter 18:1-11 we read: "And he reasoned in the synagogue every sabbath and persuaded the Jews and the Greeks." . . . . "And he continued there a year and six months teaching the word of God among them." Here we find Paul making tents during the week, and preaching to both Jews and Gentiles on the sabbath. He remained there a year and six months; consequently, we have here 76 sabbath days the apostle Paul preached. It could not be said that he was visiting these synagogues preaching on Saturday just because the Jews met on that day, for he was preaching to Gentiles also. Furthermore, he was an apostle to the Gentiles and not to the Jews; hence, his making it a custom to hold meetings on the sabbath shows his regard for God's day, and proves that he was not using it for a secular purpose as he was the other days upon which he made tents. The sabbath which was the seventh day of the week was consequently observed by Paul and his followers, both Jews and Gentiles, at this period of the gospel age about 66 A.D. It therefore is the day for rest and worship today.

Further evidence, found in the New Testament, that God has not changed by giving another day, in the place of his day, for people to rest upon is found in the following text, "For God spake of the seventh day on this wise, And God did rest the seventh day from all his works" (Hebrews 4:4). In verse 8 he says: "For if Jesus had given them rest, then would he not afterwards have spoken of another day. There remaineth therefore a rest to the people of God, for he that is entered into his rest, he also hath ceased from his own works as God did from his" (Verses 9, 10).

Some teach that we do not have any day of rest at this time, but the sabbath still belongs to God, and not to man for secular use. Here we are told that "there remaineth," a rest to the people of God. The word rest is here taken from the Greek word sabbatismos, which means the sabbath day rest. The other words "rest" as found in these verses are derived from a different Greek word entirely. It is kataposus, and means rest. It may refer to a rest after fatigue, to the Eden rest, or the eternal rest, but the word sabbatismos of verse 9 does not refer to any of these rests, but to the sabbath day, and we are told it remains for the people of God. God has not changed, the sabbath day still belongs to him, and should not be used by man for secular work. At the beginning of the world the seventh day was "sanctified," that is, it was set apart. Webster's dictionary gives the definition for the word "sanctify": "To be set apart for religious use." This is what happened at creation with the last day of the week, the seventh day, which is Saturday. It was set apart from the other days, for God, as his holy day. Now what right has any man, or set of men, to interfere with God, and attempt to change this divine order. In Isaiah 58:13 it is spoken of as God's day, thus, "If thou turn away thy foot from the sabbath, from doing thy pleasure on my holy day, and call the sabbath a delight, holy unto the Lord, honorable" etc. Here the sabbath is again said to be God's day. It is, therefore, not ours to use for ourselves in common work. It is the day separated from the other six days at creation, and it is still thus separated. Man has made all manner of excuses, and tried in vain to alter God's order of things regarding the sabbath, but dear reader, this day, the seventh, is still God's day. It does not belong to mankind to use in their common labor, but it is for our worship and service of the creator.

Should someone give you a ten dollar bill, and tell you to keep that for them until they returned, this money would be in your hands, and in your charge just as the seventh day of the week or the holy sabbath. You would have the ten dollars. It would be in your power, you could keep it for this person, or you could use it for yourself. God has given the sabbath to mankind to keep for him. It is within our power, and we can be faithful and use this sacred time for God, or we can take it and perform our own common labor on this day, and use it for ourselves. Before you would take this money and use it for yourself, you would first covet it. You would break the commandment forbidding covetousness. Furthermore, you would take this money and appropriate it for yourself you would break the commandment forbidding stealing. It is just this way with the sabbath. This day belongs to God. It does not belong to us. When people get so busy in the things of this old world that they covet more time, and then by taking this day, which is not their own and using it for their own work, they are guilty of stealing. This is the situation of many honest people, to whom the precious truth of the sabbath has not yet gone. God will forgive them for such action when they ask him in the precious name of Jesus. He is loving and merciful, and this precious truth of the sabbath day, which is Saturday and not Sunday is going to all the world, and many dear people are seeing the true light and rejoicing to walk in this strait and narrow way.

While holding meetings in London, England, a few years ago, I purchased a little book at one of the great book stores of London which was entitled "The Weekly Cycle." In this book the "week," is traced down from one hundred years before Christ. Every change man has made in the calendar is mentioned and tables showing that the days of the week are just the same as they were in the time of Christ. This book gives tables copied from leading author- ized works on Astronomy, and contains copies of calendars from the time of Christ to the present day, showing beyond any question of doubt that the weekly cycle is just the same as it always was. Consequently, time has not been lost as so many affirm, and the seventh day of the week is still just as it was anciently.

As further proof that we are observing the real ancient sabbath, the same day that God blessed and made holy, we find in Matthew 28:1 as follows: "In the end of the sab- bath as it began to dawn towards the first day of the week, came Mary Magdalene and the other Mary to see the sep- ulchre." Here the Holy Spirit has told us very clearly that in the New Testament times the sabbath was not "the first day of the week," but it was the day just pre- ceding it. Therefore, the sabbath as verified by the Holy Spirit for the gospel age, was not Sunday, but the day be- fore, which was Saturday.

Furthermore, the sabbath is one of God's ten command- ments, and it is of just as much importance as the other nine. People who confess Jesus, and try to live right, are usually quite strict about keeping all of the other ten commandments, but some seem to believe that the keeping of importance. Yet to covet this time which is God's time, and then to take it and use it for ourselves, is committing two of the prominent sins forbidden in the ten commandments. The sabbath is just as important as any of the other nine, and should be kept for God and regarded as his day for worship and rest.

The ten commandments were formerly the standard of right and wrong. To break any one of them in the Old Testament time was such an offense against heaven that something had to die. Either the person offending, or he had to get an animal and have the priest kill it in his stead. The Lord says the blood is the life, and that "without the shedding of blood, there is no remission" (Heb. 9:22). When any one of the ten commandments were broken under the administration of death at the time of Moses, the man or the woman was stoned to death, when two or three witnesses testified against them. They could have an animal killed in their stead or two turtle-doves (Lev. 5:7) if the offender was too poor to furnish a lamb. This law of pardon by the blood of the animal was given by Moses to deliver people from the penalty of the ten commandment law, and now we have the new law of pardon through Jesus Christ, known in the New Testament as the "Testimonies of Jesus" (Rev. 12:17).

The entire old system of pardon with its ceremonies, bloody sacrifices, feasts on holy days, new moons, and yearly sabbaths given to Israel, and spoken of as "Her" sabbaths were done away with and nailed to the cross. Ephesians 2:15, and Col. 2:14 to 16. Paul speaks of this law of pardon in Gal. 3:19 and says: "Wherefore then serveth the law? It was added because of transgression until the seed should come." This seed was Jesus, and this law of pardon was only to last till Jesus came when, according to God's plan, he had provided something better. It was not the same old system of pardon by the killing of animals, but through the precious blood of Jesus, the lamb of God, slain from the foundation of the world (Rev. 5:6).

It was not the ten commandment law that was nailed to the cross and abolished through the work and death of Jesus, but it was the old sacrificial law of pardon. The Lord said of Jesus that when he came into the world, he would magnify the law and make it honorable (Isa. 42:21). Jesus said: "Think not that I came to destroy the law or the prophets, I came not to destroy but to fulfill" (Matt. 5:17-19). Jesus did not destroy any law, or any prophecy. His life and work fulfilled the old law of pardon, and also fulfilled many Old Testament prophecies, and therefore finished them. But he never destroyed any law or any prophecy. His life which was our example taught us to keep the sabbath. See Luke 4:14-16, where it says his custom was to keep the sabbath day. We are told that "In him was life, and his life was the light of men" (St. John 1:4). Also: "If we follow him we will not walk in darkness but will have the light of life" (St. John 8:12). Jesus made it his custom to keep the sabbath, and he also "Kept his father's commandments," (St. John 15:10), and repeatedly tells us to "Keep the commandments of God" (Rev. 14:12; also 12:17 and 22:14). He says those who are saved are the ones "keeping the commandments of God and the faith of Jesus" (Rev. 14:12).

In the New Testament we are repeatedly told to keep the law of God, the ten commandments. Notice the following: "Whosoever therefore shall keep the whole law and yet offend in one point is guilty of all. For he that said, Do not commit adultery, said also, Do not kill. Now if thou commit no adultery, yet if thou kill, thou art become a transgressor of the law" (James 2:10, 11). Here we have the law of ten commandments mentioned and two of them quoted. We also find that in the New Testament gospel age this law of ten commandments is still the great measuring standard of righteousness. We cannot be saved by keeping any law, neither by our own works, but when we are saved before heaven, it will be our very nature to keep all of these holy commandments including the 4th which is the seventh day sabbath.

The Lord says further that the "remnant" of the seed of the woman, or the remnant people called out during the gospel age are those who "keep the commandments of God, and have the testimonies of Jesus" (Rev. 12:17). Here we have the commandments of God as the standard just as it was in the Old Testament time, but we have the new law of pardon spoken of as "the testimonies of Jesus." It is the New Testament. It testifies of the birth, life and death of Jesus and gives us the new law of pardon.

Jesus tells us in Matt. 24th chapter and also in Luke 17th that when Jesus returns to earth again, there will be but very few people saved. He compares it to the time of Noah and the days of Sodom. We are now in a very wicked sinful age, as everyone knows, and the great majority of people are traveling the broad way that leads them to destruction. Jesus said that "strait is the gate and narrow is the way that leadeth to life, and but few there be that find it, because broad is the gate and wide is the way that leadeth to destruction, and many there be that walk therein" (Matt. 7:13, 14). He also says: "Fear not little flock for it is your father's good pleasure to give you the kingdom" (Luke 12:32). We are living in the closing days of this age, when Jesus is soon to return and judge the world. There are but few going to be saved compared to the many. Jesus says it is going to be those who "Keep the commandments of God" (Rev. 14:12). John also says: "This is the love of God that we keep his commandments and his commandments are not grievous" (John 5:3, 4).

PORTER'S FIRST NEGATIVE

It gives me pleasure to enter into this discussion with my friend, A. N. Dugger, in an effort to determine by the Bible the day of religious service enjoined upon Christians. While he failed to define the terms of his proposition, I take it that the subject is easily understood, and the important thing is to test the proposition by the things said in the Bible. My friend is undertaking to prove that "the Scriptures teach that the seventh day of the week as a Christian sabbath is enjoined upon God's people in this age of the world." There is no discussion between us as to whether the seventh day of the week was ever enjoined upon anybody as a sabbath. We both agree that such is true. But the question is this:

Is it a Christian sabbath? Is it binding upon Christians? That I emphatically deny while my opponent ardently affirms. So that is the issue between us. I shall now take up the arguments in order as introduced by him and see if they sustain his proposition.

Our attention is first called to the six days of creation and the Lord's rest on the seventh day as recorded in Gen. 2:1-3. The seventh day was certainly "classed with the other days" in that it was mentioned as one of the days of the week. I readily grant that the seventh day of the week was sanctified—set apart to a sacred use—and in that sense it was not like the other days; but the question that confronts us here is: When was it sanctified? Was it sanctified, set apart, at the creation? Was it sanctified at the time God rested or did the sanctification take place some time after he rested? What does the passage say? "And God blessed the seventh day, and sanctified it: because that in it he **had rested.**" "Had rested" is past perfect tense of the verb and refers to an action completed sometime in the past. But if we regard it as simple past tense, the fact still remains that the day was sanctified some time following the rest. There is nothing to indicate that it was set apart at the creation. Moses wrote the record of it about 2500 years after God rested, and at the time he wrote the day was sanctified; but it is up to friend Dugger to prove that it was sanctified about 2500 years before Moses was born. Until he does this, the passage is of no value to him. Neither do I agree that "God told us to keep this day for him in many places throughout the Scriptures." God told somebody to keep it, but Elder Dugger must give the passage that shows that God told **us** to do it. Nor has he "always tested the loyalty of mankind over the way they regarded the sabbath." The loyalty of some men has thus been tested in one age of the world; but when my friend puts "always" into his comments, I deny and call for the proof. Mere assertions are not sufficient in a discussion like this.

The argument that Israel were keeping the sabbath day in Egypt when Moses and Aaron made them "rest from their burdens," according to Ex. 5:5, is a very weak effort on the part of my friend. The word from which "rest" comes simply means "to cause to cease." It does not indicate that they were keeping the sabbath. The work of Moses and Aaron had filled them with a desire to leave Egypt, and as a result they quit their work, or ceased from their burdens. This is clearly shown in verse 4 in which we are told that the king of Egypt said: "Wherefore do ye, Moses and Aaron, let the people from their works? Get you unto your burdens." God did not make known to the people in Egypt anything about the sabbath, but after he brought them out of Egypt and into the wilderness he gave them the sabbath law. This is definitely told us in Ezek. 20:10-12. There in the wilderness, God said, "I gave them my sabbaths, to be a sign between me and them." Then he did not give them the sabbaths in Egypt, and my friend's argument is all wrong.

That Israel's loyalty to God was tested in the wilderness in connection with the mann and the sabbath is readily granted. But I want to remind my friend that the first time the sabbath is mentioned in all the book of God is in this connection in the sixteenth chapter of Exodus. According to verse 4 it was given to "prove them," whether they would walk in God's law. This is sufficient evidence that they had not been previously keeping the sabbath; for if they had been, they would have been proven already. Also when Moses introduced the sabbath he said: "Tomorrow is the rest of the holy sabbath unto the Lord" (Ex. 16:23). This manner of introducing it shows they were unacquainted with it; and they had to be instructed in the smallest details of it. When the next day arrived Moses said: "Today is a sabbath unto the Lord" (Ex. 16:25). All this reveals to us that the sabbath was now being introduced for the first time; here in the wilderness in the region of Sinai it was first made known. In Neh. 9:13, 14 we read: "Thou camest down also upon mount Sinai, and spakest with them from heaven, and gavest them right judgments, and true laws, good statutes and commandments: and **madest known unto them** thy holy sabbath, and commandedst them precepts, statutes, and laws, by the hand of Moses thy servant." So they did not know the sabbath through the past years of

their history—it was **made known** to them in the region of
Sinai—and the argument of my friend fails. But I might
grant all he claims for this incident, and it still would do
him no good, for it contains no proof that Christians are required to keep it now.

Elder Dugger next assumes that Abraham kept the sabbath, for God said: "Abraham * * * kept my charge, my commandments, my statutes, and my laws" (Gen. 26:5). But
he could just as well assume that Abraham was baptized
and observed the Lord's supper, for both of these are commandments of God. However, Abraham did not keep the
sabbath law, for Moses, while speaking of the covenant that
contained the sabbath commandment, said: "The Lord
made not this covenant with our fathers, but with us, even
us, who are all of us here alive this day" (Deut. 5:3). Abraham was one of the fathers with whom God did not make
that covenant; neither was he alive the day Moses spoke.
But suppose Abraham did keep the sabbath. Would that
prove that it is binding on Christians now? Abraham kept
the law of circumcision (Gen. 17:10-14) and offered animal
sacrifice (Gen. 22:13); but my opponent would not be willing to take this as authority to bind such upon Christians.

I agree with my friend that God's people have always been
known by their keeping his commandments; but to indicate
that this means the sabbath is pure assumption. His quotation of Ex. 20:8, 9 in this connection, in which God said,
"Remember the sabbath day to keep it holy," with emphasis
being placed by Dugger on the word "remember," is to indicate that they had been long keeping the sabbath, or they
could not **remember** it. God said to Israel in Egypt: **"Remember** this day, in which ye came out from Egypt" (Ex.
13:3). Yet they had never before observed the day. How
could they **remember** this? The explanation of one is the
explanation of the other. I do not deny that the seventh
day was the sabbath of the Lord, but it was for the Jews in
the Jewish age and not for Christians in this age.

In an effort to prove that the sabbath commandment is
binding on Gentile Christians today, my friend introduces
Isaiah 56:6 in which the "sons of the stranger" (Gentiles)

were mentioned as keeping the sabbath. And relative to this Elder Dugger says: "God's people of all nationalities, whether Jew or Gentile, were duty bound to observe the sabbath * * * in order to enjoy the blessings of heaven." But he could have as well said: "God's people of all nationalities, whether Jew or Gentile, where duty bound to observe the law of circumcision" for the very same reason; for God said: "And when a **stranger** shall sojourn with thee, and will keep the passover of the Lord, let all his males be circumcised * * * for no uncircumcised person shall eat thereof" (Ex. 12:48). But what did the "sons of the stranger," mentioned in Isa. 56:6, have to do to be eligible for sabbath keeping and entrance into God's house of prayer? They had to "join themselves to the Lord"; to "love the name of the Lord"; to "be his servants"; to "take hold of God's covenant." But in doing this they had to be circumcised, for God said: "No stranger, uncircumcised in heart, nor uncircumcised in flesh, shall enter into my sanctuary, of any stranger that is among the children of Israel" (Ezek. 44:9). But when Gentiles thus "joined themselves to the Lord" they ceased to be Gentiles and became proselytes to the Jewish religion; then they kept the sabbath, not as Gentiles, but as Jews. What my opponent needs to find is where any Gentile **as such** was ever commanded to keep the sabbath. If he can produce such a passage, let us have it. And while he is looking for that, he might also tell us why, if the sabbath was of universal application, the Gentiles were called "strangers." Here is a task for him to undertake. And why did Paul, speaking of them during the Jewish age, say they were "**strangers** from the covenants of promise, having no hope, and without God in the world"? (Eph. 2:12). And why did God, when he gave the sabbath commandment at Sinai, make it binding only on "thy stranger that is **within thy gates**"? (Ex. 20:10). Let my friend find where it was binding on the stranger without their gates. All this shows the sabbath was not of universal application; if it had been, there would have been no "strangers."

My opponent next presents Jer. 17:21-25 to show that God was "testing Israel and bringing rebuke upon that na-

tion" because of their attitude toward the sabbath. But
that is the wrong reference for my friend's proposition; for
he needs to find the passage where God "tests Christians,"
not Israel, by that means. Since, as Dugger tells us, Israel
and Judah were "scattered among the nations" because they
failed to keep the sabbath, why did he not, for the same
reason, scatter the nations among Israel? It is right in this
connection that our attention is called by my friend to Rom.
2:11 and Eph. 6:9 to prove that "God is no respecter of persons." If the sabbath applied to all nations, why did not
God bring the Babylonians into Judean captivity for their
failure to keep the sabbath? My friend's position makes
God a respecter of persons. He sent the Jews into Babylon because they did not keep the sabbath; but he did not
send the Babylonians into Judea for the same reason. I
challenge my friend to clear up this situation in the light
of his position on the sabbath.

The statement of Isaiah 24:5, 6, which is introduced to
prove the sabbath of general application, has no reference
to the Gentiles. "The earth," as there mentioned, is used
interchangeably with "the land" in verse 3. This refers
to "the land of Judea," "the land of Canaan," and to punishment upon Israel, as a reading of the entire chapter
will plainly disclose.

Following my friend in all the arguments he has introduced, we come now to his references in the New Testament. Luke 4:14-16 is given to show that Jesus kept the
sabbath. Many passages might be given to prove this.
But Jesus also was circumcised (Luke 2:21) and kept the
passover (Matt. 26:17-25); but my opponent does not
observe these because Jesus did. Why did Jesus observe
the law of circumcision, the sabbath and the passover?
Because "God sent forth his Son, made of a woman, made
under the law" (Gal. 4:4). And since he lived "under the
law" he kept these requirements of the law. But Paul
tells us that Christians "are not under the law" (Rom.
6:14). So there is the difference.

Elder Dugger thinks that the sabbath was a holy day in

A. D. 70 when Jerusalem was destroyed—long after the crucifixion of Jesus—because Jesus told his disciples to "pray ye that your flight be not in the winter, neither on the sabbath day" (Matt. 24:20). But if this passage proves the sabbath was a holy day in A. D. 70, it also proves "the winter" was a "holy season," for he told them to pray that their flight be not in the winter. It was not the sacredness of the day or the season that Jesus had in mind, but the safety of his disciples. Flight in the winter time would be difficult. Also the Jews, who had not accepted Christianity, would still be keeping the sabbath and would have the gates of Jerusalem closed on that day. Therefore, escape on that day would also be difficult; so they were to pray that they not have to flee on the sabbath or in the winter. You will have to try it over, Elder Dugger.

Then to "the sabbath" in the book of Acts. My friend finds where Paul went into the Jewish synagogues on the sabbath day to preach as recorded in Acts 13:14-44. But had it ever occurred to him that the Jews who were conducting their services on the sabbath were not Christians. There were no Christians in these places when Paul went there. But did Paul keep the sabbath with them? Not a word said about it. He went there to preach. I have often gone to places to preach on Saturday, but I did not observe the sabbath. And even those Gentiles who requested "the word to be preached to them the next sabbath" were not Christians. Let Dugger find where they requested Paul to keep the sabbath, not to preach, and where he responded. This he cannot find. The same is true of his going out to the riverside (Acts 16:13, 14) and to Corinth (Acts 18:1-11). In both these he preached —he "spake unto the women" and "reasoned in the synagogues," but not a word about "keeping the sabbath." My friend says he finds "76 sabbath days the apostle Paul preached." Well, he needs to find one sabbath day that he kept holy. But Paul left the Jews and turned to the Gentiles in Acts 18:6 before the "year and six months" are mentioned. Friend Dugger skipped this point. He connected verse 4 with verse 11, ignoring this point altogether.

But "the Holy Spirit called Saturday the sabbath day in this age" when Luke wrote the book of Acts. And don't forget that the Holy Spirit still called a certain day "the day of Pentecost" (Acts 2:1) and the passover week "the days of unleavened bread" (Acts 12:3). Yet Dugger does not regard this as proof that he should keep the passover and Pentecost. Did "the Spirit deceive him" in thus designating these days in the gospel dispensation? And why does he not keep them? If this plan, on the one hand, proves the sabbath is binding; on the other, it proves the passover and Pentecost binding.

In Heb. 4:9 Paul says: "There remaineth therefore a rest to the people of God." Elder Dugger thinks this means the sabbath. But note that it is "a rest," not "the sabbath." But he tells us that the word comes from the Greek "sabbatismos," whereas the word "rest" in other connected verses is from the Greek "katapausis"; hence the heavenly rest, he thinks, cannot be the rest of verse 9. But the word "rested" in verse 4, referring to God's rest on the seventh day, is from katopausin. So, according to Dugger, verse 9 cannot be the seventh day rest. Besides, the word sabbath in our New Testament comes from sabbaton, not sabbatismos. They had entered the seventh day rest and the Canaan rest, but a rest yet remained to be entered. It is the heavenly rest, for Paul said: "Let us labor therefore to enter into that rest, lest any man fall after the same example of unbelief" (Heb. 4:11). This is the rest spoken of a long time after the other rests. Read Heb. 4:7, 8.

My friend returns to his argument relative to the "sanctifying" the seventh day at creation. But since I have already noticed that, I shall not return to it here. I readily grant that God in Isa. 58:13, referred to the sabbath as "my holy day," but what my friend needs to find is a reference that calls it **God's holy day** in the Christian age of the world. In this particular he has failed, but it is the thing he must do to have any support for his proposition.

His effort to prove that those who do not keep the sabbath now are guilty of covetousness and theft is a complete failure. He tries it by a "ten-dollar-bill" illustration. But for this ilustration to serve his purpose he will have to find where the Lord gave mankind the sabbath "to keep until he returns." But such a passage cannot anywhere be found. Certainly, God commanded the Jews to keep the sabbath, but he didn't even command **them** to keep it till the Lord's return. If my friend thinks so, let us have the passage. There is no need to argue that the sabbath day is "not our own" but "belongs to God" unless he will give a text of Scripture that says the sabbath is God's holy day in this age of the world.

Elder Dugger next refers to "The Weekly Cycle," a book he bought in London, England, a few years ago, to prove that no time has been lost and that we now may keep the same day that Israel did in the long ago. But, as far as this discussion is concerned, his effort on that is lost, for I can grant him all of that without giving him any support whatever for his proposition. Just grant that the days of the week are the same as they were anciently, would that prove the sabbath binding on Christians? What my opponent must do is to find some passage in the Bible that requires Christians to keep the sabbath. His proposition reads: "The Scriptures teach."

His reference to Matt. 28:1, to prove that Sunday is not the sabbath but that the sabbath was the day before the first day of the week, is also a misspent effort. Elder Dugger has had enough debates with my brethren to know that we do not claim Sunday to be the sabbath. We fight that idea as valiantly as my opponent. Denominational preachers are wrong when they refer to Sunday as the sabbath; the sabbath was the seventh day of the week (Ex. 20:10), the day which we call Saturday. On this Elder Dugger and I agree; the fight is over whether the sabbath requirement extends to Christians today.

And now we are informed by my opponent that the sabbath commandment is as important as the other nine of the ten commandments, and is, therefore, just as binding on Christians as the other nine. But the burden of proof is on his shoulders. We read in Ex. 31:13-16 that God told Israel to keep the sabbath "throughout their generations." This very expression proves the commandment to be temporary—that it would pass away. Do you ever read of the other nine commandments being thus required? Where did God say, "Thou shalt not kill **throughout your generations"**? Or, "Thou shalt not commit adultery **throughout your generations"**? Did God say, "Thou shalt not covet, steal, bear false witness, and so on, **throughout your generations"**? No, but he did say to "keep the sabbath throughout your generations." This proves there was a difference between the fourth commandment and the other nine. Keeping the sabbath was spoken of in the same terms that God used concerning many of the ceremonies of the Jewish law. The passover, burnt-offerings, circumcision, the Levitical priesthood, and such like, they were told to keep and observe "throughout your generations." Just so with the sabbath, but not so with the other nine commandments of the ten.

And why say that "the ten commandments were formerly the standard of right and wrong"? Notice it: **"The standard** of right and wrong." Friend Dugger makes this claim because he finds a death penalty attached to the violation of those commandments. Bu⁺ the sons of Kohath, who did service for the sanctuary, were told that they should not "touch any holy thing, lest they die" (Num. 4:15). Was this a standard of right and ·wrong? It was no part of the ten commandments. Even wizards were to be put to death (Lev. 20:27). If a man should lie with a beast, he suffered the penalty of death (Lev. 20:15). Other commandments carried the death penalty too. Why, then, say the ten commandments were **the standard** of right and wrong? They **were a part** of the standard, but not **the standard.** Many things were wrong that were not forbidden in the ten commandments. The ten commandments forbade bearing "false witness against thy neighbor," but they did not forbid bearing false witness for thy neighbor or against thy enemy. So they were not so inclusive, after all.

My opponent claims that the law that was done away was merely the "old system of pardon, with its ceremonies, bloody sacrifices, feasts," etc., and not the law containing the sabbath at all: Gal. 3:19 does not merely refer to the sacrificial system, but it was the law which was given "four hundred and thirty years after" God made the promise to Abraham concerning his seed (Gal. 3:17). The promise to Abraham is recorded in Gen. 12:1-3. Check your chronology, and you will find that 430 years brings you to Sinai and the giving of the ten commandments. It was this law that was to last "till the seed should come." And in Col. 2:14-16 Paul enumerates the set order of Jewish services: daily, weekly, monthly and yearly, and shows that all of them are done away, for they were nailed to the cross.

I believe, with friend Dugger, that Christ would "magnify the law" (Isa. 42:21), and that he "came not to destroy the law, but to fulfill it" (Matt. 5:17-19). But this is true regarding the whole Mosaic system; he did not dishonor any of it. Does that prove it all to be binding on Christians? But his statement made in Matt. 5:18 shows the law was to cease. He said: "One jot or one tittle shall in no wise pass from the law, till all be fulfilled." This shows it would pass when it was fufilled, and my opponent says the Lord fulfilled it. That settles it, then; it passed away. When the record tells us that Joseph knew not Mary "till she had brought forth her firstborn son" (Matt. 1:25), it does not mean that he never knew her. And when Paul's enemies bound themselves under an oath "that they would neither eat nor drink till they had killed Paul" (Acts 23:12), they did not mean they would never eat or drink any more. So when Jesus said the law will not pass "till all be fulfilled," he did not mean that it would never pass. One passage shows that Joseph knew Mary after she brought forth her firstborn son; another shows that Paul's enemies planned to eat after they had killed Paul; and the other shows that the law passed after it was fulfilled.

Yes, Jesus kept his father's commandments (John 15:10). And we are to follow him (John 8:12). But Elder Dugger does not think this means we should do all that Jesus did. Jesus was circumcised and kept the passover; but Dugger does not regard either of these as binding on us now. As Jesus obeyed the commandments of the law under which he lived, we must obey the commandments of the law under which we live; in that way we follow him. And then a list of passages from the book of Revelation are given that show the importance of obeying "the commnadments of God." The passages given are Rev. 14:12; 12:17; 22:14. It is claimed that these mean "the ten commandments." Who said so? Elder Dugger. Let him prove it. I demand that he answer this question: Does God have any commandments besides the ten? I predict that he will not answer the question, but if he does, he will ruin his own arguments. Please, Elder Dugger, tell us if God has any other commandments except the ten commandments. Paul said: "The things that I write unto you are the commandments of the Lord" (1 Cor. 14:37). I fully agree with friend Dugger that only a few will find the narrow way that leads to life (Matt. 7:13, 14), and that those who do will be those who keep God's commandments (Rev. 14:12), and that God's commandments are not grievous (1 John 5:3, 4) ; but I deny that these refer to the ten commandments as such. When he has answered my question, this matter will be fully taken care of in his own answer.

My opponent thinks we must keep the sabbath because James said: "Whosoever shall keep the whole law, and yet offend in one point, he is guilty of all" (James 2:10). Then verse 11 quotes two of the ten commandments. So my friend says this means all of the ten must be kept. But did he ever notice that in verse 8 James quoted a commandment not found in the ten but in what Dugger would call the law of Moses. Does this mean that all of the Mosaic law is to be kept now? But James did not quote the sabbath commandment at all. He did not say to keep it. The law he referred to was "the law of liberty" (verse 12).

The distinction which Dugger makes between "the commandments of God" and "the testimony of Jesus Christ" in Rev. 12:17 is amusing. "The commandments of God," according to Dugger, means the ten commandments, and "the testimony of Christ" means the law of pardon through the sacrifice of Christ. Such reasoning would distinguish between "the word of God" and "the testimony of Jesus Christ" in Rev. 1:9, and would make "the testimony of Christ" no part of "the word of God." But "the things concerning the name of Jesus Christ" and "the word of God" are used interchangeably by Luke in Acts 8:12, 14. This shows the absurdity of his whole argument.

Having replied to all the arguments introduced by the Affirmative, I now present to you some

Negative Arguments

1. **The sabbath was given to Israel only.** In Deut. 5:1-5 Moses addressed Israel and said: "The Lord our God made a covenant with us in Horeb." And in Ex. 31:13 God said: "Speak thou also unto the children of Israel, saying, Verily my sabbaths ye shall keep." In the same verse God said: "It is a sign between me and you throughout your generations." How could it be a sign between God and Israel if all other nations were included too? Let my friend answer this for me. Hence, the sabbath was never given to Gentiles.

2. **Ministration of death, written and engraven in stones, was done away.** In 2 Cor. 3:7-11 Paul refers to that which was written and engraven in stones at the time the face of Moses shone. This refers to Sinai and the giving of the ten commandments. These commandments were placed upon "tables of stone, written with the finger of God" (Ex. 31:18). "The writing was the writing of God, graven upon the tables" (Ex. 32:16). This, Paul says, was done away. We hear him say: "For if that which was done away was glorious, much more that which remaineth is glorious" (2 Cor. 3:11). This ends the sabbath, written and engraven in stones, unless Dugger can find it re-established in the New Testament.

3. **Christians are not under the law.** Sabbatarians con-

stantly refer to "the law" as meaning the ten commandments, including the sabbath. My friend has done the
same in his argument on Jas. 2:10, 11. But if "the law"
means the sabbath, we are no longer under the sabbath, for
we are not under the law. In fact, "the law" refers to the
Old Testament system, sometimes called "the law," sometimes, "the law of God," and sometimes, "the law of Moses."
Since the sabbath belonged to that, we are not required to
keep it longer. Note the following facts about "the law."

(a) "We are not under the law" (Rom. 6:14; Gal. 5:18).
(b) We are dead to the law (Rom. 7:4). (c) We are delivered from the law (Rom. 7:6). (d) Christ is the end
of the law (Rom. 10:4). (e) "Wherefore the law was our
schoolmaster to bring us to Christ . . . . we are no longer
under a schoolmaster" (Gal. 3:24, 25). (f) "The law"
has been abolished (Eph. 2:15).

4. **The sabbath is gone.** In Amos 8:5 the Jews said:
"When will the new moon be gone, that we may sell corn?
and the sabbath, that we may set forth wheat?" Two questions are here presented: When will the new moon be
gone? And when will the sabbath be gone? My friend
says the sabbath will never be gone, but God said it would,
for in answering their question in verse 9, he declared:
"And it shall come to pass in that day, saith the Lord God,
that I will cause the sun to go down at noon, and I will
darken the earth in a clear day." This was fulfilled when
Jesus died on the cross (Mark 15:33). There the sun went
down at noon—at noon darkness covered the earth and
remained for three hours. At that time the feast of new
moons ended. My friend will agree to this. But the sabbath also ended, and since that time, no inspired man ever
commanded any one to keep the sabbath holy.

5. **The sabbath blotted out at the cross.** In Col. 2:14,
16, Paul makes this statement: "Blotting out the handwriting of ordinances that was against us, which was contrary to us, and took it out of the way, nailing it to his
cross; . . . . Let no man therefore judge you in meat, or in
drink, or in respect of an holy day, or of the new moon, or
of the sabbath days." We are not to be judged, therefore,

concerning sabbath days, for the handwriting concerning them has been blotted out, just as it has with respect to meat, drink, holy days or new moons. All of these were blotted out when Jesus died. Not one has been re-instituted since his death.

DUGGER'S SECOND AFFIRMATIVE

We wish to first notice our friend's reference to Amos 8:5-9 where he claims the prophet foresaw the time when the sabbath would cease, but he is mistaken as the entire prophecy of Amos is given. We will begin with verse 5 and quote to verse nine and let the reader be the judge if this shows the sabbaths were to cease. It reads: "When will the new moons be gone that we may sell corn? and the sabbaths that we may set forth wheat making the ephah small and the shekel great, and falsify the balances by deceit? That we may buy the poor for silver, and the needy for a pair of shoes, yea and sell the refuse of the wheat. The Lord hath sworn by the excellency of Jacob, Surely I will never forget any of their works. Shall not the land tremble for all of this, and everyone mourn that dwelleth theren? And it shall rise up wholly as a flood, and it shall be cast out and drowned, as by the flood of Egypt. And it shall come to pass in that day, saith the Lord that I will cause the sun to go down at noon, and I will darken the earth in a clear day" (Amos 8:5-9).

Because Israel became corrupt and wanted the sabbaths to end, so they could sell and cheat by making the ephah small and falsifying the balance by deceit, the Lord said the land would tremble, and everyone mourn that dwell therein, and this punishment would begin when the sun went down at noon, etc. This was the terminating point of Israel's sins, and after the crucifixion of Jesus the nation was smitten. The Lord did not promise them that the sabbath would end and that they could falsify the balances by deceit when the sun went down at noon, but rather that judgment would come upon the nation because of their corrupt desires of wanting the sabbaths to end and desiring to falsify and cheat.

We next answer his second argument that the ten commandments ended according to 2 Cor. 3:7-11 where it says: "The ministration of death written and engraven on stones was glorious," but that it had no glory by reason of the ministration of the Spirit which was more glorious, and that the ministration of death passed away. We agree that the old ministration of death written and engraven on stones has ended, but this comes a long way from saying that the ten commandments ended and were abolished, as so many people would like to have it say. There is much difference between the words "ministration of death," and "the ten commandments." They come far short of being synonymous terms. Everyone knows that the old administration ended, and we have a new and more glorious one through Jesus Christ. This refers to the whole system back there. The ten commandments were written on tables of stone by the finger of God and also the law of pardon by the blood of the animal or the Mosaic law of blood sacrifice was written on stones. Note the following, in Joshua 8:31, 32 the Lord gave instructions for Israel to erect an altar of whole stones and to offer their burnt offerings thereon, and also to write the law of Moses on these stones. Verse 31 reads: "And he wrote there upon the stones a copy of the law of Moses, which he wrote in the presence of the children of Israel." This was the law of Moses and not the ten commandments. God wrote the ten commandments with his own finger on tables of stone (Exodus 31:18; Deut. 9:10). God also wrote the second tables (Deut. 10:1-5). Moses wrote the old law of pardon through the blood of animals and this law was written in a book (Deut. 31:24-26). And this is the law that was written on the stones of the altar. Then why say that 2 Cor. 3:7-11 teaches that the ten commandments were abolished, when we know the old law of pardon through the bloody sacrifices ended, and that the new order of pardon through the precious blood of Jesus, took its place, which is indeed a more glorious ministration accompanied as it is by the presence of the Holy Spirit, is far more glorious. When the Republican ministration of laws gives away to the Democratic administration, it does not do away with the constitution of our nation, or the fundamental basic laws. Neither did those fundamental, organic, basic laws of heaven end, known as the ten commandments, when the old ministration which was written on stones, cease, and give place to the new and more glorious ministration of the spirit.

Our friend believes because Christians are not under the law, they do not need to keep the commandments, but it is sinners who are under the law. They are under its power, and under its penalties when they break it. Being dead to the law by the body of Christ shows that our sins have been forgiven us, and the law has no more effect upon us. Its grip of death has been released by our acceptance of Jesus Christ (Rom. 6:14). Delivered from the law by the body of Christ (Rom. 7:6) again shows our release or deliverance from the penalty of death hanging over us while sinners, and while breaking the law. Christ being the end of the law (Rom. 10:4), for righteousness, means that the power of the law to condemn and destroy us has no more dominion over us because we have accepted Jesus Christ and his blood law of pardon. Our sins hence are forgiven and the law has no more dominion over us. Notice that Paul is careful to say that Christ is the end of the law for righteousness. If we could break the law because Christ came and was crucified, then he would be the end of the law for wickedness, and acts of violence which the law forbids. But he is the end of the law for righteousness. He has released us from the death cell in which we were bound while sinners. We were waiting our execution, just as the murderer in the death cell of our prisons. When we accepted the pardoning favor (grace) of Jesus Christ we were turned loose and set free, just as the criminal is when granted a pardon by the governor of state. That prisoner set free, by the pardon power of the governor has his freedom, to do acts of righteousness, and not violence. He is under the grace or favor of the governor, and no longer under the power of the law. Just as we who were once sinners, were bound in the death cell awaiting our sentence of judgment, but when we accepted the grace offered by the pardoning power of Jesus Christ are made free. We are no longer under the law but under the grace or favor of heaven, and are free. Not free to break the law, any more than the prisoner is free to break the law and commit murder again, because he is pardoned by the governor, and under his grace and favor.

These foregoing scriptures, about being dead to the law by the body of Christ, and not being under the law but under grace, etc. are from Paul's writings. Peter in speaking of Paul's writings says they are hard to be understood, and "they that are unlearned and unstable wrest them to their own destruction" (2 Peter 3:15, 16). We do not believe our friend interpreted these scriptures wrong because he is unstable, for we believe he is honest, but he has surely wrested them in such a way that people believing in them as he herein set them forth will be led to sin. and destruction. Those who believe Christ is the end of the ten commandment law, so we can break it, and those who believe because we are under grace, we do not need to keep the ten commandments of God, will surely meet the doom of sinners and are in the category spoken of by Peter, who are "wresting Paul's writings to their own destruction."

The last one of our friend's arguments is found in Col. 2:14-16, where he again confuses the law of God, or the ten commandments, with the old law of pardon, or law of Moses. It reads: "Blotting out the handwriting of ordinances that was against us, which was contrary to us, and took it out of the way nailing it to his cross. . . . . Let no man therefore judge you in meats or in drinks or in respect to an holy day, or the new moons, or sabbath days which are a shadow of things to come, but the body is Christ." Whatever this was blotted out it was something against the apostles and contrary to them. How could the ten commandments be against any good men like the apostles were? Notice this was the hand-writing of ordinances that was blotted out. It was contrary to the apostles, and, the ten commandments are in harmony and not against any good man. Good people with whom the

Holy Spirit is dwelling are in harmony with the ten commandments, and they have no desire to commit the acts of violence which that law forbids. Hence, this law nailed to the cross was not the ten commandment law of God, but it was just as these verses say, "the law of ordinances." It was the old law of pardon by the blood of animals which Moses wrote in a book, and placed in the side of the ark. This law contained over one hundred commandments and was only to last until Jesus came. It was a law against the beloved apostles because they had accepted Jesus, and found no virtue in killing animals and practicing all the ritual and endless ceremonies taught by the old pardoning system of the law of Moses, with its meats, drinks, and new moons, and yearly sabbath days. In Leviticus 23rd chapter we are told about the holy days, new moons, and yearly sabbaths, which have no connection whatever with the weekly sabbath. On these yearly sabbaths, of which there were many, they had to kill from 18 to 45 animals each day. The blood of these animals pointed forward to the blood of Jesus. When Jesus died upon Calvary and shed his blood, this old system ended. They had no need of these sabbath days any more because the killing of animals was past. These days set apart for these bloody sacrifices were ended. The apostles understood all of this and that is why the law herein mentioned was against them and contrary to them. Dear reader, the Lord says: "Study to show thyself approved of God, a workman that needeth not to be ashamed, rightly dividing the word of God" (2 Tim. 2:15). The holy ten commandments were not included in what was nailed to the cross, neither was the weekly seventh day sabbath, for it plainly says it was the law that was against the apostles and contrary to them, which was not so with the law of God's ten commandments. They are not contrary to, or against any good man.

The ten commandments were written on tables of stone (Exodus 31:18). The law of Moses, with bloody offerings for pardon of sin was written in a book (Deut. 31:24). God's ten commandments were written with his own finger (Exodus 31:18), while the law of animal sacrifice, or the

law of Moses, was written by Moses (Deut. 31:9). The
ten commandments were placed in the ark (Deut. 10:5),
while the other law that was against the apostles and
contrary to them was placed in the side of the ark (Deut.
31:25, 26). The ten commandment law of God was to
continue forever, and not one commandment cease (Psalms
111:7, 8), but the other law, the law of pardon by the
blood of animals, ended (Eph. 2:15). This is why the law
of God and the commandments of God are mentioned so
often in the New Testament, and we are told to observe
them in the following texts (Matt. 5:17, 19; Rom. 2:13;
Rom. 7:1, 12, 22) ; also Rom. 8:7 where it says "the natural
or carnal mind is enmity against God and is not subject to
the law of God, neither indeed can be." We do not make
void the law through faith (Rom. 3:31). We are not pardoned or justified by the deeds of the ten commandments,
for this law is the knowledge of sin (Rom. 3:20). New
Testament circumcision is keeping the commandments of
God (1 Cor. 7:19). We are to keep this whole law and
not offend in one point (James 2:10, 11). If we sin, we
transgress the law, for "sin is the transgression of the
law" (1 John 3:4). "He that saith I know him and keepeth
not his commandments is a liar and the truth is not in
him" (1 John 2:4). "This is the love of God that we keep
his commandments" (1 John 5:3). The remnant church
against whom the dragon beast is to make war are the
people keeping the commandments of God and having the
testimonies of Jesus (Rev. 12:17). Those saved in the
judgment are the ones keeping the commandments of God
(Rev. 14:12). And those who enter the city of gold and
eat of the tree of life are the obedient who keep the commandments of God (Rev. 22:14).

Furthermore, Jesus Christ, knowing that the sabbath
was going to remain, said not a jot or tittle would pass
from the law, as long as heaven and earth were here (Matt.
5:17, 19), and he also told his beloved disciples to pray
that their flight would not be on the sabbath day, or in
the winter time. It was not because the winter was holy
that he did not want them to flee at that season as my

friend says, but it was because of the hardships and suffering in the mountains during the storms, snows and rain of that season. I lived in that country myself and therefore know something about the winters in the mountains there. Another very amusing dodge my friend took of this strong text was, that the gates of Jerusalem would be closed on the sabbath and they could not flee on that day, but if he will examine the text again, and more carefully, he will see that Jesus was telling the people of Judaea to pray that their flight would not be on the sabbath day, and not to those just in Jerusalem, and there was no wall around the country of Judaea, or no closed gates. Surely he will have to correct this error on his part and find a better excuse for Jesus teaching the sacredness of the sabbath down in this dispensation.

My friend has agreed that the sabbath was sanctified, and set apart for a sacred use, by God Almighty according to Genesis 2:1-3, but he assumes that it was thus made sacred 2500 years after creation, because he says it is not mentioned until after Israel came out of Egyptian bondage. Because God says he showed Israel his judgments and gave them his sabbaths after he had brought them out of Egypt, my friend assumes that God had never given them his judgments and sabbaths before this time. His assumption, however, is wrong because we find that God gave his laws, statutes and judgments to Abraham long before Israel ever went into Egyptian bondage (Gen. 26:5). While God rested on the sabbath at the creation of the world, a fact our friend admits, yet he passes this by lightly as only a trifling incident in the concourse of events. Jesus said "The sabbath was made for man, and not man for the sabbath" (Mark 2:27). Man was made at creation, and so was the sabbath, which my friend admits. If his contention is true, dear reader, then God rested on the sabbath, and the race of men he created failed to follow God's example, and on for 2500 years they desecrated the sabbath day until God made a special race of men for the sabbath which he called Israel. But this is contrary to what Jesus said. He said the sabbath was made for man, and not a special race of men for the sabbath. Our claim is that because God set the example of resting from his creative work on the seventh day, he immediately set 'it apart, or sanctified it for man. Also that God's people have so regarded it in every age of the world. As God is "no respecter of persons" (Rom. 2:11; Eph. 6:9), and as he never changes (Mal. 3:6), his divine purpose has remained the same from the beginning, and he never gave Israel any different requirements to meet from what he gave Abraham and all men created from the beginning. That his divine purpose pointed with precision to the birth of Jesus when the system of pardon was to be changed, from the blood of the animal to that of Jesus Christ, but the laws which constituted sin were never changed or altered. His commandments containing the sabbath were to remain forever (Psalms 111:7-9).

There were more than two million of Israelites who came out of Egypt, from the bondage of slavery, where they could not worship God as they wished to do. Therefore, when God brought them out where they had the liberty to keep his holy day, he gave it to them again for he said "remember." It was an institution previously given or he would not have said "Remember the sabbath day to keep it holy." Then again when he rained the manna (Exodus 16), and before they had reached Sinai, he did not rain it on the sabbath which he said was the "rest of the holy sabbath." God also said: "How long refuse you to keep my sabbaths and my laws," showing that these had been given at some previous date, and they were not keeping them. The reason was they were in bondage, and the word "remember" in this case referred to something they had previously known about, for God said: "How long refuse you to keep my commandments and my laws" (Ex. 16:28). When they broke the sabbath they broke a law that contained the sabbath, for God says so. These were the same laws that Abraham kept, because Israel had not yet reached Sinai; therefore, Abraham kept the sabbath that God blessed at creation. Abraham was chosen because he kept God's commandments and laws (Gen. 26:5).

There is no question whatever that God has one system of salvation for all mankind. It is the same for the Gentile as it is for the Jew, for God says there is neither Jew nor "If ye be Christ's then are ye Abraham's seed, and heirs Gentile, bond or free, but all are one in Christ Jesus, and according to the promise" (Gal. 3:28, 29). Just as the Gentiles had to join themselves to the Lord in the Old Testament (Isa. 56:6), and keep the sabbath to be saved, so it is in the New Testament. The Gentiles must indeed join themselves to the Lord, as our friend says, and when they do this, they are adopted into the family of Israel, and become Jews, or Israel. No doubt my friend will object to this but it is gospel. Paul says: "He is not a Jew which is one outwardly, but he is a Jew which is one inwardly, and circumcision is not outward in the flesh, but the circumcision of the heart" (Rom. 2:28, 29). Then, he further tells us that circumcision is nothing but the keeping of the commandments of God (1 Cor. 7:19). The commandments of God are to be written in the fleshly tables of the heart with the spirit of the living God, and then they will actuate our life. It is not in the letter but in the spirit that counts, for the letter killeth but the Spirit giveth life. Salvation is not won by dead works, but it is through the Spirit of God operating on the hearts of mankind through prayer that changes their lives, and they have a desire and possess power to do God's will, and by nature to keep all of God's commandments including his holy sabbath day. In Romans eleventh chatper we are told clearly of how the Gentiles are broken off of the wild olive tree, and as branches they are grafted into the tame olive tree, or adopted into the family of Abraham contrary to nature (Rom. 11:24). They no longer bear the fruit of the Gentiles, but resemble the fruit of the stock of Israel. If you graft buds of the peach tree on to the plum, according to nature, the peach will continue to bear the fruit of the old stock while grafted into the plum tree, but Gentiles are grafted contrary to nature (verse 24), therefore they leave off the old fruit of Gentileism and bear the fruit resembling that of the tame olive tree, or Israel, and the Lord said of the sabbath:

"It is a sign between me and the children of Israel forever, for in six days the Lord made heaven and earth, and on the seventh day he rested and was refreshed" (Ex. 31:17). The word Israel means an overcomer, and the Lord never intended for sinners to keep the sabbath. It is for his people.

In Hebrews 4:4 to 9, we are plainly told that "There remaineth therefore the keeping of a sabbath to the people of God." In verse 4 we are told that the sabbath spoken of here is the seventh day, and it is this sabbath that remains for God's people. Our friend says it is the rest in Canaan, but God says it is a sabbath rest. The Greek word sabbatismos is the same as sabbaton, only used gramatically in the sentence to derive a different ending. It means the sabbath day rest as anyone familiar with Greek understands, and, furthermore, all we need to do is to believe God. He plainly says here: "There remaineth therefore a rest for the people of God, and he that has entered into his rest, he also hath ceased from his own work, as God did from his," and we are told that God ceased from his work on the seventh day of the week in the 4th verse of this chapter.

We are commanded many times in the New Testament to keep the commandments of God in order to be saved, but my friend says we are to keep only nine of them. I keep just one more, making ten, and that is the difference between us. If I am under the law for keeping ten, and fallen from grace, then he is nine tenths as bad off, for he claims to keep nine. The commandments of God, mentioned in the New Testament, when referring to our moral duty toward God, mean the ten commandments just as in the Old Testament. When we are told in 1 John 3:4 that sin is the transgression of the law, it means the ten commandment law, for sin was the transgression of that law in the Old Testament; and just because some other acts were also considered to be sin, this does not do away with the fact that breaking the commandments was sin then, and is sin today. If God gave another law to take the place of the ten commandments, surely we would have some history of the event. Anciently when he gave laws he did it with wide publicity, but no mention whatever is made of any great gathering or event in the New Testament where he gave new laws. The day of Pentecost would have been an excellent opportunity for such a noble work, but not one word is said about any new laws, but it does say that they continued steadfastly in the apostles doctrine (Acts 2:42). No new laws or new regulations were given. My friend thinks it would be absurd to think about the commandments of God mentioned in Rev. 12:17, being the ten commandments, but when he believes in keeping nine of these same commandments and claims they are binding on Christians, and we have no record of them ever being done away with, then why does he think it absurd to believe when God speaks of the commandments of God, that he means what he says. Surely the whole world knew, throughout the entire Bible period, that the commandments of God were always spoken of as the ten commandments, and vice versa. We therefore claim that when the Lord tells us to keep the commandments of God in the New Testament he refers to the ten commandments just as he did in the Old Testament. Jesus said: "If you will enter into life keep the commandments" (Matt. 19:16-19), and he meant the ten commandments, for he quotes a number of them to show what he did refer to. He did not mention the sabbath and our friend may emphasize this point, but if he claims the sabbath is not binding because Jesus did not expressly mention it here, then he will have to concede that the other commandments not mentioned are equally not binding, and there were several of the others not mentioned also. Jesus again meant the ten commandments when he used the expression "the commandments" in Matt. 22:35-39. Here he said the whole law hung on two commandments, love to God and love to man, and that the first and great commandment was to love the Lord thy God with all thy heart, soul, and mind. This takes in the first four of the ten, as they are all love to God, and the sabbath is one of them. The last six are love to our fellow-man, and embrace the second commandment as Jesus says.

The whole law of ten commandments hangs on that one great principle, "love," love to God being first, and love to man, second. Consequently, Jesus teaches us that the commandments of God mentioned in the New Testament are the ten commandments.

We have also shown previously that it was the custom of Paul to preach on the sabbath day, and he was not preaching entirely to Jews either, for Acts 17:4 says a great company of Greeks or Gentiles believed. Then they were Christians, and Paul made it his custom to preach to them on the sabbath. In Acts 18:4 we read how Paul reasoned every sabbath in the synagogue persuading both Jews and Gentiles, and nothing is said about them wor· shiping or meeting on any other day. In verse 8 it says many of the Corinthians believed and were baptized; hence, there were Christians here, and Paul stayed a year and six months preaching in a house joining against the synagogue. Here he labored making tents (verse 3) during the week, and nothing is said about them holding meetings on any other day excepting the sabbath. Furthermore, the Holy Spirit said the day they were meeting was the sabbath day, and my friend admits it was the seventh day of the week; hence, this alone establishes my proposition that the seventh day is the sabbath in this age. The Holy Spirit would not deceive us by telling us it was the sabbath if it had ceased to be at the cross. We know that Paul speaks of the pass-over and of Pentecost also in the New Testament, as my friend says. Yes, it is evident that the early Christian church observed these seasons by holding meetings, but· not as the Jews observed them. Both of these are to be continued in the kingdom as we are plainly told, and so is the sabbath to continue over there. The prophet Isaiah assures us that the sabbath will be kept in the new heaven and the new earth (Isa. 66:23). The passover was to be perpetuated as an ordinance, just as Jesus introduced it, forever. It was never to end, and Jesus says he is going to eat it anew with the apostles in the kingdom. It was kept once a year, at the time, and on the day Jesus shed his blood up to 321 A.D. when Constantine put Easter or passover on a fixed Sunday. This anyone can find in different histories and encyclopedias. Paul says: "Christ our passover was sacrificed for us, therefore let us keep the feast" (1 Cor. 5:7, 8). They kept it once a year on the very night Jesus introduced it, on the very day Jesus shed his blood. These institutions were kept in the New Testament with the sabbath, but they were all modified and observed according to the teachings of Jesus. Jesus taught them to keep the sabbath by performing God's work and doing good on that day. The old restrictions put on it by Moses in which they were forbidden to kindle fires or pick up sticks, etc., were removed by Christ. It was the same way with the passover and Pentecost, but they both continued to be kept and observed. When Jesus through the Spirit called the seventh day the sabbath repeatedly in the New Testament it surely is the sabbath.

In the New Covenant dispensation, God says he writes his laws on the hearts and in the minds of his people (Heb. 8:10), consequently God's laws remain as a part of this covenant. The primary meaning of the word "covenant" is an agreement. This was entered into between Israel and God before Israel got to Mount Sinai. Hence, when the old covenant ended it was the covenant or agreement. See Exodus 19th chapter, verses 1 to 8. In verse 8 it says all the people answered together and agreed. The agreement or covenant was on their part, they were to obey God, and keep his commandments. On God's part the agreement was that he would make of them a great nation, and continue with them protecting them in Canaan forever. The old covenant passing away was not the ten commandments ending. The ten commandments are spoken of as a covenant, but never as the one that ended. They were what Israel were to keep and they agreed to keep them; then when they failed to keep their part of the agreement, God withdrew his power and protection and they have been scattered all over the earth and lost their Canaan land. God has made a new covenant with his people based on better promises. It is not the land of Canaan we are to possess, but it is an eternal home in his kingdom; but we have to comply with the very same terms, as did Israel. What was sin then is sin now, and all of the commandments are to be kept, for the ten commandments are declared to be a perpetual covenant. They constitute his declared covenant and were given for a thousand generations (Psalms 111: 8, 9). There are more than fifty different covenants in the Old Testament and we must not confuse these in a way to do violence to such a righteous code of law as we find in the ten commandments.

Our friend has frankly admitted that the seventh day is the sabbath; then why not keep it together for the Lord, and not substitute some other day in its place. We appreciate this admission, Elder Porter, for it is right. The seventh day was, and is the sabbath of God. It is his holy day and does not belong to man to use for himself (Isa. 58:13; also Ex. 20:8-11). May the Lord through the power of his blessed Spirit direct us all and give power to separate from the world and walk as Jesus walked in the way of God's commandments.

PORTER'S SECOND NEGATIVE

I appreciate the effort made by my opponent in his second affirmative to establish the idea that the seventh day of the week as a Christian sabbath is enjoined upon God's people in this age, but the farther he goes, the more apparent becomes his failure. Before replying to the things he has said in this affirmative, I want to call attention to some things he overlooked. These are things of vital importance, and the readers are going to wonder why he said nothing about them.

1.   In an effort to prove that the sabbath was of universal application—binding on the Gentile as well as the Jew—Dugger introduced Isaiah 56:6 in his first affirmative. I countered by asking him why the Gentiles were called strangers. He made no reply whatever to my question. Please tell us, Elder Dugger, why the Gentiles were called strangers. Are you afraid to answer?

2.   I also asked him this question: "Why did not God

bring the Babylonians into Judean captivity for their failure to keep the sabbath?" My friend says it was as binding upon the Babylonians as upon the Jews. Then why send the Jews into captivity and let the Babylonians go free? Please tell us something about this.

3. In every place in the New Testament where he found "commandments of God" he said it meant the ten commandments. I asked him this: "Does God have any commandments besides the ten?" I predicted that he would not answer. And he passed the matter in complete silence. Elder Dugger, what is the matter with you? Won't you please answer this question for me? The readers are going to see that you are evading these important matters.

4. I showed from Exodus 31:13-16 that the sabbath was to be kept by Israel "throughout their generations." This is the very kind of language used concerning the passover, burnt-offerings, circumcision, their priesthood, and so on, that proves they were temporary. Such language is never used regarding the other nine commandments. I wonder why my friend said nothing about this.

These difficulties will have to be cleared up by my friend or the readers are going to see his failure. There are other things that he overlooked that I shall emphasize again as I reply to his second affirmative. And now I am ready to make that reply.

My opponent says that Amos 8:5-9 began to be fulfilled at the crucifixion of Christ, but that it refers to the punishments upon Israel and does not mean the sabbath would be gone. I know there is punishment involved in the prophecy. And it matters not about their evil desires to cheat and defraud. The fact remains that they asked when the new moon and sabbath would be gone. And God told them when it would be so. My friend admits that the feast of the new moon ended at the cross. Well, when the new moon was to be gone is the same time the sabbath was to be gone. God said so. Dugger denies it.

His effort to set aside my argument on 2 Cor. 3:7-11 is amusing and absurd. This refers to the "ministration of death written and engraven in stones" being done away.

My friend tells us that it was the "ministration" that was
done away, not the ten commandment law. Well, whatever
it was that was done away was the thing "written and
engraven in stones." Dugger, please tell us what it was
that was "written and engraven in stones." Was it the ten
commandments? Now, don't pass this question in silence
like you have a number of others, but give us an answer.
The thing "written and engraven in stones" was the thing
that was done away. The ten commandment law was
"written and engraven in stones" (Ex. 31:18; 32:16). I
challenge him to find anything else written on those stones.
But my friend calls attention to the law that Moses wrote in
a book (Deut. 31:24-26) and says: "This is the law that
was written on the stones of the altar." He had just introduced Joshua 8:30-32 to show that Joshua wrote "a copy
of the law of Moses" upon the stones of the altar. And
he insists that it was this law, instead of the ten commandment law, that Paul referred to in 2 Cor. 3:7-11 as being
done away. Yes, I know that Joshua wrote a copy of the
law of Moses on the stones of the altar. But did Paul
refer to that in 2 Cor. 3:7-11? Did he say "the law written
on the stones of the altar" was done away? What stones
did Paul mention in 2 Cor. 3? Let us read it in verse 7:
"But if the ministration of death, written and engraven in
stones, was glorious, so that the children of Israel could not
steadfastly behold the face of Moses for the glory of his
countenance." Was the countenance of Moses so glorious
when Joshua wrote the law on the stones of the altar that
Israel could not behold his face? Is that the time when
the face of Moses shone? If so, then Paul referred to that.
But Moses was dead when Joshua wrote the law on the
stones of the altar. This was done after they had crossed
the Jordan into Canaan (Josh. 4:1; 8:30-32). But Moses
died before they entered Canaan (Deut. 32:5, 6). Hence,
his face did not shine so glorious that Israel could not behold
it when Joshua wrote the law on the stones of the altar.
But when and where did that incident occur? We have
the record in Ex. 34:29-35. Verse 29 says: "And it came
to pass, when Moses came down from Mount Sinai with

the two tables of testimony in Moses' hand, when he came down from the mount, that Moses wist not that the skin of his face shone while he talked with him." The following verses show that he had to put a veil over his face while he talked with Israel because they were afraid to come nigh when they saw the glory of his face. When did this occur? When Moses came down from Mount Sinai with the two stones on which God had written the ten commandments. Paul referred to this very incident in 2 Cor. 3 and declared that the "ministration of death written and engraven" in these stones was done away. My friend made a colossal blunder when he tried to switch this statement to the stones of the altar on which Joshua wrote. My friend's illustration of the Republican and Democratic administrations does not fit, for those things are not written in that which contains our fundamental, basic laws; but the ministration Paul referred to was written in the stones.

My friend did as I expected him to do with my argument that ."Christians are not under the law." I showed this by Rom. 6:14; Gal. 5:18; Rom. 7:4-6; Rom. 10:4 and Gal. 3:24, 25. Dugger says Christians are not under the law, and admits that the law embraces the ten commandments, but he says: "It is sinners who are under the law." Well, that just about fixes things for him. Let us see the consequences of his position. 1. It makes Jesus a sinner. Paul tells us he was "made under the law" (Gal. 4:4). If Dugger's position is right, the Bible is wrong when it says he did no sin, for he was "under the law." Dugger says that means he was a violator of the law and, therefore, under its condemnation. 2. It makes Christians irresponsible. In Rom. 3:19 Paul says: "Now we know that what things soever the law saith, it saith to them who are under the law." According to my friend, this means that the law speaks only to sinners, to those under condemnation. Then the law says nothing to God's people, to Christians; they are not under the law, and the law says nothing to them. In that case they would not be responsible at all if this law continues in force today. And if the sabbath is contained in "the law," and if Christians are not "under the law," then the law of the sabbath says nothing to them, inasmuch as it speaks only to them that are under the law. Later on Dugger says: "The Lord never intended for sinners to keep the sabbath." Then to whom does the sabbath law speak? It speaks to them who are under the law, says Paul, but Dugger says Christians are not under the law; so it does not speak to them. Yet sinners were not to keep the sabbath; so it does not speak to them. I ask my friend to please explain his predicament here. 3. It makes men desire condemnation. Paul said: "Tell me, ye that desire to be under the law, do ye not hear the law?" (Gal. 4:21). According to my friend these people were desiring to be condemned. 4. And finally, when the answer of my friend is carried to its legitimate conclusion, it condemns all Christians, for in 1 Cor. 9:21 Paul said Christians are "under the law to Christ." Does this mean all Christians are condemned by Christ? It must, according to my friend's position. The man in the death cell who is pardoned by the governor is just as much under the law of the state after his pardon as he was before he committed his crime. The grace of the governor does not remove the restriction of the law. To be under the law means to be amenable to the law. Those who live in Oklahoma are under the law of this state; those who live in Oregon are under the law of that state; those who lived in the Mosaic dispensation were under the law of that age. But we who live in the gospel age are "no longer under the law" that governed men then (Gal. 3:24, 25). And since the sabbath belonged to that law, we are not under the sabbath—it is not binding now. Any man who makes that law binding ·in this age is the man who is "wresting the Scriptures" to his own destruction. I do not claim, according to Rom. 10:4, that "Christ is the end of the law for wickedness." Any one knows a man cannot break a law that has been abolished.

Now, to Col. 2:14-16. My friend says this cannot refer to the sabbath law but to a law that was "against the apostles and contrary to them." This, he says, was not true with the ten commandment law. To what law, then, did Paul refer? Dugger answers: "It was the old law of par-

don by the blood of animals which Moses wrote in a book."
And why was this against them? My friend says: "It was
a law against the beloved apostles because they had accepted Jesus, and found no virtue in killing animals." Furthermore, he says: "When Jesus died upon calvary and
shed his blood, this old system ended." And now, of course,
since it is ended, it would be against Christians who have
reached Jesus the antitype. Well, if that is what Paul had
in mind, he should have made a different statement. He
should have said this law "is against us and is contrary
to us." Certainly it is contrary to us since Jesus has died.
But Paul did not say it is contrary to us; he said it **was.**
That refers it to the past. While it was in force it was
against us and it was contrary to us. And because it **was**
against them, it was blotted out. And the "us" referred
to Jews, not to the apostles. Paul was not an apostle while
that law was in force, but he was a Jew, and he refers to
the past and says "the handwriting of ordinances was
against us." This referred to the whole law system of the
Jewish age. It was against them because it demanded perfect
obedience (Gal. 3:13). But does Col. 2:14-16 concern the
sabbath law? Read it for yourself. He mentions "the
handwriting of ordinances" concerning meat and drink, holy
days, new moons and sabbath days. Yes, the handwriting
concerning sabbath days was blotted out, according to Paul.
But Dugger denies it. I prefer to stand with Paul. My
friend claims "the sabbath days" in this passage refers to
the yearly sabbaths. That is untrue; for the yearly sabbaths are listed as "holydays." Note the set order of services they had—daily, weekly, monthly, and yearly. Let
us read 1 Chron. 23:30, 31: "And to stand every morning
to thank and praise the Lord, and likewise at even; and to
offer all burnt sacrifices unto the Lord in the sabbaths, in
the new moons, and on the set feasts." Note the things
here specified. There was the service for morning and
evening (daily), in the sabbaths (weekly), in the new moons
(monthly), and on the set feasts (yearly). This same set
order of services is mentioned in 2 Chron. 2:4; 8:13; 31:3;
Neh. 10:33 and other passages. And that is exactly the

same order given by Paul in Col. 2:16. "Let no man therefore judge you in meat, or in drink, or in respect of a feast
day or a new moon or a sabbath day." Revised Version.
Note the order: "in meat, or in drink" (daily), "in respect
of a feast day" (yearly), "of a new moon" (monthly), "or
a sabbath day" (weekly). What the King James translation calls a "holyday" the revised translation calls a "feast
day." And that means the yearly services mentioned in
Lev. 23. So the yearly sabbaths that my friend has in
mind are mentioned as feast days, or holydays, and the
weekly sabbath is shown to be abolished. The argument
stands that no man has a right to judge Christians with
respect to sabbath keeping, for the handwriting concerning
such has been blotted out and nailed to the cross of Christ.

The distinction which Elder Dugger makes between the
law of God and the law of Moses is absurd. He calls the
ten commandments the law of God and the remainder of the
Old Testament system the law of Moses. Hence, he claims
the law of God was written on stones (Ex. 31:18) ; the law
of Moses was written in a book (Deut. 31:24) ; the law of
God was written with his own finger (Ex. 31:18) ; the law
of Moses was written by Moses (Deut. 31:9) ; the law of
God was placed in the ark (Deut. 10:5) ; the law of Moses
was placed in the side of the ark (Deut. 31:25, 26). And
then he concludes that the law of God is to continue forever
(Ps. 111:7, 8), but the law of Moses was done away (Eph.
2:15).

I shall fully blast this argument he makes on the two laws.
Did it never occur to my friend that what he calls "the law
of God" was also written in the book by Moses and was
placed in the side of the ark? The ten commandments in
full were written twice by Moses in the book (Ex. 20:1-17;
Deut. 5:1-21). So if that written in the book by Moses
and placed in the side of the ark was done away, that does
away with the ten commandment law too. And the statement in Ps. 111:7, 8 does not specify the ten commandments,
but it refers to "all his commandments." Did God have
any commandments besides the ten? But you don't need
be disappointed if Dugger does not answer this question.

I predict again that he will not. Now, I want to show you that "the law of God" and "the law of Moses" were the same thing. Consider the following: 1. God gave "the law of Moses" (Ezra 7:6). And Moses gave "God's law" (Neh. 10:29). This ruins my friend's argument. He claims Moses gave the law of Moses, and God gave the law of God, and they are two separate things. 2. God gave "the book of the law of Moses" (Neh. 8:1). Moses gave the "book of the law of the Lord" (2 Chron. 34:14). This shows them to be exactly the same thing. 3. Some things written in "the law of Moses." Remember that my opponent says the law of Moses refers to all that law of the Old Testament dispensation except the ten commandments. Jesus declared: "Moses said, Honor thy father and thy mother." But this is one of the ten commandments. Again, "Did not Moses give you the law, and yet none of you keepeth the law? Why go ye about to kill me?" (John 7:19). So Jesus refers to the law against murder and says Moses gave it. 4. The things contained in the law of God. Dugger says it contains only the ten commandments. But what does the Bible say? Burnt offerings are contained in "the law of the Lord" (2 Chron. 31:3). The acts of Josiah are written in the same law (2 Chron. 35:26). And Luke makes the following statement: "(As it is written in the law of the Lord, Every male that openeth the womb shall be called holy to the Lord;) and to offer a sacrifice according to that which is said in the law of the Lord, a pair of turtledoves, or two young pigeons" (Luke 2:23, 24). None of these things are in the ten commandments; yet they are all in "the law of the Lord." 5. The expressions are used interchangeably in the eighth chapter of Nehemiah. The book from which Ezra read is called "the book of the law of Moses" in verse 1. Verse 2 calls it "the law." Verse 3 calls it "the book of the law." And verse 8 says "they read in the book of the law of God." So "the law," "the book of the law," "the book of the law of Moses," and "the law of God" are all the same thing. I challenge my opponent to explain all these things in the light of his position. His reference to Rom. 2:13; 7:1, 12, 13; 3:31 and such like to prove the ten commandments binding on us is thus exploded. Yes, "sin is the transgression of the law" (1 John 3:4), but this has no reference to the ten commandment law.

My friend mentions again a number of verses that speak of the necessity of keeping God's commandments, such as 1 Cor. 7:19; 1 John 2:4; 5:3; Rev. 14:12; 12:17; 22:14. He assumes these are the ten commandments. I am asking him again: Does God have any commandments except the ten? I asked him that before, but he wouldn't answer. I wonder if he will leave it alone this time. If he answers, he ruins his argument.

Jesus did not say in Matt. 5:17-19 that the law would not pass "as long as heaven and earth are here." But he said it would not pass "till all be fulfilled." My opponent admitted that Jesus fulfiled it. So it passed away. I gave him a number of similar statements, but he silently passed them by. I call upon him to notice the argument I made on this in my first negative. Will he do it? I seriously doubt it, but we will wait and see.

As to the flight in the winter or the sabbath day (Matt. 24:20), I am fully aware of the fact that there was no wall around the land of Judea, but it is also true that Jerusalem was not the only city that was walled, and escape on the sabbath would be difficult because their gates would be closed. Certainly such flight on the sabbath among Jews who were strict in their attitude toward the sabbath would be difficult for the disciples of Christ. But my friend surrenders his argument by admitting that the statement, "pray that your flight be not in the winter," did not make the winter holy. Then to pray that their flight be not on the sabbath day would not make the sabbath holy. If such a statement makes the sabbath holy in A.D. 70, it also makes the winter a holy season, and my opponent cannot escape the conclusion here.

Elder Dugger says that I assume that the sabbath was made sacred 2500 years after creation, but he must not forget that the laboring oars are in his hands. It is up to him to prove that it was set apart before that time. He

is the man who is assuming that during the first 2500
years of the history of the world the sabbath was kept.
Let him produce one passage that mentions such thing! He
cannot do it. It was God who said he "gave the sabbaths"
in the wilderness (Ezek. 20:10-12) and "made known" the
sabbath in the region of Sinai (Neh. 9:13, 14). If God
made it known then, what right has Dugger to say he made
it known 2500 years before then? His dispute is with
God, not with Porter. I gave these scriptures in my first
negative; why didn't he pay some attention to them? The
race of men could not "desecrate the sabbath" during 2500
years before it was enjoined upon man; it must be enjoined
before it can be desecrated. And my friend cannot find
where it was enjoined on anybody during that 2500 years.
I do not believe, as charged by my opponent, that God
made a special race of men for the sabbath; but I believe
"the sabbath was made for man" (Mark 2:27). However,
the sabbath was not "made for man" until it was sanctified,
set apart, or enjoined upon man. In other words, it was
"made for man" when God "gave" it to man, but God said:
"I gave them my sabbaths" after he brought them out of
Egypt (Ezek. 20:10-12). This was long after the race of
Israel had come into existence. I called my friends' attention to the fact that God sanctified the seventh day because in it he "had rested" (Gen. 2:1-3), which shows the
sanctification of it took place after he rested, not when he
rested. But he paid no attention to this fact. He contends
that since God is no respecter of persons (Rom. 2:11; Eph.
6:9) and never changes (Mal. 3:6), he has had the same
commandments for men in every age. This is not true,
however, for God has changed his law (Heb. 7:12) and has
given commandments in this age that he never gave in any
other. Did God command Abraham to be baptized? He
has commanded men in this age to be. But suppose God
did set it apart at creation; that would not make it binding
on Christians now, and that is what my opponent is required
to prove.

When God said **"remember** the sabbath," did he mean the
sabbath had been previously given? Not at all. The state-

ment simply means "I am giving you the sabbath; now remember to keep it." God told Israel to remember the day they left Egypt (Ex. 13:3), but that does not mean they had been previously keeping the passover. I have already shown that the sabbath is first mentioned in Ex. 16:23, but my opponent thinks when God said, "How long refuse ye to keep my commandments?" (v. 28), it proves the sabbath requirement of long standing. But one such refusal would be sufficient to bring forth such a question, especially since they had been rebellious in other matters. Besides, I have already shown that God dealt with them here to "prove them," whether they would keep his laws. If they had the sabbath for years before, they would have been proven already.

Reference is made to Abraham's seed (Gal. 3:28, 29), to the "Jew which is one inwardly" (Rom. 2:28, 29), to the grafting in of the Gentiles (Rom. 11), and to circumcision (1 Cor. 7:19), to prove that Gentiles must become Jews, in order to make the sabbath binding on them. But one of the references given says that in Christ "there is neither Jew nor Greek" (Gal. 3:28). Why use a passage to prove the very thing the passage says is not true. Certainly Christians are sometimes called Israel, or Jews, but this refers to spiritual Israel, not to fleshly Israel. In Ex. 31:17, the Israel to whom God gave the sabbath was fleshly Israel. The argument of Dugger, if true, would bind upon Christians every other commandment God gave to fleshly Jews, as killing the passover lamb (Ex. 12:6), offering other animal sacrifice (Lev. 17:5), the burning of incense (Ex. 30:8), and so on. Will my friend make all these binding on the Gentiles who "become Jews, or Israel"? If not, his argument is worth nothing.

Again we consider Heb. 4:4-9. In my friend's first affirmative he said the word "rest" in all these verses except verse 9 was from the Greek "katapausis" and meant "rest after fatigue, the Eden rest, or the eternal rest." Turn back and read his statement. But now he says the "rest" of verse 10 is the sabbath rest. Yet it is from the Greek word "katapausis." Now, which of these positions does Elder Dugger want; in one affirmative he says it is not the sabbath rest; in the other, he says it is. Both statements cannot be true. Let him tell us which he wants. And he says the Greek word "sabbatismos" is the same as "sabbaton", except the grammatical use gives a different ending. I deny this emphatically and challenge him to tell the grammatical use of the two words. But lest he will not, I shall show them to be the same in grammatical use. In Heb. 4:10, "there remaineth a rest (sabbatismos) to the people of God." Sabbatismos is a singular noun, third person, nominative case, used as subject of the sentence. In Mark 2:27, "the sabbath (sabbaton) was made for man," sabbaton is a singular noun, third person, nominative case, used as subject of the sentence. Their grammatical use is the same. What is the difference? Sabbaton is of neuter gender; sabbatismos is of masculine gender. The word "sabbath" in the New Testament always comes from "sabbaton" (neuter gender). The word "sabbatismos" (masculine gender) is used only one time in the New Testament and does not refer to the seventh day. They are two different words. The rest of Heb. 4:10 is the eternal rest that we must labor to enter (Heb. 4:11). And to cease from work "as God did from his" does not say "on the day God did."

I keep nine of the ten commandments, not because they were in the ten commandments, but because they have been required in the New Testament law in an enlarged form. And if my opponent will show the commandment for keeping the sabbath, I'll keep that too. But no one has ever been commanded to keep the sabbath since the cross of Christ. So I am not nine-tenths fallen from grace, for I do not go to the old law for justification. And 1 John 3:4 does not refer to the ten commandments. The transgression of any divine law was sin. I ask Dugger to answer this: Would violation of other commandments, except the ten, be sin? Watch and see if he answers this. And it is claimed by the affirmative that no new commandment was given even on the day of Pentecost. Read Acts 2:38. This is the first time men were commanded to be baptized in the name of Christ. It was a new commandment. God means what he says when he "speaks of the commandments of God." But when Dugger says that means only and always the ten, he says something that God neither says nor means. His claim that through the entire Bible "the commandments of God were always spoken of as the ten commandments" is not true. To set fire to Ai was a "commandment of the Lord" (Josh. 8:8). To destroy Amalek, their flocks and herds, were "commandments of God" (1 Sam. 15:11). Preaching the gospel was a "commandment of the everlasting God" (Rom. 16:26). Not one of these is in the ten commandments. And you can find many others by checking your concordance. Dugger is wrong on this point.

Although Jesus did not mention the sabbath when he told the rich young man to keep the commandments (Matt. 19:16-22), I gladly admit that it was included, for he was still living under the law. But we are living since the law was abolished at the cross (Col. 2:14-16). The young man was told to "love thy neighbor as thyself." This is not one of the ten but belonged to what Dugger calls the law of Moses. All those commandments were binding on him.

Neither did Jesus mean the ten commandments when he mentioned the two great commandments of the law in Matt. 22:35-40. The first was: "Thou shalt love the Lord thy God with all thy heart, and with all thy soul, and with all thy mind" (verse 37). The second: "Thou shalt love thy neighbor as thyself" (verse 39). No matter if the principle of love is embraced in the ten commandments (it is embraced in all divine commandments), these are two definite, specific commandments, and neither is found in the ten. They are found in Deut. 6:5 and Lev. 19:18, in what my friend calls "the law of Moses." In Matt. 19, after naming five of the second group of the ten commandments, Jesus said: "**And,** thou shalt love thy neighbor as thyself." Thus he shows this is not the second group of the ten commandments, but in addition to it. And Paul, in Rom. 13:9, mentioned five of that second group, and then said this is "another commandment." My friend, therefore, cannot

make them the same thing. The two greatest commandments of the law were not in the ten commandments.

My friend argues that the only day on which meetings
were held in Corinth for a year and half, during which
time many believed and were baptized, was the sabbath
day. At first Paul preached in the Jewish synagogue on
the sabbath (Acts 18:4), but after he turned from the Jews
to the Gentiles in verse 6, there is not a word said about
any sabbath meeting. Let my friend notice this. And not
a word said about Paul's keeping the sabbath at any time.
I have often preached on the seventh day, but I did not
keep the sabbath. I was a little surprised that Dugger
said the passover and Pentecost are still binding under the
gospel, but he was hard pressed. The passover was a type,
and he would have it kept after the antitype, Jesus, our
passover, has been sacrificed. That reverses type and antitype. But, he says, they did not keep these feasts according to original requirements, but in modified form. If
they did not keep them as the law said, they did not keep
them at all. In Acts 12:3 and 20:6 it was still called "the
days of unleavened bread." That was **as the law required.**
Does that bind it on us? Does Dugger keep it? Let him
tell us. I challenge my friend to produce the proof that
the passover and Pentecost are binding on Christians. 1
Cor. 5:7, 8 has to do with purging evil characters from the
church, and not to a keeping of the Old Testament passover.

If Isa. 66:23 means the sabbath will be binding in the
new heaven and the new earth, it means the feast of the
"new moon" will be binding too. Read it for yourself. Does
Dugger keep the feast of the new moon?

Yes, I know, according to Heb. 8:10, that God has laws
in his new covenant. But that does not say they were the
same laws of the old covenant. Verse 9 says the new
covenant was "not according to" the old one. And the
covenant was more than their agreement in Ex. 19:1-8.
God does not refer to their agreement which **they made**
with him, but to the covenant which **he made** with them.
And that covenant which **God made** was the old covenant

that was done away (Heb. 8:13; Jer 31:31-34). God said in Ex. 19:5: "If . . . . ye will keep **my covenant.**" He did not say: "If you will keep **your agreement.**" He also said they broke **his covenant** (Jer. 31:32; Heb. 8:9), not merely their agreement. So **their arggreement** was not **his covenant,** but his covenant which they broke was taken away (Heb. 8:7, 11). What was the covenant that God made? Deut. 4:13 says the Lord "declared unto you **his covenant,** which he commanded you to perform, **even ten commandments.**" The tables on which they were written were called "the tables of the covenant" (Deut. 9:9). The ark in which they were placed was called "the ark of the covenant" (Deut. 31:26). The ten commandments are called "the words of the covenant" (Ex. 34:27, 28). And this covenant Israel broke and God took away.

Another negative (Gal. 4:22-31). Abraham's son by bond-woman represents covenant from Sinai. Isaac represents new covenant. Bondwoman and her son were cast out (verse 30). That ends covenant from Sinai. Children of that covenant are not heirs with son of free-woman. But Christians are not children of the covenant from Sinai (verse 31). Hence, are not under dominion of the sabbath law.

DUGGER'S THIRD AFFIRMATIVE

Before giving further affirmative argument in proof that the seventh day of the week (Saturday) is still God's time, and holy to him, we will answer the negative arguments set forth by our opponent. He says that I claim the commandment to love the Lord our God, and to love our neighbor as ourselves, are separate and do not pertain to the ten commandments. He is mistaken, however, for it is Jesus who made this statement and not myself. Jesus said plainly "On these two commandments hangs all the law" (Matt. 19:16-22). Jesus never did teach the people to keep the old sacrifices of the law of Moses, but his teachings against them was one thing that set the ministers in that day against him (the Jewish priests), for they received their money and their living through this old system which both Jesus and Paul condemned. It was the old law of pardon by the animal's blood, and the whole system of pardon through Moses that Jesus and the apostles were against. Therefore, when Jesus said the whole law hung on the two commandments to love God, and love our neighbor, he did not include the old animal sacrifices, but the ten commandments. The first four of these are love to God, and the last six, love to man; and if Elder Porter will love God as he should, he will not only try to keep three of these first four commandments, but he will also "Remember the sabbath day," which is just as binding on God's people as it ever was. He said Jesus did not mean the ten commandments when he told us to love the Lord our God with all our heart, which was the first commandment, and to love our neighbor was the second; but Jesus said the whole law hung on these two commandments. Anyone knows that by the very nature of the first four commandments they are love to God, while the last six are love to man. If we through prayer and contact with God, receive enough of that heavenly virtue within our hearts and souls, we will love God, and by nature keep all of these commandments. The keeping of a law will not save anyone, but when the heart is really regenerated by the presence and power of God, then it will be our nature to keep all of God's commandments whether they be the ten commandments or all that he has given through Jesus Christ. As the apple tree bears nothing but apples, and never lemons, because it is contrary to its nature to bear the lemons, so will we bear nothing but the fruits of the Spirit, because it is our nature to bear nothing else. If we "love God we will keep his commandments, and his commandments are not grievous" (1 John 5:3). Paul says "the carnal mind is enmity against God, for it is not subject to the law of God, neither indeed can be" (Romans 8:7).

Our opponent says Paul never said anything about the sabbath after he announced that he was going to turn to the Gentiles, but he is again mistaken. Paul makes this statement a number of times when laboring with different Jews. In Acts 13:46 he says: "Lo we turn to the Gentiles."

Then later in chapter 16:12-14, we find him holding meetings on the sabbath as it was their custom to do out by the river side. This was not a Jewish synagogue either. Then again in chapter 17:4, and in 18:1-4 we find him teaching on the sabbath, and the Holy Spirit calling it the sabbath.

Elder Porter says if the feasts are not to be kept according to the old law, then they are not to be kept at all; but this is what he says, and not what God says. God says Pentecost is to be kept. The apostles kept the first Pentecost, and God honored it by sending the Holy Spirit on that day. The Lord also speaking of a time after Armageddon when the wicked powers of earth are to fall, and when the glorified state of his kingdom is established here on earth, and the Lord will be king, that the nations left who will not worship the king the Lord of hosts and will not keep the feast of Pentecost, upon them will be no rain (Zechariah 14:9-17). Now, this is what God says. He also says the sabbath is to be kept then, too, and calls it the new earth (Isa. 66:23). If we are to honor God at each new moon time then, it will be fine; and who are we, that we should deny God's word, and say it is not true, just because we cannot fully understand the significance of it. We know that these services will not be the same as under the old "administration of death" which Paul tells us has been done away. It will be a new order. God's sabbath is to be kept now, but not as it was under the old administration when they could not pick up sticks or build a fire. Jesus himself removed those restrictions, when the old Mosaic law was abolished containing these things. Jesus did change the manner of keeping the sabbath but he never did abolish the institution.

Our opponent says the old covenant that was done away was the ten commandments, and he is positively sure about this; but then he puts back all of this covenant but just one precept and claims we are subject to nine tenths of it just as was Israel. He forgets that if his theory is true, then the "New Covenant" was made according to the old one. But the Lord plainly says the new covenant was "not according to the old one" (Heb. 8:9). Elder Porter says it was just the same only the sabbath was left out of the new covenant. Now who are we to believe? If the old covenant was the ten commandments as he seems positive about, then the new covenant with all of these commandments but one, was made very much like the old covenant indeed. Now, the Lord tells us the difference between the old covenant and the new covenant and does not leave us in doubt of the matter. He says: "This is the covenant that I will make with the house of Israel after those days saith the Lord, **I will put my laws into their minds and write them in their hearts**" (Heb. 8:10). This is the difference, says God. Under the old covenant they had the law written on two tables of stone and carried it about the camp in the ark. Under the new covenant this same law is to be written on the fleshly tables of the heart by the Spirit of the living God. Remember, God does not change. He is the same yesterday, today and forever (Malachi 3:6; Heb. 13:8). The English definition for the word "covenant" is agreement, and everyone uses the word this way. The old covenant was the agreement clearly recorded in Exodus 19th chapter where the Lord agreed to make. Israel a great nation and continue them as such, if they would keep his commandments. His part of the covenant was to watch over them, bless and protect them on certain conditions. Their part of the agreement was that they would keep all of his commandments. These were the conditions. The ten commandments were therefore the words of the covenant. The ark contained these tables of stone embracing the terms of Israel's agreement. God did not fail on his part, but they failed and desecrated the sabbath day, breaking all of God's commandments by idolatry, blasphemy, and adultery, just like the Gentiles are doing today. God "found fault with them" (Heb. 8:8) and cast them away as a nation. The covenant ended because they broke their part of the agreement, but God does not change. He requires the same of any nation or people that he required of Israel. He requires obedience to the ten commandments.

In Galatians 4:22-31 we have the contrast between Abraham's two sons, Isaac and Ishmael, or Sarah and Hagar.

It is the same lesson exactly and shows the contrast between the works of the flesh and the works of the spirit. Abraham through his own works and by a lack of faith in the power of God to perform what God promised, took Hagar to obtain the promised seed. As a result we have today the Arabs or Canaanites possessing the old promised land, as the offspring from Hagar. Hagar represents the futile efforts of man through his own strength and power, which gendereth to bondage. It represents Israel's fleshly effort to keep God's commandments without prayer and without seeking God for help. It resulted in failure. Israel broke the commandments. Their fleshly weakness was manifest immediately, when they worshiped the golden calf, and there were slain in that day about three thousand (Exodus 32:28). But under the administration of the Spirit through Jesus Christ the descendant from Isaac, there were saved and baptized on the day of Pentecost three thousand souls. The old covenant from Sinai, wherein Israel entered into the agreement with God, is represented by Hagar. They promised and in vain attempted to keep the commandments of God in their own strength. They failed on their part of the agreement, as everyone will fail when vainly trying by human strength to obey God and do his will. "The carnal mind (natural mind) is enmity against God. Is not subject to the law of God neither **indeed can be**" (Rom. 8:7).

The new covenant was made with Israel, the Lord says, and not one word is said about the Gentiles in it. The Gentiles, as Gentiles, cannot be saved; but they must become Israel, as we have shown. This is why the ancient Babylonians were not condemned because they did not keep the sabbath. There always has been one salvation for all men, not two ways. It was so then, and is true to-day. The Gentiles who came into the salvation of God did keep the sabbath then, or they had no promise. See Isa. 56:6 as given previously. He says I did not answer these questions as to why the Gentiles were called strangers, etc. The Lord says the Gentiles were strangers because they had no hope, and were without God in the world (Eph.

2:11, 12). The Lord says there is no difference between the Jew and the Gentile (Rom. 10:12). To Abraham and his seed were the promises made (Gal. 3:16). The Lord said the Gentiles were strangers, having no hope; consequently, they were not expected to keep the sabbath. It is the same way to-day; if they want salvation they must come and accept a Jewish Christ, and an atonement by Jewish blood, and be adopted into the Jewish family through Jesus (Rom. 2:28, 29 and 1 Cor. 7:19 and Rom. 11).

Now, we have set forth certain definite arguments for the continuation of the sabbath day in this age of the world for God's children, and every argument thus far set forth stands. Elder Porter tries in vain to explain them away, and tells us that he has blasted them, etc. But God's word reads just the same. God tells us to "Study to show thyself approved of God, a workman who needeth not to be ashamed, rightly dividing the scriptures of truth" (2 Tim. 2:15).

1. We set forth the truth that God gave a law of ten commandments which he wrote on tables of stone, and one of these commandments tells us the seventh day is God's time, and holy to him, commanding it to be kept holy, as a day of rest. Furthermore, it has been clearly proven that this was the only portion of the Bible God wrote with his own finger on tables of stone, and that it is repeatedly spoken of in the Old Testament as the commandments of God and the law of God; that it' was the law measuring sin in that time and, furthermore, that these same commandments are spoken of repeatedly in the New Testament, just as they are in the Old, and called the law of God and the commandments of God. We have given already many scriptures in proof of this. As the sabbath was part of this law then, it is part of it now; and wherever we are told to keep the commandments of God in the New Testament, these ten are included, and we are commanded, therefore, to keep the seventh day sabbath many times in the New Testament.

His only answer to this is to challenge me to prove that the commandments of God in the New Testament mean the ten commandments. I have given much proof, and it is now up to him to prove the sabbath is not included as one of the commandments. This he has failed to do so far.

In James 2:8-11 we have two of the ten commandments mentioned; and then we are told that if we keep all of this law and offend in one point we are guilty of all. Our opponent, therefore, in breaking the 4th commandment which enjoins rest on the seventh day, is breaking one of these commandments. In Romans 7:7 Paul is discussing this same law, for he says: "I would not have known lust except the law had said, thou shalt not covet." It is, therefore, this same ten commandment law he is speaking of and his conclusion is found in verse 12 as follows: "Wherefore the law is holy and the commandment holy and just and good." Our opponent says the law is done away with and is no good any more. Now who shall we believe? Paul says it is holy and just and good.

Again Paul discusses the law in Romans 2:21 to 25 and mentions stealing, blasphemy, adultery and worshiping of idols, and says: "Thou that makest thy boasts of the law, through breaking the law dishonorest thou God?" This surely fits all who boast themselves above the law, just to get rid of the one precept, God's true sabbath day. God says those who break the law dishonor God, so reader be very careful how you deal with Paul's writings, of which Peter says some are wresting to their own destruction. Paul says here if we break the law that contains these commandments we dishonor God.

He attempts to answer my arguments on this by stating that the ten commandments were also written in the book of the law, but this does not erase the fact that God did make a distinction between the two, even if our opponent denies the fact. Had we been there and seen God write the ten commandments on two tables of stone and then write the other in a book there would be no further doubt, for we would know that God divided the law into two distinct codes. Their very nature is also different. One was a law that constituted sin, and the other was to pardon the transgressor, as we have clearly shown. We gave

Psalms 111:7, 8 where God says all of his commandments
are sure, that they stand fast forever and ever, and he
challenges me to prove that this is the ten commandments;
but he is the one to prove they are not the ten commandments. I affirm they are, for the ten commandments are
the commandments of God, and this says all of his commandments are sure, etc. Certainly a code of outstanding
commandments like all of the ten would be in this category
and would be included in all of his commandments. He
puts in one whole page endeavoring to show that God speaks
of the law of Moses as his law, and endeavors by this to
prove that they were all one and just the same; but the
facts remain that God separated them himself when he
made them, and when he gave them to Moses, and furthermore, their very nature separates them into two separate
codes, which every reasonable mind will easily acknowledge.
Those given through Moses would of course be God's law
too, but one ended and one continued.

Our proposition is forever sustained in the one fact that
there were two separate and distinct laws given at the
beginning, the very nature of one being a temporary means
for pardoning sins, while the nature of the other is absolutely perpetual and everlasting. The principles involved
in the ten commandments are organic principles of righteousness expressing the true relationship between man to
his God, and man to man. They stand by reason of their
nature, regardless of his efforts to put them all together
and erase them. Then the New Testament abundantly
sustains our claim, in the following scriptures and many
more. "Whosoever committeth sin transgresseth the law,
for sin is the transgression of the law" (1 John 3:4). "This
is the love of God that we keep his commandments and
his commandments are not grievous" (1 John 5:3). "Circumcision is nothing, and uncircumcision is nothing but the
keeping of the commandments of God" (1 Cor. 7:19). "The
law is holy, and the commandment holy and just and good"
(Romans 7:12). "Do we then make void the law through
faith? God forbid, yea, we establish the law" (Rom. 3:31).
"Whosoever shall keep the whole law, and yet offend in

one point is guilty of all. For he that said, Do not commit adultery, said also, Do not kill. Now if thou commit no adultery, yet if`thou kill, thou art a transgressor of the law" (James 2:10, 11). Of those who are saved at the judgment, it says: "Here are they that keep the commandments of God, and the faith of Jesus" (Rev. 14:12). Those that the beast makes war on, who, we are told, are the remnant of the seed of the church, are those who "keep the commandments of God, and the testimonies of Jesus" (Rev. 12:17). Now if this is not that special law of ten commandments occupying such an outstanding position in the Old Testament age, he must prove positively it is not. This he has failed to do. One of the commandments of this law enjoined rest on the seventh day of the week, and that law being binding on both Gentiles and Jews under the New Testament order, they are both alike duty bound, to keep God's sabbath day if they are recognized as his children. Yes, we surely admit that God has given different commandments at different times, but never did he give such a law as this, either before or since. He wrote these ten commandments with his own finger on tables of stone and spoke them with a voice that shook the earth. They constitute the complete relationship between man and man, and man and God. The law of ordinances, the law that was "against the apostles," is the law that was done away, as previously shown with Israel's yearly sabbaths.

He says I admit that Jesus fulfilled the law which my opponent says concluded or abrogated it, but he is mistaken. I said that Jesus fulfilled the bloody sacrificial law of pardon given through Moses, and he did when he shed his own blood for our sins. What he fulfilled in this way, of course, brought it to an end; but he said himself he came not to destroy. Hence, he did not destroy anything that his mission into the world did not complete. As he completed the old Mosaic law of pardon it ended. Paul said this law was added because of the transgressions of the people until the seed which is Christ should come. See Gal. 3:19. Not one jot or tittle was to pass from the law as long as heaven and earth is here, says Jesus (Matt. 5:17-19). His conclusion of this saying is found in the context, that for this reason anyone breaking the least one of the commandments and teaching men so will be the least in the kingdom. My opponent better take earnest heed to this warning, for he is surely teaching men to disregard these commandments, and the least in the kingdom are to be gathered out as tares and cast into the fire.

2. The command that Jesus gave to honor the sabbath down on this side of the cross, also stands just as he gave it in Matt. 24:20. My opponent has come far short of explaining away this solemn warning and command of our Saviour. Jesus told his followers to pray that their flight from Jerusalem would not be on the sabbath day or in the winter. Jerusalem as Jesus knew would not be destroyed until long after his crucifixion. It was not destroyed until 70 years down in this age. Therefore, the sabbath by a command of Jesus was regarded and observed by his followers then. Why does not our opponent just admit this, and tell the people that the sabbath is still holy, and that God still wants us to regard it? He has tried to answer this, first by saying the gates of Jerusalem were closed on the sabbath was why Jesus told them to pray that they would not have to flee on that day. Then we showed that Jesus was speaking of the land of Judea and not of Jerusalem, and there was no wall around Judea; but now he vainly tries to make it appear that if it were because the sabbath was holy that Jesus did not want his followers to flee on that day, that the winter would also be holy as he also mentioned the winter, but surely the readers will be able to see the folly of such an answer. His people would be subject to wind, rain and snow and have much suffering in the winter, and he knew God's sabbath was still the sabbath and therefore commanded them to pray that they would not have to break it by fleeing on that day, and having to carry burdens from their homes, which God had repeatedly forbidden them to do on the sabbath.

3. Another argument fully sustaining my proposition has not been overthrown; viz., That the seventh day sabbath is traced through the scriptures from the beginning

of the world, and even into the age to come, is proof that God.still regards this time holy and expects us to regard it as such for him, not using it for our own selfish purposes. Elder Porter seems to believe that the prophet Amos spoke of a time when the sabbath would end (Amos 8:5-9), but the prophet **did not** say the sabbath would end when the sun went down at noon. This is a far fetched conclusion. God spoke definitely here of when his judgments would come upon the Jews because they wanted the sabbath over that they might sell and get gain through deceit. Amos was not speaking here of when the institution would end. The people were wicked at heart, and keeping only the law according to the letter. They could hardly wait until the sun went down, ending the sabbath day, so they could open their stores and go on with their dishonest business. Please read this scripture, and prayerfully judge for yourself, if God promised them the sabbath would end when the sun went down at noon, or if he promised to bring judgments upon them for their wickedness when the sun went down at noon. The judgments upon the Jews and persecutions ever since is proof that God still regards his sabbath and commandments, and now destruction is coming upon the Gentile nations for the same offenses. The Jews, however, are returning to Jerusalem and keeping the sabbath and accepting Jesus as their Saviour. He also claims that as the sabbath is not mentioned from Adam to Moses it was not kept as an institution during this period, but the sabbath is not mentioned either from Moses to Elijah which is a longer period than from Adam to Sinai, but he will not deny that it was observed during this time. The Passover is not spoken of either for over a thousand years after being given; circumcision from Joshua to John the Baptist; sabbatical year for 900 years; then why assume that because the sabbath was not mentioned from Adam to Moses it was not kept then? It is up to him to furnish proof that it was not kept. The fact that God made the sabbath and blessed it at creation (Gen. 2:1-3), and then Jesus tells us it was made for **man** (Mark 2:27, 28) is sufficient proof to those who want the truth. Jesus did not say it was made for the Jew, but for man, and man was made at creation. The sabbath was observed by Jesus and all of his apostles and is to be observed in the new heaven and earth (Isa. 66:23); therefore, this evidence still stands and the sabbath should be kept, and is being kept by God's children today, as he leads them into the light. Many are accepting the true sabbath all over the world, and many more are going to do so, as the Holy Spirit takes up its abode in their hearts and leads the honest ones into this precious truth.

4. Another argument set forth for the continuation of the sabbath commandment in this age is found in Heb. 4:4-9. Our opponent claims this does not mean the sabbath of the commandments, but as we have shown that the word sabbatismos is used in verse 10 which refers to a sabbath rest, we have the word of God on our side in this point of contention. He admits that the word "sabbatismos" is used here instead of "katapausis," but concludes by saying, "it does not refer to the seventh day." He does not deny it refers to a sabbath rest, for the marginal reading says "the keeping of a sabbath." Hence the text does teach that there remains the keeping of a sabbath for the **people of God.** It does not remain for anyone else, and when the Gentiles take hold of the covenant relationship with God that gives them life eternal, they will keep this sabbath "that remains for the people of God." He cites Mark 2:27 where sabbaton is used and says it is the subject of the sentence, singular number, third person, and nominative case, the same as the word sabbatismos in the text under question; and then he admits that one is neuter gender, while the other is masculine. The fact remains exactly as I stated previously that this word refers to a day of rest, and my opponent will not deny this. The next verse then tells us to enter into this rest as God did his. The 4th verse tells us that God rested on the seventh day; hence, we are here commanded to do likewise and to rest on the sabbath day, the seventh day of the week in this age. He says the rest spoken of in verse 10 means the eternal rest. How does he know? The margin of my Bible says it means "the keeping of a sabbath." Why and on what authority

does he say it means something else? This text is such strong argument that he must put forth great effort to destroy it. It adds great weight in sustaining my proposition. What he says about it meaning the future rest does not change the reading of the scripture, for it says God entered into his rest on the seventh day of the week (verse 4) ; so it is the seventh day of the week God is talking about, for that is what he says. Then he tells us to enter into our rest as 'God did his, because there remains a rest for the people of God. Dear reader, if you are one of the people of God, you will be spending some time every day in prayer and thanksgiving to God, seeking him for wisdom and power, and you will be led into keeping all of God's commandments. The natural mind is not subject to the law of God and cannot be (Rom. 8:7), but the spiritual mind is subject to the law, and it does not find the commandments of God to be grievous (1 John 5:3).

The ten commandment law, of which the sabbath is one precept, stood out prominently in the Old Testament above everything else in the religious rites pertaining to salvation. It was the dial around which true relationship between man and man, and man and God rotated, and there is nothing in the nature of any part of this law that would give it a limited jurisdiction, or necessitate its abolition. Every text of Paul's writings which might at first seem to teach that the ten commandments were made void through Jesus Christ will have an entirely different setting when given careful study and consideration. Peter is right when he says Paul's writings are hard to be understood, and certain ones wrest them to their own destruction. Anyone knows that to interpret Paul's writings of the law in such a way to make it void would increase wickedness, but to interpret them as I am doing which shows the perpetuity and binding force of the ten commandments will increase righteousness and godliness. Paul's teaching throughout the New Testament is that sinners are under the law, and those who keep the law are not under its condemnation. He speaks to sinners who desire to be under the law, and we have many of them today, who walk after their own lusts because they enjoy this life. These are the ones the law was made for. The Lord plainly says the law was not made for a righteous man but for the sinner. If all were righteous, there would be no need for the law, as Paul says. Our opponent does not like this explanation, and as negative argument gives the text where Jesus was made under the law. Now, it is true that Jesus was not a sinner, but the Lord does say plainly that Christ was "made to be sin for us who knew no sin, that we might be made the righteousness of God in him" (2 Cor. 5:21). In Gal. 4:4, 5 it says: "Jesus was made of woman, made under the law to redeem them that were under the law." This does show clearly that he died to redeem sinners, and that sinners are the ones under the law, and not the righteous people. Righteous people have been redeemed from sin by the blood of Jesus and brought out from under the law. Be careful, reader, that we do not wrest these writings of Paul to our destruction, as Peter gives us warning. Why did not our opponent refer to all of the text instead of just part? The rest of it shows clearly why Jesus was made under the law, or made sin for us, that he might redeem them that are under the law. Christians are not under the law but under grace, as Paul says, because they have been brought out from under it, from under its penalties. Paul says "The flesh lusteth against the spirit and the spirit against the flesh, and these are contrary the one to the other, so that ye cannot do the things that ye would, but if ye be led by the spirit ye are not under the law" (Gal. 5:17, 18). In the next verse he gives a list of the manifestations of the works of the flesh, adultery, murder, hatred, etc., which when people do they are under the law, for when they by following the spirit bear the opposite fruit they are no longer under the law. This is absolute proof that my explanation of Paul's writings on this law subject is correct, and that I am not wresting them to my destruction. We will now examine his other negative text: "And unto the Jew I became a Jew that I might gain the Jews: to them that are under the law as under the law that I might gain them that are under the law." This proves that it was another class other than the Jew as a nation who were under the law, and again confirms the truth of my interpretation of the law question. Paul goes right on in the next verse as follows: "To them that are without law, as without law (being not without the law to God, but under the law to Christ), that I might gain them." This further establishes the strength of this truth, as those under the law to Christ are lost, for Paul says he desires to save them. Hence, being under the law, as expressed in the New Testament does not mean being under its dominion or jurisdiction, but it means more than that—it means under its power and condemnation because of having broken or disregarded it.

5. We have previously proven that the Holy Spirit, in this age, called the day the Jews were worshipping on **"The sabbath day"** (Acts 13:42, 44; also Acts 17:2, and 18:4 and other scripture). Furthermore, the Holy Spirit spoke in this age as follows, telling us definitely that the day preceding the first day of the week is the sabbath. It reads: "In the end of the sabbath as it began to dawn toward the first day of the week, came Mary Magdalene and the other Mary to see the sepulchre" (Matt. 28:1). Hence, the day before the first day of the week is the sabbath in this age just as it was in the old. It was because of these scriptures and others equally as strong, that Elder Porter, in his previous negative, admitted that the seventh day of the week was the sabbath, and that it still is the sabbath. A frank admission indeed. As he now agrees with us on the sabbath question, surely he will keep it. His objection has been that he could not find a command where we were told to keep it in the New Testament, but now we have given him an abundance of scripture showing:

1. That Jesus kept it (Luke 4:14-16), and commanded it to be regarded and kept in this age (Matt. 24:20), when Rome conquered Palestine, 70 A.D.

2. Paul commanded us to enter into our rest as God did his, after telling us plainly that God rested on the seventh day of the week (Heb. 4:4-9).

3. Paul made tents on the other days of the week, but

kept the sabbath and preached to both Jews and Géntiles on that day (Acts 18:1 to 11; also Acts 13:42, 44 and 16:12-15 and 17:2).

4. We are commanded to keep the commandments of God in this age, and the law of God of which the seventh day sabbath always composed a prominent part, since God's commandments were given (James 2:10, 11; 1 John 3:4 and 5:3; Rev. 14:12; 22:14). We have given abundance of proof that it was the law of pardon through Moses with many yearly sabbaths and bloody sacrifices that ended and not the ten commandment law of God, and have thus made harmony and not contradiction in the New Testament teaching regarding the law.

PORTER'S THIRD NEGATIVE

I did not say that Elder Dugger said the two commandments—to love the Lord, and to love thy neighbor—were separate from the ten. But my friend says that "Jesus made this statement." I thank you, Dugger, for that admission. That is the very thing I was contending for and the thing you deny. So Jesus made the statement that you deny. You say reference is made to the ten commandments but that Jesus made a statement to the contrary. That is true, of course, and you could not meet the arguments I made. Jesus mentioned five of the second group of the ten commandments, and then added "Thou shalt love thy neighbor as thyself" as a distinct commandment (Matt. 19: 18, 19). And Paul called it "another commandment" after specifying five of the second group of the ten (Rom. 13:9). Why didn't Dugger make an effort to answer these arguments? He knew it was better to let them alone. Neither commandment is contained in the ten, as Dugger well knows, but they are distinct, separate commandments found in Deut. 6:5 and Lev. 19:18, in what Dugger calls the law of Moses. So the greatest commandments are not in the ten. "On these two commandments hang all the law and the prophets" (Matt. 22:40). He did not say "these two commandments make all the law." And where can

Dugger find room for "the prophets" in the ten commandments, if that is all Jesus referred to? He'll not answer;
so don't be disappointed. Certainly love for God and man
is embraced in the ten commandments, but love is included
in all of God's commandments; and Jesus and Paul distinguish between "these two" and the ten commandments.
Dugger is hopelessly lost at this point.

My friend says: "Jesus never did teach the people to
keep the old sacrifices of the law of Moses." When Jesus
cleansed a leper he told him: "Go thy way, show thyself to
the priest, and **offer for thy cleansing those things which
Moses commanded**" (Mark 1:44; Luke 5:14). The sacrifices
required by Moses can be found in Lev. 14. Elder Dugger,
read these verses and be ashamed of yourself! Jesus did
not teach against the sacrifices of the law during his personal ministry. Sacrifices were made for him (Luke 2:21-
24) and he told his disciples to observe the requirements of
Moses (Matt. 23:2, 3). He lived under the law (Gal. 4:4).
He was subject to the law. And I challenge my friend to
prove that the Jewish priests were against him because he
opposed the sacrifices required by Moses. He said such was
true; now let him prove it! But I'll not be disappointed
if he fails to produce the proof, for I know he cannot find
it.

Neither did I say that Paul never mentioned the sabbath
after he announced that he was turning to the Gentiles.
I said that no mention is made of any meeting **in Corinth** on
the sabbath after Paul turned from the Jews to the Gentiles
(Acts 18:4-6). The sabbath meetings in Corinth were in
the Jewish synagogues, and if such meetings were held on
the sabbath there after he turned to the Gentiles, why
did not my friend give us the proof. Certainly Paul mentioned the sabbath on other occasions. It was after this
that Paul said the sabbath had been taken away and nailed
to the cross (Col. 2:14-16). The meeting by the riverside
(Acts 16:12-14) was not in a Jewish synagogue, Dugger
claims. I gladly admit that. But they were Jewish wor-
shipers—not Christians—for they had never heard the gos-

pel. Paul preached to them and converted them to Christ
after they had been holding such meetings on the sabbath.
Why can't he find a group of Christians who were keeping
the sabbath? It is not on record.

Friend Dugger still claims Christians are required to
keep the Old Testament feasts. He says: "The apostles
kept the first Pentecost." My! My! What is the matter
with my friend? The first Pentecost was kept in the days
of Moses, hundreds of years before the apostles were ever
born. But perhaps he meant the first Pentecost after
Jesus arose. But he will have to prove they kept that.
His reference, Zech. 14:9-17, to prove Pentecost will be
kept in the new earth, **does not even mention Pentecost.**
It mentions "the feast of tabernacles"—not Pentecost. My
friend must be excited. But the application he makes of
this passage will require the re-establishment of those
shadows and figures in the eternal age that belonged to
an age and a system that was inferior even to the Christian
age. He reverses type and antitype. He would re-institute
the old Jewish system, inferior to the gospel, for the
eternal age. Any man's position is wrong that demands
such an interpretation of scripture. Neither does Isa. 66:23
give him any help. This was formerly introduced to prove
the sabbath binding in the next age. If so, it binds also
the feast of "new moons." Dugger is willing to have the
new moon feast over there if he can manage to get the
sabbath in. But Paul says the "new moon" was done
away, and that it was a shadow of things to come (Col.
2:14-17). Dugger said it belonged to the law of Moses.
But now he thinks it will all come back in the next age.
Well, verse 21 mentions the priests and Levites. Will
Dugger say the Levitical priesthood will be brought back?
If so, what about animal sacrifice? What good will the
priesthood do without the sacrifices that go with it? You
can see my friend's position will require a "let-down," a
returning to an inferior system, in the eternal age. "From
one new moon to another, and from one sabbath to another"
does not mean that either will be kept. But "from one to

another" may easily include all the time between them; hence, a daily, a perpetual service, instead of sabbath keeping.

My friend is still in trouble about the two covenants. He thinks my position would make the New Covenant nearly like the Old Covenant, for only one commandment would be left out; but God said the New Covenant was "not according to the old." Since, then, Dugger would have the same ten commandments, he would have the new covenant **exactly like the old.** The ten commandments were the very heart of the old covenant, but there were many commandmnts in that old covenant besides the ten. So my position does not even make the new resemble the old. The difference between the two, Dugger says, is that laws of God were written in stone under the old, but written in the heart under the new. That is one of the differences. But Heb. 8:9-12 shows a number of other differences. Dugger says: "Under the new covenant this same law" is written on the heart. That is the point he must prove. The Bible says "God's laws" would be written in the heart, but where does it say, "this same law"? Dugger said that; the book of God says no such thing. If so, let him give it! He still contends that the covenant done away was Israel's agreement in Ex. 19. I showed him that God said: "If . . . . ye will keep **my covenant**" (Ex. 19:5). God did not say: "**Your** agreement." Furthermore, God said they broke the covenant which **he made** with them—not the agreement which **they made** (Jer. 31:32). And it was the covenant that **God made**—not Israel's agreement—that was done away (Heb. 8:7, 13). I introduced all of these points in my other negative. What did my friend say about them? Absolutely nothing! He knew the argument was unanswerable. But the reader will wonder why he did not at least try. His utter silence with respect to many of my arguments will react upon him when the discussion is read.

We are informed that Jesus removed the restrictions concerning the sabbath and changed the manner of keeping it. Indeed! What, then, must men do to keep the sabbath? Let Dugger tell us the new manner of sabbath keeping since all the restrictions are removed. Watch and see if he says anything about it.

My opponent's position on Gal. 4:22-31 is amusing. He says: "Hagar represents the futile efforts of man through his own strength and power." But Paul says Hagar is the covenant from Mount Sinai (Gal. 4:24, 25). Now, take which you will. I believe Paul is right. And regarding that covenant from Sinai, Dugger says in this third affirmative: "The ten commandments were therefore the words of the covenant." But the new covenant, according to Paul, was represented by Sarah. And he says, "We are not children of the bondwoman (the covenant from Sinai) but of the free" (Gal. 4:31). However, my friend and his people are children of the Sinai covenant, and are, therefore, not heirs with the children of the freewoman. Hagar was cast out; and the old covenant was done away. No need to still hold to it.

My opponent tells us that the Gentiles, as Gentiles, cannot be saved today. They must first become Jews. There is not a passage in all of God's book that even intimates that Gentiles must become fleshly Jews in order to be saved. Rom. 10:12 is given to prove "there is no difference between the Jew and the Gentile." I fully accept that, but it upsets my friend's argument. He is insisting that there is a difference; that the Jew is favored and the Gentile must become a fleshly Jew. If that is so, there is a difference and Paul was mistaken about it. The New Testament plainly teaches that fleshly Jewish relationship means nothing under the gospel. Paul said: "There is neither Jew nor Greek . . . . for ye are all one in Christ Jesus." Dugger says: "Paul, you are mistaken. There is no Gentile in Christ, but all are Jews." Well, I'll take Paul; you can take Dugger if you want to. Both Jews and Gentiles become spiritual Israel in Christ; but the Jew, as a fleshly Jew, is no more that than is the Gentile in the flesh. Both Jew and Gentile become "Abraham's seed" by being baptized into Christ (Gal. 3:27-29). But neither Jew nor Gentile is Abraham's spiritual seed until baptized into Christ. Both must do the same thing and become "Abraham's seed" in exactly the same way. Hence, there is no difference between them. But there is a differnce, according to my friend. "The seed of Abraham" to whom the promise was made, according to Gal. 3:16, was Christ. The very verse says so; so it fails to help my friend Dugger. At last Dugger tells us why the Babylonians were not sent into Judean captivity for failing to keep the sabbath. It was because they were not Jews, and the law could not apply to them till they became Israel. Good! That ruins all of his arguments regarding the sabbath requirement being of universal application. In his first affirmative Dugger said: "God's people of **all nationalities,** whether Jew or Gentile, were duty bound to observe the sabbath." But now he **backs out** of that and says that no such duty existed unless they first became Jews. I wonder which of these positions he wants. Likewise he said in his first affirmative: "The **Gentiles** must realize that divine ownership, and keep God's day." Were the Babylonians Gentiles? Then they had to keep the sabbath or suffer the consequences; but Dugger said they did not have to suffer the consequences because they had not become Jews! My friend is so terribly mixed he will never get straightened on this proposition until he gives up his false theory. He also said in that affirmative: "The Gentiles today . . . . will soon be victims of his wrath" because they are failing to keep the sabbath. Why subject Gentiles today to his wrath and let the Babylonians go free? Is God a respecter of persons? The Gentiles were strangers, my friend says, because they had no hope, "consequently, they were not expected to keep the sabbath." God does not say in Eph. 2:12 that the Gentiles were strangers "because they had no hope." Rather, they had no hope as a result of being strangers. They "were strangers from the covenants of promise." This shows they were not included in the covenants then. And Dugger admits all of this by saying "they were not expected to keep the sabbath." That being true, he gives up his former arguments that the Gentiles were to keep the sabbath day. If it applied to them, why did not

God expect them to keep it? I challenge him to answer this question.

Dugger says the ten commandments are included "wherever we are told to keep the commandments of God in the New Testament." That is his statement—not the word of God. He wants me to prove the sabbath is not included, and he seems to forget the laboring oar is in his hand. He must prove that it **is included!** He has admitted that God had other commandments beside the ten. Then why is the sabbath always meant? I might as reasonably say: "To destroy Amalek, their flocks and herds, were commandments of God. Therefore, wherever we are told to keep the commandments of God in the New Testament these are included." That would have just as much sense and reason in it as the argument of Dugger for the ten commandments.

But "James 2:8, 11 mentions two of the ten commandments." Yes, but it **does not mention the sabbath.** Besides, it mentions one of the commandments in "the law of Moses" (verse 8). Compare Lev. 19:18. So if mentioning two of the ten binds all the ten on us, then mentioning one of the commandments of Moses would bind all the law of Moses on us. There is no way to escape this conclusion. Although I called his attention to this fact in my first negative, Dugger has passed it by in utter silence. He feels the force of it and knows he cannot answer it.

In Rom. 7:7 is found the statement: "Thou shalt not covet." Then in verse 12 Paul says: "The law is holy, and the commandment holy, and just, and good." Dugger thinks this binds the sabbath on Christians, although not a word is said about the sabbath. All commandments that God gives are holy, just and good. And "Thou shalt not covet" is a holy commandment. It is a part of "the law of liberty" now (Jas. 2:12), and the law that contains it is holy, just as the law that contained it in the Old Testament was holy then.

Paul's reference to the law in Rom. 2:21-25 was for the purpose of showing the Jew that his attitude was wrong even while he was under the law of the Old Testament, for he was then a violator of the law, but claimed justification on the mere fact that he had the law. The context clearly shows this. But just admit for argument's sake that reference is made to Christians. What then? Not a word is said about the sabbath. However, it refers to the Jewish attitude under the law. Verse 25 says: "For verily circumcision profiteth, if thou keep the law." Is my friend willing to bind circumcision on men because of this statement? Paul says that circumcision in this age avails, or profits, nothing (Gal. 5:1-6). Hence, the statements of Rom. 2 refer to the Jewish attitude while he was under the law.

I have already shown that Psa. 111:7, 8 cannot be limited to the ten commandments, but it refers to "all his commandments." I have two questions for my friend. 1. Did God have any commandments besides the ten? 2. Has any of God's commandments ever been discontinued? I demand that he answer these questions. He has one more chance to do so. But if he answers them, he ruins his argument; so watch him ignore them as he has so many others.

Friend Dugger dies hard on the "two laws." He has affirmed that the ten commandments was the law of God, and all the rest was the law of Moses—that the law of Moses was done away, but the law of God remains. I showed that God gave "the law of Moses" (Ezra 7:6). And Moses gave "God's law" (Neh. 10:29). I also showed that God gave "the book of the law of Moses" (Neh. 8:1). And Moses gave "the book of the law of the Lord" (2 Chron. 34:14). I proved from Neh. 8: 1, 2, 3, 8 that the two expressions are used interchangeably; therefore, mean the same thing. I gave 2 Chron. 31:3; 35:26; Luke 2:23, 24 to prove the law of God included many things besides the ten commandments. What reply did he make to all of these arguments? Absolutely none! He insists there is a distinction between the two laws but made no effort to meet my arguments. He does admit this: "Those given through Moses would, of course, be God's law too." This admission ruins his whole argument. If that given through

Moses is "God's law," as Dugger now admits, then that
fanciful distinction he has tried to make between "the
law of Moses" and "the law of God" blows up from within.
Thank you, Dugger, for bidding your argument "good-bye."

My friend claims the ten commandments "constitute the
complete relationship between man and man, and man and
God," but "the other was to pardon the transgressor."
Note the words "complete relationship." That means it
covers the whole thing. Dugger, answer this: Is it wrong for
a man to "bear false witness for his neighbor"? Is it wrong
for him to "bear false witness against his enemy"? Don't
dodge now. Come right on and answer. If you don't answer, the reader will think you are afraid. Here is a relationship between man and man, and I challenge you to
find it in the ten commandments. You know you can't
do it, and the reader will know it when you fail to answer.
God said in the law of Moses: "Thou shalt not lie with
mankind, as with womankind" (Lev. 18:22). Did that
"pardon the transgressor"? Or did it not constitute sin?
Don't answer, for if you do, you will ruin your entire
argument. All this shows how badly mixed my friend is
about the "two laws."

He returns to 1 John 5:3; 1 Cor. 7:19; Rev. 14:12 and
Rev. 12:17, which show the importance of keeping the
"commandments of God." Then he says I must prove this
is not the ten commandments. But he immediately says:
"Yes, we surely admit that God has given different commandments at different times." It took me a long time
to get him to say whether God has any commandments
beside the ten, but he has finally said, "Yes." That puts
the burden of proof right back on him. As he admits God
has other commandments he will have to prove these passages refer to the ten. That is his task, and it is begging
him to begin. I deny that the ten are referred to. Let
him offer his proof. Reference is to the commandments
of the gospel—not to Old Testament commandments.

A return is made to 1 John 3:4; Rom. 7:12; Rom. 3:31 and
James 2:11, 12 to prove "the law" is binding. One question
will settle this. Does "the law" in the New Testament

always mean the ten commandments? If he answers this, his argument is gone. Just note how he lets this question alone.

Dugger now insists that the law that Jesus fulfilled, and therefore ended, was the bloody, sacrificial law of pardon. Well, the law that Jesus said he "came to fulfill" was the same law about which he said "one jot or one tittle shall in no wise pass from" it "till all be fulfilled" (Matt. 5:17, 18). If the reader will read this passage, he can easily see that. My friend says that Jesus said one jot or one tittle would not pass from the law "as long as heaven and earth are here." But Jesus did not say that. He said "as long as heaven and earth are here" (till heaven and earth pass), "one jot or one tittle shall in no wise pass from the law, **till all be fulfilled.**" But my opponent leaves out the modifying clause, "till all be fulfilled"; and when he leaves that out, he changes the meaning of the passage completely. Saying it will not pass "till all be fulfilled" is saying that it will pass **when fulfilled.** And the text says that Jesus "came to fulfill" that very law. If he did what he said he came to do, that law was fulfilled, and then it passed. Dugger admits that whatever law Jesus fulfilled passed away. All right, then, Jesus said he "came to fulfill" this law that Dugger says would never be done away. I called his attention to the meaning of "till" in such expressions, in my first negative, but so far he has never had enough courage to try to answer the argument made. Joseph knew not Mary **"till she had brought forth her firstborn son"** (Matt. 1:25). Does this mean that Joseph never knew Mary? Tell us, Dugger. And Paul's enemies bound themselves under an oath "that they would not eat nor drink **till they had killed Paul"** (Acts 23:12). Does this mean they would never eat nor drink? When Dugger leaves out "till all be fulfilled" from Matt. 5:18, he changes the Lord's meaning; when he leaves it in, he ruins his argument.

And he is still ruined on his argument on Matt. 24:20. If "pray that your flight be not on the sabbath" makes the sabbath holy in A.D. 70, then "pray that your flight be not in the winter" will make the season holy too. Dugger thinks the reader can see the "folly of this answer." Well, it is a poor rule that won't work both ways; and if it makes one holy, it makes the other holy. But Dugger says it means there would be difficulties in the winter. Exactly so. And there would be difficulties facing them if they had to flee on the Jewish sabbath. And the passage proves neither a holy day or a holy season. And the argument is still lost to Dugger.

I am perfectly willing for the reader to decide if Amos 8:5-9 says the sabbath would "be gone" when the sun went "down at noon." Read it for yourself and compare Mark 15:33.

Dugger now admits the sabbath was not mentioned from Adam to Moses, but he says it was neither mentioned from Moses to Elijah, a longer period; nor was the Passover mentioned for over a thousand years after given; and circumcision was not mentioned from Joshua to John the Baptist. This is a wonderful (?) argument. Any one knows that a law once given remains in force till repealed, even if it is never mentioned again, but that does not prove it was in force before it was given. My friend reasons the sabbath was in force for 2500 years before mentioned and tries to prove it by its not being mentioned any more from Moses to Elijah. By the same argument you can prove the passover existed during the first 2500 years of the world's history, for Dugger says it was not mentioned for a thousand years after it was given. If it existed during that thousand years, it would prove, according to Dugger, that it also existed during the 2500 years in which it was not mentioned before Moses. If it works this way on the sabbath, it will work the same way on the passover and on circumcision. So we could prove circumcision existed for two thousand years before Abraham's day. A man is hard pressed for an argument to depend upon a matter of this kind. Not only is the argument weak, but my friend shows a lack of Bible knowledge in making it. Is it true that the passover is not spoken of for over a thousand years after being given? It was given in Exodus

12. In Num. 9:1-5, in the second year after it was given, it was mentioned and kept. In Deut. 16:1-5, shortly before Israel entered Canaan, it is mentioned again. And in Josh. 5:10, 11, forty years after it was given, it is mentioned again. My opponent should compare his ideas with the Bible before making such reckless statements and save himself some embarrassment. And what of circumcision? He says it is not mentioned "from Joshua to John the Baptist." However, Jeremiah, who lived about 800 years after Joshua and 600 years before John the Baptist, mentioned it (Jer. 9:25). Hence, Dugger's argument, besides being weak, is based upon a misstatement of facts.

Yes, Mark 2:27, 28 says "the sabbath was made for man." But it does not say it was made **when** man was made. And I wonder if my friend thinks the Jew was not man. When made for the Jew it was made for **man,** for the Jew was not a horse or a turkey gobbler, but he was man.

As to Heb. 4:4-9 my opponent says that Paul "commands us to enter into our rest as God did his." There is no such commandment found in this text. The statement of Dugger is a perversion of what the passage says. Here is what it says: "For he that is **entered** into his rest, he also **hath ceased** from his own works, as God did from his" (Verse 10). Can't my friend distinguish between this and a commandment? On another occasion God said: "Blessed are the dead which die in the Lord from henceforth: Yea, saith the spirit, that they may rest from their labors; and their **works do follow them**" (Rev. 14:13). So the man who thus "hath ceased from his works," according to Paul, "is entered into his rest," even as God entered into his rest when he ceased from his work. Our attention is called to the marginal reading of verse 9, "the keeping of a sabbath." But to help my friend it would have to read: "The keeping of **the sabbath.**" That is what even the marginal reading does not say. But it is claimed that I will admit that this refers to a day. I will admit that it refers to "the day of eternal rest" but not to a 24-hour day. It is that rest that we must labor to enter (verse 12), which we may fail to enter just as Israel failed to enter Canaan. This is the rest that remains for the people of God. No man would ever have thought of anything else if he had not been searching for proof of a theory that lacks New Testament sanction.

If any man ever wrested the writings of Paul, Elder Dugger has done that regarding the expression, "under the law." Paul said Christians "are not under the law, but under grace" (Rom. 6:14). Dugger says "under the law" means under condemnation for violating the law. In John 1:17 we read: "For the law was given by Moses, but grace and truth came by Jesus Christ." So the law means the system given by Moses, and grace means the system that came by Jesus. If "under the law" means under condemnation of the law, then "under grace" means under condemnation of the system Jesus gave. If not, let Dugger tell us why. So his interpretation of Paul's writings puts all Christians under condemnation. Of course, Christians are not under the law, because the law has been abolished (Col. 2:14-17). And Dugger makes Jesus guilty of sin, for he was "under the law" (Gal. 4:4). He tries to fix this by an appeal to 2 Cor. 5:21 that Jesus "was made to be sin for us." Jesus was made to be sin for us when he bore our sins on the cross, or became our sin-offering. However, the word "made" in Gal. 4:4 is from the Greek "genomenon," which means "born." He was **"made** of a woman, **made** under the law"—**"born** of a woman, **born** under the law." So Jesus was under the law as soon as he was born, and not merely when he became our sin-offering on the cross. Dugger has not even touched the argument. To be under the law was to be under its jurisdiction, or authority, and Christians thus are **not** under the law. Certainly those "under the law" needed to be redeemed, according to Gal. 4:5, for that law could not give them life (Gal. 2:21; 3:21). Hence Jesus died "for the redemption of the transgressions that were **under the first testament**" (Heb. 9:15), as well as for others. And when a man goes back under the law now, he still needs redemption. I agree with Paul's statement in Gal. 5:18 that "if ye be led of the spirit, ye are not under the law." That proves that Dugger and his

people are not being led by the spirit, for they desire to
be under the law (Cf. Gal. 4:21). In 1 Cor. 9:20-22 Paul
clearly showed that while "to them that are without law"
he became "as without law," yet he realized that he was
"not without law to God, but under the law to Christ."
If "under the law" means condemnation, then Paul stood
condemned, for he referred to himself as being "under the
law to Christ." He mentions the Jews, them that are
under the law, them that are without law, and the weak.
If the Jews and them that were under the law were not
the same people, let Dugger tell us who they were, and
then tell us who the other two classes were. But I want
to give my friend a question that will settle this matter.
Paul said: "What things soever the law saith, it saith to
them who are **under the law**" (Rom. 3:19). Hence, the
law says **not one thing to any body** except those who are
under the law. I ask my friend: Does the law say **anything**
to you? No evading this question. It will clarify the whole
situation. So tell me, please. Does the law say **anything**
to you? If not, then upon what principle do you claim
the sabbath to be binding on you? If so, then you are
under the law; and you will have to admit you are under
condemnation or change your position on the meaning of
these words. So face the question with courage and give
us an answer. I don't believe you will answer the question,
for it is a death blow to your theory if you do. But I am
willing to be surprised and I await your answer. If you
don't come through with an answer to this question, the
readers will easily see who is wresting the writings of Paul
to his own destruction.

The fact that the seventh day of the week still retained
the name, "the sabbath," after the cross of Christ does not
prove it still binding. The passover and Pentecost still
retained their names, but they are not binding on men.

Yes, Jesus kept the sabbath, but he was under the law
(Gal. 4:4). For the same reason he was circumcised. But
that does not bind it on Christians.

And Paul did not command any one "to enter into rest
as God did" in Heb. 4:4-9. Read this for yourself and

find the commandment. This has already been discussed.

Dugger says: "Paul kept the sabbath **and** preached on that day." His references say he **preached**; not a one of them says he "kept the sabbath."

And I agree that we are "to keep the commandments of God in this age." But my friend has admitted that God has many commandments besides the ten. So it is up to him to prove that any of these references, Jas. 2:10, 11; 1 John 3:4; 5:3; Rev. 14:12; 22:14, include the ten. This he has failed to do.

Now for another negative argument. Paul speaks of "the law" which was given "four hundred and thirty years after" the promise, or covenant, made with Abraham regarding his seed (Gal. 3:17). Then he tells us "the law . . . . was added because of transgressions, till the seed should come to whom the promise was made" (Gal. 3:19). But in verse 16 he said the seed was Christ. So "the law" given 430 years after the promise to Abraham was to last till Christ should come. But what law was given 430 years after the covenant with Abraham? The promise to Abraham was given in 1921 B.C. (Gen. 12:1-3). Then 430 years later than that would be 1491 years B.C. At that very time "the law" from Sinai was given (Ex. 20:1-17). And this was to last till Christ should come. He came and fulfilled it (Matt. 5:17, 18) and took it out of the way (Col. 2:14-17). That ended the sabbath unless Dugger can find it given this side of the death of Christ.

DUGGER'S FOURTH AFFIRMATIVE

I said it was Jesus that made the statement "On these two commandments hangs all the law and the prophets" (Matt. 22). On the commandment to love the Lord our God, etc. Elder Porter misquotes me by saying I said the ten commandments hung on the two commandments of love to God and love to our neighbor, but this was Jesus who said this instead of me (Matt. 19:16-22). Now for Porter to deny that the whole ten commandment decalogue does not hang on these two principles of love, is to deny the plain statement of the Lord Jesus.

Elder Porter makes another mistake by saying "to love God" is not mentioned in any of the ten commandments. Let us quote a part of one as follows, "Showing mercy unto thousands of them that **love** me and keep my commandments." This shows that the principle of love is the foundation of all the ten commandments just as Jesus said. The trouble is that people are "lovers of their own selves," as Paul said they would be in the last days (Timothy 3rd chapter), and they do not care for God, and will not honor his holy day. The carnal mind is "enmity against God, for it is not subject to the law of God, neither indeed can be" (Rom. 8:7). This is why people fight the law of ten commandments is because they are carnal, and cannot be subject to the fourth one, or keep the sabbath, for it is too unlike the popular customs of the world. Porter says. "Certainly love for God and man is embraced in the ten commandments." Then we ask why leave out the ten commandments, and take only the two commandments "love to God and love to man"? The only reason is to try to get rid of the sabbath of God, the day our heavenly Father blessed. But Jesus said the whole law and prophets hung on these principles. Then neither the law or prophets were done away with. Now we know fully that God has frequently commanded the people to love God and love their neighbor. Also that these are mentioned separate and apart from the ten commandments. But when Jesus gives them again and plainly says the whole law and prophets hang on them, and the greater is love to God, let us believe just what he says. Yes, Paul mentions five of the ten commandments, and then says, "If there be any other commandment it is briefly comprehended in the saying, "Thou shalt love thy neighbor as thyself" (Rom. 13:9, 10). God is included here as our neighbor, for surely one so good and one who has done so much for all of us would be included as our neighbor, and if we love him as we do ourselves, we will not commit any of the deeds against him such as taking his name in vain, worshiping other gods, or using the day he blessed and sanctified for our own personal secular work. We are commanded to keep it for

God, and God has repeatedly said he never changes, but is the same yesterday, to-day and forever.

Jesus did not teach the keeping of the old law of animal sacrifices for the forgiveness of sins, for he and the apostles always taught the people to believe on the Lord Jesus Christ and to keep the commandments to be saved. In the case of healing of the leper he did refer him to the priest. Elder Porter knows that with the preaching of John the Baptist, we were entering a new order of things, and a new system and plan for pardon was being established. It was through the blood of Jesus and not by the blood of animals, that people were to receive pardon and forgiveness of their sins, but the ten commandments of God are mentioned over and over again in the New Testament as the standard of right and wrong, and as the foundation of sin. Porter admits he keeps nine of them, then why not just go one step further and keep them all? Why leave just one out? We know why. It is because Sunday is the popular day of rest, and it is easy to be with the world and keep it. The fourth commandment is too much of a cross, too much of a separation from the world, and he cannot bear it. We have shown plainly that Gentile as well as Jewish Christians held meetings and observed the sabbath in the New Testament and previously given many passages in proof. In Acts 18th chapter Paul stayed a year and six months in one place and preached every sabbath to Jews and Greeks, and worked on the first day making tents. Surely this is sufficient proof.

Elder Porter claims that I am teaching the binding of the Old Testament feasts on Christians now, but he again misquotes and misrepresents me. Please re-read what I did say previously about this. The old feasts will not be kept as they were under the Mosaical order; far from that. God has his own plan about these things, and let us not question the word as he gives it. I said the apostles kept the first Pentecost, meaning of course the first one after the crucifixion of Jesus. I proved this by giving Acts 2nd chapter. Then again to prove that another would be kept in the kingdom I simply gave the scripture. If

Elder Porter wishes to deny this scripture as he has done, he must bear the responsibility of the matter. It is there, and it is God's plan, not mine, but I have shown that the services would not be the same, that blood sacrifices have ended and all the yearly sabbath days whereon they offered these things have also ended according to the law of Col. 2:14, that was against the apostles. This was the old law of pardon that was against them, and not the law of ten commandments. This Porter well knows.

As to the covenants, again we repeat, that the word covenant means "agreement" according to the English definition of words. We showed from the scriptures (Ex. 19) that God and Israel did make an agreement, or covenant which Israel broke and became scattered among all nations as a result. The agreement between God and Israel was the old covenant. They were to obey his voice, and he was to make of them a great nation. They failed to obey just as Adam and Eve did, and Israel was cast off. In this gospel age in the new covenant relationship God says he writes his laws in their minds and hearts (Heb. 8:8-10). Hence, God's laws (not animal sacrifices) but the ten commandments which included the sabbath, God writes on the hearts and minds of his people. Be careful, dear reader, lest you are cast off for the same reason that Israel was— disobedience. He repeatedly says I will not answer his argument. I am answering every argument he has put up, but they have been so few, and so flimsy, in his futile attempt to do away with God's law and God's sabbath, that we have had much repeating to do.

Yes, Jesus taught us to do good on the sabbath day, and not to carry burdens out of our houses or out of Jerusalem on that day. He told the apostles to pray that they would not have to flee from Judaea on the sabbath, when the land was surrounded by hostile armies.

Hagar represents the covenant from Sinai, because Israel tried to obey God in her own strength, and failed; thus she was cast off. This is how the comparison is made and Paul is exactly right about it too. The covenant from Sinai was the agreement between God and Israel. Israel agreed to do all that God commanded them to do, but they tried in their own strength just as Abraham tried to bring about the promised seed through Hagar instead of believing and trusting in the power of God. Had Israel prayed for the Holy Spirit to give them strength and power to do all that God commanded them to do, they could have kept their part of the agreement, and not been cast off as a nation. Gentiles today, who have become Israel through adoption, will also be cut off and cast away if they depend on their own strength to stand, for they will fail. The carnal mind is enmity against God; it is not subject to the law of God neither indeed can be, and that is why people want to get away with the ten commandments; and then when pressed admit they keep nine of them. Admitting they oppose the law because of the sabbath precept that separates them from the world. May God have mercy and give them the spirit of prayer that they may find grace and power and be found keeping all of the commandments and be saved, and not cast off as was Israel.

As to Gentiles being saved, we gave just what the New Testament said about this matter and no more. Elder Porter makes all kind of fun and ridicules what he says that I said, but is only scripture. Anyone knows, however, that Gentiles do not become fleshly Jews. I never said they did, but when God says we are Jews inwardly, and we are Israel, why try to deny it and make fun of it, and ridicule this gospel teaching? Elder Porter, this will get you nowhere with the readers of this book, and much less with God. In Romans 11th chapter we are plainly told how the Gentiles are saved. It is by adoption into the family of Abraham through Jesus Christ, and then we are Israel by adoption, and spiritually. The promises to Israel are ours, and the law to Israel is for us, and the sabbath to Israel is for us, for there is no difference between the Jew and the Gentile; we are all one in Christ Jesus (Gal. 3:27-29).

Everyone acquainted with the scriptures knows that the ten commandments of God occupy a prominent and outstanding place through the entire Bible. These ten commandments was the only part of the Bible God wrote himself and they were written on tables of stone as we have previously shown. They measured sin throughout the entire Bible and occupying, as these ten precepts do, a very prominent place, then why try to put them down on an equality with a local commandment given at a special time and for a special war to "destroy Amalek," as Porter mentions. This comes far short of proving that in the many places throughout the New Testament where we are told to keep the commandments of God that the sabbath is not included. You have failed, Elder Porter, to prove that the seventh day sabbath is not included, when I have positively proven and shown from many scriptures that the seventh day of the week was always included as one of these ten commandments of God. You must prove beyond any question of doubt that the sabbath is not included when the commandments of God are mentioned in the New Testament, or this argument stands just the same as other arguments you fail to disprove.

In James 2 the Royal Law in verse 8 is the ten commandment law, and not the law of Moses. Elder Porter, you know that the apostle James would not be teaching people to observe the law of Moses with all of its ritual and bloody sacrifices. You know they were ended, and why infer such a ridiculous thing, or accuse this beloved man of God of such. The prophet James speaks of this same law in chapter 1:24, 25 comparing it to the looking-glass. The ten commandment law always held this position and place, and it always pointed out sin. Then the Lord tells us if we keep the whole law and offend in one point, we are guilty of all. He means the very law he is speaking about, and from which he quotes two of the commandments; hence, the seventh day sabbath is included, and you better be careful, and get lined up with God. Jesus says if you break the least of these commandments and teach men so, you will be called least in the kingdom of heaven (Matt. 5:17-19), and the least are the tares to be plucked up and burned, he says. You are teaching men to break the fourth commandment which tells us plainly to keep the seventh day of the week, for God, as it is his holy day. You are therefore guilty before heaven, and will surely be one of the tares, according to the words of Jesus, unless you repent and change your ways.

He claims I have bidden good-by to my argument that there are two distinct laws set forth in the Bible. But, dear reader, how could I do this, when we read that God wrote one law on tables of stone with his own finger, and then wrote the other through Moses, by dictating it to him. I have given these references repeatedly (Exodus 24:12; 31:18 and 32:15; Deut. 10:1-4). How deceptive are the tactics of the enemy to blind the eyes of God's children to the truth. The history of the giving of all of these laws shows that God did make a separation. God did it, and not Dugger. Now Porter, or millions like him, cannot change it, and God's true children who pray to him daily for wisdom and guidance will see and understand it. Those who lean on their own understanding and do not seek God for wisdom will be deceived and lost. They will not be subject to the law of God, neither can be (Rom. 8:8). Now Porter says I have bidden good-by to my argument on the two separate codes of law, just because I admitted a truth I have always taught and always known, that God speaks of all his laws as his laws, for they are his laws, but the two were separated when given. Their very nature makes them different and separates them. The ten commandments stand forever just as Jesus and all the apostles teach us, and they will always stand; but the law of pardon under the Old Testament by the blood of animals is what ended. We have always known and taught that God had other commandments besides the ten, and have given scriptures to prove that many of his commandments ceased. Their very nature limited their period of service, and they were given only until "the seed should come" (Gal. 3). The commandments against the apostles ended at the cross as we have shown (Col. 2:14-16). The ten commandments were not against the apostles, and they are not against any other good person; hence, they were not the commandments or not the law that ended at the cross. As some law did end, and some commandments did cease, why claim it was the ten, or that the ten were even included, when God did have other commandments and other laws that were of a limited nature, and given only until Jesus came? Why mix them all together? Why try to do away with such just and righteous commandments as the ten? It is just to get rid of the 4th, and keep a day popular with the world, the counterfeit day of rest Sunday. There is no other motive that could be back of such an attempt. He admits that God brought back nine of these commandments. It seems strange indeed that he would blot out a law, and then resurrect all of it but just one commandment.

When the ten commandments of God were written with the finger of God on tables of stone, and are just seven times so declared in the Bible; when they constituted the fundamental basic law of mankind; when they measured the guilt of the transgressor all through the Old Testament age, and stood out pre-eminently above all other laws, as determining sin, and when every offender of any one of these commandments was stoned to death for the offense unless he had the priest kill an animal and use its blood for a means of pardon, anyone knows that these ten commandments stood out pre-eminently above all other laws and commandments. Therefore, when they are mentioned in the New Testament as the law of God and as the commandments of God just as in the Old Testament, and people are determined righteous for keeping them and as unrighteous for breaking them, Porter is the one to prove that when the commandments of God are mentioned in the New Testament they do not include the sabbath just as they did in the Old Testament. I have already proven that in every place where the law or commandments are spoken of as being abrogated in the New Testament, it always means the law of pardon, the law of animal sacrifices, and not the ten commandments. Therefore, as far as any evidence remains that any law is done away, there is none whatever that the ten commandments are abolished. He must therefore prove that the commandments of God, mentioned in the New Testament are not exactly the same ten commandments as mentioned the same way in the Old Testa-

ment. This he cannot do, for he had failed to give even
one text teaching they were abolished. In 1 John 3:4 it
reads: "This is the love of God that we keep his commandments, and his commandments are not grievous." Anyone
knows the commandments referred to here were not those
Paul said were against the apostles and contrary to them,
containing the yearly sabbath, and new moons, meat offerings, drink offerings mentioned in Col. 2:14, 16. Therefore,
these commandments spoken of here, and in the following
texts, were the ten commandments which God said were to
stand forever, and which Jesus said would not pass away as
long as heaven and earth were here. This law remains and
Elder Porter will have to prove beyond any question of
doubt that these commandments are not the ten, and that
the weekly sabbath is not therefore one of them (Romans
7:13 and 3:21; also James 2:10, 11; Romans 2:13, etc.).

He quotes the scripture that "Joseph knew not Mary till
she had brought forth her first born," and then asks: Does
that mean that he never knew her? No, dear reader, it
does not. He gives this to answer the argument set forth
by Jesus himself (Matt. 5:17-19) where he says not one
jot or tittle will pass from the law till heaven and earth
pass away. Joseph did not know Mary till she brought forth
her first born, but she brought forth her first born, then
he knew her. The difference is that heaven and earth have
not yet passed away, therefore every jot (abbreviation like
a period) and every tittle (the smallest letter) of the ten
commandment law remains. Jesus says those who teach
anyone to break the least of these commandments will be
the least in the kingdom. Porter is guilty, and he better
repent, or he will be one of the least, that is, one of the
tares to be gathered out and burned in the fire. The expression "Till all is fulfilled" which he tries to make us
believe refers to Jesus fulfilling the law and thus ending
it, is another deception. If fulfilling means to end the law,
then when Jesus was baptized it means baptism and all
righteousness is ended, for the exact expression is used.
See Matt. 3, last verses. The Lord does not teach that
baptism is ended, and all righteousness is gone; neither

does the same expression teach us that the law of commandments ended. Remember heaven and earth are still here.

Those who follow Jesus in daily prayer, for the Holy Spirit (Luke 11:11-13) will not want to do away with the ten commandments; neither will they rebel against the sabbath day that God blessed and made holy, but will find joy in doing God's will in every precept. Paul tells us that the natural mind is not subject to the law of God; neither indeed can be (Romans 8:8). This is why so many people want the law done away with, to get rid of the sabbath day, which is not popular to observe.

SUMMARY

We have fully established the fact that the sabbath of God was instituted at creation (Gen. 2:1, 2), and that it was made for **man** (Mark 2: 27, 28), and not for the Jew or any other special race. The scriptures from beginning to end mention this weekly sabbath as God's day, as belonging to God exclusively, and that he has given it to man to keep for God, and for his spiritual work here on earth. We have shown that God has tested man's loyalty to heaven and to God by their treatment of this particular day, blessed and made holy by the divine touch of the Almighty.

We have shown that Israel while in Egyptian slavery could not keep it, but as soon as God brought them forth from there, thus delivering them from bondage, he told them to keep his holy sabbath, and rained manna from heaven for forty years every day of the week, but the sabbath. Thus showing Israel what day the sabbath was, and proving that the entire system of God recognized this day as holy, by stopping the flow of manna on the sabbath for 40 years (Exodus 16th chapter). He thus proved again that this was not the day for temporal gain, or for obtaining the things needed for physical food, but it was, and still is, the day to receive spiritual refreshment from heaven, and engage in the work of God. It is not our day to use for personal work in any way, for it belongs to God, and we are to keep it for **him.**

We have shown that when the people went out on the seventh day to gather the manna they found none, and God condemned them saying :"How long refuse ye to keep my commandments and my laws" (Exodus 16:28). Israel had not yet reached Sinai; therefore, the ten commandments had not yet been given in their written form on stones. This proves therefore that the sabbath of creation, on the seventh day of the week was part of that law existing before Sinai, because in breaking the sabbath, Israel had broken God's commandments and laws.

We have shown also that over 400 years before Sinai Abraham was chosen because he kept God's commandments (Gen. 26:5). This scripture reads: "Because that Abraham obeyed my voice, and kept my charge, my commandments, my statutes and my laws." The commandments and law which Israel broke when they went out to gather manna on the sabbath, was the law of commandments existing before Sinai; and as it was these commandments, and this law which Abraham kept, what right has anyone to say with certainty that Abraham did not also keep God's sabbath, which is God's day, blessed and hallowed at creation? Such statements without scriptural proof come with rather an ill-grace to praying men and women who commune daily with their God, receiving divine power and heavenly wisdom, with which to judge and decide spiritual matters.

The very nature of every one of the ten commandments is such that those who love God will rejoice over them instead of finding them grievous. They cover fundamental, organic principles of righteousness that never can be altered or changed. This perfect relationship between man and God, and between man and man, set forth in this code of law is marvelous. The sabbath is the central hub around which the others cluster, for if we remember God's day and keep it for **him,** praying, studying, talking to neighbors about God, doing acts of brotherly love and kindness on that day, and worshiping God on the day **he** made holy, we take our minds away from the worldly cares, we rest our bodies physically, and have time to love God and think about him and eternity; and thus coming in contact with heaven's influences, we become magnetized more and more with his goodness and love, so the keeping of the other nine commandments becomes our very nature. We thus find ourselves doing God's will from the heart, and keeping the commandments because we are in a saved condition, and not trying vainly to keep them to get saved. It was evidently the same law of commandments which Abraham kept, that certain ones of Israel broke when they wanted to gather manna on the sabbath. As many scriptures tell us that God never changes, but is the same yesterday, to-day and forever, let us be careful, for if we even want to carry on our own work for temporal or physical gain, we may be sinning against God as Israel did when they wanted to gather more manna on his sabbath day. The ten commandment law evidently existed from the beginning of the world, because the same acts and deeds of mankind then against one another and against God would have been offensive to him just as they were a thousand or two thousand years later, because of his unchanging nature. He was just the same then as he is now. When Cain killed his brother he committed a sin. This sin is forbidden in the ten commandments. When Joseph first went to Egypt he was made overseer of a rich man's house, whose wife tried to entice Joseph to lay with her, but Joseph refused saying: "How can I do this great wickedness, and sin against God?" (Gen. 39:9). We find another of the ten commandments which was generally known to God's people to be a sin to transgress. It is further evident that Joseph and all other good men kept every one of these ten commandments at that time, for the acts these commandments forbid and condemn are such that all mankind knows them to be wrong, against one another or against God.

Now Elder Porter's argument is that because the sabbath is not particularly mentioned from Adam to Moses it did not exist, but we only have a very few pages of Bible history during this period, and we have shown that a number of other things required in the law of pardon under Moses were not mentioned either during long periods, even longer than this, yet they existed; therefore, such argument is not dependable, and makes nothing certain. Other evidence, some of which I have given, shows that the sabbath by its very nature, and being placed in the law and with other **commandments of an unchangeable** character did exist and was a part of the law and commandments that preceded Sinai.

I said the passover was not mentioned for 1000 years after it was given but it existed just the same. Now Porter gives texts to show it was mentioned 40 years after it was given, and vainly tries to destroy my argument, but reader, what is forty years in comparison to 1000 years. I knew it was mentioned for a brief period after it was instituted, but when mention of it ceased in the holy scriptures after it was given, it is not spoken of again for around 1000 years, and this is true. Circumcision he says was also mentioned (Jer. 9:25, 26), but here you will find it is not the old law of circumcision of the flesh, but the prophet promises punishment for those who are uncircumcised at heart. This is also true today. In 1 Cor. 7:19 we are told that circumcision is the keeping of the commandments of God, and those today who are uncircumcised at heart, will not have these commandments written there, and will claim they are abolished. Those who teach as Elder Porter does the abolition of the ten commandments, and tries to get others not to keep this law, it is surely evident that he is uncircumcised at heart, because he does not have the commandments of God written there. While he may say he has some written there, but James says if you keep the whole law and yet offend in one point, you are **guilty of all** (James 2:10, 11) ; therefore, he is guilty of their violations, as he is not keeping the fourth; and being guilty of all, he is uncircumcised at heart, and bound for punishment by the Almighty, unless he repents and keeps God's sabbath.

Porter admits that a law is in force until it is repealed, but he has not found one text yet showing the ten commandments of God were repealed. Therefore, they stand, and those breaking one are guilty. The seventh day sabbath is one of them, and for anyone to rebelliously break it in wilful defiance of Almighty God, will surely suffer the penalty of sinners, for "Sin is the transgression of the law" (1 John 3:4).

We have proven, furthermore, that Jesus commanded the sabbath to be kept when he commanded the apostles to pray that their flight from Judaea would not have to be made on the sabbath. This also he has utterly failed to explain away. He made the ridiculous answer, that if this proved the sabbath to be holy, it also proved the winter was holy. There is no answer to this statement of our Saviour, only to leave it as it is, that the sabbath was still God's holy day just the same as it always had been, and Jesus did not want his followers to have to break it by packing up their belongings and flee on that day. Every reader who has been seeking God for the Holy Spirit to lead him in the ways of God's will, and to eternal life, will not only see that the sabbath is still holy, but the Holy Spirit will give him joy and boldness to keep it for God, and to teach this great truth to their friends and neighbors.

We have further proven beyond any doubt that the expression "under the law," means under the condemnation of law. Mr. Porter has tried in vain to show that Paul condemns all who try to keep the law by saying they have fallen from grace, but Mr. Porter seems to forget that he himself is keeping nine of these same ten commandments; hence, he is nine-tenths fallen from grace too. If I am fallen from grace because I keep the sabbath, the 4th commandment, then surely he is also fallen from grace when he keeps the other nine. How absurd and ridiculous is such argument. Jesus teaches us that we are all born in sin; hence, we are all under the law, and sinners by nature, being human, and we need the grace of God. We need the pardoning power of the blood of Jesus to bring us up out of the death cell, forgiving our transgressions of this law, putting us right before God. Then we stand no longer under the condemnation of law, but under the grace and favor of God.

We have proven that the Jews, and all others not accepting the grace of God through Jesus Christ, were under the law, and that the other class who are without law, are the Gentiles (heathen), who have never heard of any law; consequently, they were without law (Rom. 2:13 to 16). And, furthermore, that the ten commandments stand as a looking glass (James 1:22-25 and 2:10-12) given for sinners. It reads: "Whatsoever the law saith it saith to them that are under the law, that every mouth may be stopped and all the world may become guilty before God. Therefore by the deeds of the law there shall be no flesh justified (or pardoned) in his sight, **for by the law is the knowledge** of sin." This proves that the law was made for sinners to show them their guilt, and it shows all sabbath breakers their guilt too, but many will not heed. How sad it will be in the day of judgment for such. They will surely be condemned for not having done the will of the Father in heaven. I know you will feel more secure, dear reader, when you know you are keeping all of God's commandments instead of just part of them. The Lord tells us further: "Know this that the law is not made for a righteous man, but for the lawless, and disobedient, for the ungodly and for sinners, for the unholy and profane," etc: (1 Tim. 1:9, 10). This shows conclusively that it is the ten commandments in question and it is this law that shows people their guilt. Sabbath breakers can see in this law what God's will is concerning the day he blessed and reserved for himself, and the Holy Spirit will give you strength and boldness to keep the sabbath day.

PORTER'S FOURTH NEGATIVE

Since no new matter can be introduced in this final negative, it will be devoted to a final look at things already introduced. A number of times in his final affirmative Dugger has passed judgment on me and consigned me to hell (which, according to him, wouldn't last but a minute anyway) because I do not keep the sabbath. But this passing of judgment on me does not disturb me, for Paul: **"Let no man judge you * * * in respect of * * * the sabbath days"** (Col. 2:16). So I'll just take my stand with Paul and be satisfied. Also his constant quotation of Rom. 8:7 that "the carnal mind is not subject to the law of God, neither indeed can be" serves him to no purpose. He assumes that "the law of God" means the sabbath; yet he has admitted that God has given laws that did not include the ten commandments. This admission is fatal to his argument.

My friend insists that I misquote him, saying he did not say that the ten commandments hung on the two commandments mentioned in Matt. 22:36-40, but that it "was Jesus who said this." But Jesus did not say it; Dugger is the guilty man. Read it for yourself. "On those two commandments hang the ten"? Is that the way it reads? No! Jesus said: "On these two commandments hang **all the law and the prophets.**" "All the law" means much more than the ten commandments. And there were "the prophets" too. The statement shows that love is included in all of God's commandments. I did not say "to love God" is not in the ten—I said **the specific commandments** that Jesus mentioned in Matt. 22:36-40 are not in the ten, and Dugger did not produce them. They are found in Deut. 6:5 and Lev. 19:18, in what Dugger calls "the law of Moses," which he says was abolished. So the "two greatest commandments" were not in what he calls "the law of God." This fact he can never set aside. But if love is embraced in the ten, as I have said, Dugger wants to know why I don't keep them all. For the same reason that Dugger does not keep many of the commandments given by Moses in which love was embraced. Either love to God or love to man was embraced in all Old Testament commandments, but there are many of them that my friend does not try to keep. But he makes himself amusing and ridiculous when he tries his hand on Rom. 13:9, in which Paul said to "love thy neighbor as thyself" was **another commandment** distinct from the second group of the ten. Dugger says: "God is included here as our neighbor." If that is so, then why did you say before that this referred to love to man and the other to love to God? If what you now say

is true, both mean love to God and must refer to the first
four of the ten commandments, and that cuts you loose from
the last six. Where will you get them in? Furthermore, to
love our neighbor as ourselves is to have the same amount
of love for him that we have for ourselves. Is that the way
we are to love God? God must be first; we must love him
more than we love ourselves. But I wonder what wild statement my friend will next make.

In his third affirmative my friend said: "Jesus never did
teach the people to keep the old sacrifices of the law of
Moses." But he got into trouble for Jesus told the leper to go
and offer for his cleansing the things Moses commanded (Mk.
1:44). He also told his disciples to observe all the requirements of Moses (Matt. 23:2, 3). Dugger admits that Jesus
did refer the leper to the priest. Yes, and he told him to
make the offering also—a thing you say he never told anybody. And why didn't you say somthing about Matt. 23:2,
3? Were you afraid of it? Certainly you were; you knew
you couldn't meet it, for Jesus told them to observe all the
requirements of Moses, and that included the offering of
sacrifices. My friend is lost at this point. But he tells us
that it was through the blood of Christ, not the blood of animals, that pardon was obtained. Certainly so, but the typical
sacrifices continued till Jesus fulfilled them by his death.
Jesus never a single time opposed such sacrifices during his
ministry before his death. My friend would have produced
such evidence if he could have found it; he needed it badly.

Dugger wants to know why I keep nine of the ten commandments and leave just one out. I am not afraid of his
questions. I'll not treat them with disdainful silence like
he does mine. I keep nine of them because they are given
in the teaching of the apostles since Jesus died. I leave the
one out because Paul said it was blotted out at the cross and
to let no man judge you in respect of it (Col. 2:14, 16). The
sabbath has never been commanded since Jesus died.

He found where Paul held meetings on the sabbath. Yes,
but he failed to find where he kept **even one** sabbath holy.
Neither does the record say that he "worked on the first
day making tents." That is the language of Dugger.

As to the feasts of the Old Testament my opponent still says Christians are to keep them, as well as the sabbath, but not according to the law—that all restrictions have been removed. I do wish he had told us how they kept them then. As to his scripture, Zech. 14:9-17, which he says I deny, it does not even mention Pentecost, but the feast of tabernacles. Yet it proves Pentecost is to be kept by Christians! That is as near as he can get to it.

Dugger still thinks the covenant that God abolished was Israel's agreement made at Sinai in Ex. 19. But in verse 5 of that chapter God said: "If * * * ye will keep **my covenant.**" Not **your agreement,** but **my covenant.** Moses said "his covenant" was "the ten commandments" (Deut. 4:13). And God said: **"My covenant they brake"** (Jer. 31:32). And that covenant which they broke God took away (Heb. 8:7-13). Certainly God would not abolish **their agreement**—they did that themselves; but God took away **his covenant.** Right in this connection my friend said he was answering **all of my arguments,** but he has never said a word about these facts given to him in my second negative. He worries because I didn't give him more arguments and that he has had to repeat. I wonder if he forgot that he has been in the affirmative. Yet there are many arguments that I have made that he has not even mentioned.

I did not make fun of the idea that Gentiles must become spiritual Israel to be saved. I affirmed that. But I contended they do not become fleshly Israel. Dugger now admits that. All right, why take laws given to **fleshly Israel** and apply them to **spiritual Israel?** That is the mistake my friend has constantly made. Gal. 3:27-29 shows that both Jews and Gentiles **become** spiritual Israel—the seed of Abraham. Fleshly Jews are no more spiritual Israel than are fleshly Gentiles; they have to become such in exactly the same way that Gentiles do—by obedience to the gospel. But the sabbath was given to fleshly Israel. And the readers of the book will see Dugger's blunder here.

I know that James in James 2 did not teach that the law of Moses must be kept, and I did not even accuse him of so teaching; but Dugger's argument would prove it still binding. He argues that all the ten commandments are included because James quoted two of them. Well, in verse 8 he quoted from what Dugger calls the law of Moses. So if his argument means anything, all the law of Moses will have to be included too. This point he has definitely evaded.

I am surprised that he had the nerve to refer again to "the two laws." Any commandments that God gives constitutes law, but none of the references given by Dugger, nor any that he can find, calls the ten commandments "the law of God" in contrast with "the law of Moses." That, however, is my friend's position. Yet he bade good-bye to that argument when he admitted that the law given by Moses was also the law of God. Then there can be no such distinction as Dugger makes. No, God did not make that distinction; it is purely the distinction of Dugger and his people. If there is a verse in the Bible that says this, he would have given it, but he didn't. The two expressions, "the law of God" and "the law of Moses," are used interchangeably in Neh. 8:1-8. Read it for yourself. This shows them to be exactly the same. And Ezra 7:6 tells us that God gave "the law of Moses." And Moses gave God's law (Neh. 10:29). God gave "the book of the law of Moses" (Neh. 8:1). Moses gave "the book of the law of the Lord" (2 Chron. 34:14). I showed also that there are many things included in "the law of the Lord" besides the ten commandments (2 Chron. 31:3; 35:26; Luke 2:23, 24). Although Dugger has claimed he has answered all of my arguments, he has never **even referred** to those points, except to admit that I am correct. So his argument on the two distinct laws is hopelessly gone.

He refers again to "the commandments against the apostles" as ending at the cross (Col. 2:14-16). Paul said the handwriting "was against us." While it was in force it "was against us." That included Paul. But he was not even an apostle while that law was in force. So the "us" did not refer to the apostles but to the Jews. I called his attention to this in my second negative, but he has never said one solitary word about it. Yet he has answered all of my arguments.

Dugger says the ten commandments "stood out preemi-
nently above all other laws." Jews said the greatest commandment is this: "Thou shalt love the Lord thy God with
all thy heart, and with all thy soul, and with all thy mind"
(Matt. 22:36-38). And the second greatest: "Thou shalt
love thy neighbor as thyself" (Matt. 22:39). Just make
your choice between Dugger and Jesus.

He comes back to a study of "the commandments of God"
and insists that the expression always includes the sabbath.
When he reads of "the ten commandments" in the Old Testament, that includes the sabbath; so why not the same in
the New Testament? Well, when he reads of "the ten commandments" in either the Old or New Testament, that does
include the sabbath; but when he merely reads of "the commandments" or "the commandments of God," that does not
necessarily include the sabbath, even in the Old Testament.
In his final affirmative Dugger says: "We have always
known and taught that God had other commandments besides the ten." So that puts the burden of proof right back
on him, for the New Testament passages, as 1 John 3:4;
Rev. 22:14, etc., do not say "the ten commandments." They
simply say "his commandments," and inasmuch as Dugger
has always known that God had other commandments besides the ten, how does he know that these are not some of
"the other commandments"? The passages do not say "the
ten commandments." Of course, references are made to
God's commandments in the gospel of Christ, not to the
commandments of the Old Testament. Dugger insists that
the ten commandments must remain because "God never
changes." Yet he tells us that "some commandments did
cease." Well, if some of his commandments ceased without
making him a changeable God, why could not the sabbath
also cease and still God be unchangeable? His attention was
called to these matters in the early part of the discussion,
but he has never mentioned them. He just comes back and
says that God never changes, so we still have the sabbath.

At last he comes to consider the meaning of the word
"till" in connection with Matt. 5:17-19, after I had repeatedly begged and challenged him to notice it. I am glad he

finally got to it. But what a mess he made of it. He admits
that the statement concerning Joseph and Mary that "he
knew her not **till** she had brought forth her firstborn son"
(Matt. 1:25) does not mean that he never knew her, but that
it means he did know her after the birth of Jesus. Good!
That's exactly right. But he tells us that Jesus said: **"Till
heaven and earth pass, one jot or one tittle shall in no wise
pass from the law,"** and that heaven and earth are still here;
consequently, no part of the law has passed. But Dugger
broke off the Lord's statement at a comma and changed
completely the meaning of the Lord. His attention was
called to this before, but as usual, he answered with silence.
Jesus did not say that no part of the law would pass as long
as heaven and earth remain, but he declared that as long as
heaven and earth remain no part of the law would pass, "till
all be fulfilled." And that is the part Dugger left out because it ruined his argument to leave it in. Put the two
statements side by side. Joseph knew not Mary **till** she
brought forth her first born son; so when she had brought
him forth, Joseph knew her. Dugger admits this. Then the
law will not pass **till** all be fulfilled; hence, when it is fulfilled it will pass. No other meaning can be given to it and
retain common sense. If it is not fulfilled before heaven and
earth pass away, it will remain that long; but if it is fulfilled
before heaven and earth pass, then it will pass away and
heaven and earth can still remain. So the only question is,
Has it been fulfilled? Jesus said he came to fulfill it. If it
has not been fulfilled, Jesus did not accomplish what he
came to do. But Dugger admits that Jesus fulfilled it. So
it passed away, and Dugger hasn't even touched the argument. He ignored completely the word "till" in "till all be
fulfilled," and that is where the argument was made. But
he claims that "fulfilled" doesn't mean "passed away," for
if so, then all righteousness passed away when Jesus fulfilled it in baptism. No one has been so foolish as to claim
that "fulfilled" means "ended." But the cases are not
parallel. Jesus did not say "all righteousness will not pass
away **till** fulfilled. If he had said that, then it would have
passed away when he was baptized. But he did say the law

would pass when it was fulfilled. And remember this, the pas·
sage does not say "the ten commandments" but it says "one
jot or one tittle of the law." That includes all of the law. So if
no part of it has passed, all the law remains, including all
that God gave through Moses, and my friend should offer
animal sacrifice and burn incense and practice circumcision.
He has been afraid to say whether "the law" means simply
the ten commandments, although I have begged him to answer. I am willing for the readers to judge who is the de-
ceiver here.

HIS SUMMARY

Gen. 2:1, 2 does not prove the sabbath was instituted at
creation. The passage says God sanctified it because in it
"he had rested." This is past perfect tense and shows the
sanctification took place after God rested, not at the creation.
I pressed this in my first negative but he never even mentioned it, although he says he has answered all my arguments.

He now says Israel could not keep the sabbath while in
Egyptian slavery, but in his first affirmative he introduced
Ex. 5:5 to prove that they did keep it while there. I wonder
which position he wants.

Yes, God gave the sabbath to Israel shortly before it was
presented to them in written form, but this was after they
left Egypt (Ex. 16:23). And God did not send the manna
on the sabbath to "prove them," whether they would walk
in his law (Ex. 16:4). If they had been keeping the sabbath for 2500 years, they would already have been proven.
I gave this point in my first negative. What reply did Dugger make? His usual silence.

Abraham kept God's commandments (Gen. 26:5). My
opponent says this proves he kept the sabbath. By the
same method of reasoning I can prove that he was baptized
and ate the Lord's supper. These are God's commandments
too. But Dugger's brethren have "divine power and heavenly wisdom" that enable them to see what the Bible does not
say.

Again he says the ten commandments sets forth a "perfect relationship between man and God, and between man and man." Before he has claimed that all sin is measured by the ten commandments. Is it a sin for a man to bear false witness **for** his neighbor? Is it a sin for him to bear false witness **against** his enemies? Are these relationships between man and man? Not one word of the ten commandments covers these relationships. They forbid false witness "against thy neighbor," but not against thy enemy, or for thy neighbor. His attention was directed to this in my first negative and in others that followed. How did Dugger answer? His usual silence prevailed.

My friend thinks all the ten commandment law existed from creation because he found that Cain killed his brother and Joseph was tempted to commit adultery. Both these acts are described as sin. These certainly show that it was a sin to commit such acts at that time. He found the Scriptures that said so. Now, if he will find the Scripture during that period that says some one "broke the sabbath" and sinned in doing so, he will have his case made out. But the Scripture regarding the sabbath is lacking. No one knows it better than Dugger.

He got into trouble on his sabbath-passover-circumcision argument. He tried to prove the sabbath existed for 2500 years before it was mentioned because there is a long period after it was given during which it was not mentioned, and that for long periods the passover and circumcision were not mentioned. There is really no argument to it. **After a law** is given it remains in force whether ever mentioned again unless repealed, but that does not prove it existed **before** it was enacted. But that is the very thing Dugger tries to prove. That argument would prove the passover existed 2500 years before Moses and that circumcision existed 2000 years before Abraham. If it would prove it for the sabbath, it would prove it also for the passover and circumcision. What reply did Dugger make to this? He just called it a vain effort but didn't show why it was vain. The readers will see his failure here. But he admits he was wrong about the passover not being mentioned for 1000 years after given, for it was mentioned forty years afterward. But as to circumcision, he says Jer. 9:25, 26 does not refer to fleshly circumcision, but to circumcision of the heart. Well, verse 25 says: "I will punish all them **which are circumcised** with the uncircumcised." Did God mean he would punish those who were circumcised in heart? Those are the very ones he would not punish. But the circumcised were to be punished with the uncircumcised. This refers to fleshly circumcision. Verse 26 mentions heart circumcision, but verse 25, fleshly circumcision. Neither does 1 Cor. 7:19 say that "circumcision is the keeping of the commandments of God." If so, then the keeping of God's commandments is nothing, for the passage says "circumcision is nothing." What blunders a man will make when he tries to defend a false doctrine!

As to whether I have given any text that shows the repeal of the sabbath just read Col. 2:14-16 again. This settles the matter.

Jesus did not command his disciples, in Matt. 24:20, to keep the sabbath in A. D. 70. He warned them of the difficulties of escape either in the winter or on the day that unbelieving Jews would still be keeping. Dugger says this is ridiculous, but admits that it is true regarding the winter. If it refers to the difficulty of escape in winter, it refers to the same about the sabbath; and if it makes the sabbath holy in A.D. 70, it makes the winter a holy season in the same year. It's a poor rule that won't work both ways. You can't get out of it, Dugger, and the reader will see your predicament.

I am asked again why I am not nine-tenths fallen from grace when I keep nine of the ten commandments. Simply because I do not turn to "the law" for my authority, but I observe these because of gospel requirements. But you have to go to "the law" to get your sabbath requirement and are therefore fallen from grace (Gal. 5:4), provided you have ever reached grace in the first place.

He still contends that "under the law" means under condemnation for sin. So he says: "Jesus teaches us that we are all born in sin, hence we are all under the law." Of course, Jesus teaches no such thing. The text was not given that so teaches. But Dugger says we "are born in sin, hence we are under the law." I see. We are under the law, under condemnation, because we are born in sin. So we were under condemnation **when we were born.** Little infants, **as soon as they are born,** are under condemnation, according to Dugger. And that isn't all of it. Jesus was "made under the law" (Gal. 4:4). The word "made" is from a Greek word that means "born." So Jesus was "born under the law." So the infant child Jesus was under the guilt and condemnation of sin as soon as he was born. Dugger, the more you have fooled with this, the worse you have made it. What straits men are driven to when they undertake to defend the doctrines of men! Why has Dugger gone to such straits? Because Paul said Christians "are not under the law." Why not just admit the facts of the case, that "under the law" means under its dominion?

James 1:22, 25 and 2:10-12 do not say "the ten commandments are a looking-glass to sinners." Reference is made to "the law of liberty" (Jas. 1:25), which is "the law of the Spirit of life in Christ" that makes free (Rom. 8:1, 2), and not the Old Testament law that brings into bondage (Gal. 5:1-4).

When Dugger quotes 1 Tim. 1:9, 10 about the law not being made for a righteous man, I wonder if he means to imply that it does not **apply** to **him.** If so, why is he trying to keep the sabbath? If he admits he is embraced, then, according to his interpretation of it, he will have to say that he is not righteous but lawless and disobedient.

MY SUMMARY

Throughout the discussion I have asked Dugger many questions that he made no attempt to answer. I want to call attention to some of these.

UNANSWERED QUESTIONS

1. I have repeatedly asked him: Does the law say **anything** to you? I have begged, coaxed and challenged him to answer this question, but I could never get him to say one

single word about it. It is too late now, but he had plenty of time. It would have been better for him if he had had less time, for then the reader might think he accidentally overlooked it. But it has been pressed too often. His failure was not an accident. He saw it would not do to answer for if he said "yes," he would be "under the law" (Rom. 3:19), and according to him, under condemnation. If he said "no," he would be without any authority to keep the sabbath. So he saw his doom, backed down and said **nothing.**

2.   In view of his position that from the beginning the sabbath requirement was of universal application, to Jew and Gentile alike, I asked him: Why were the Gentiles called **strangers?** He could never find a satisfactory answer.

3.   And from the same viewpoint I asked: Why did God command "the stranger **within thy gates"** (Ex. 20:10) to keep the sabbath? Why not also the stranger without thy gates? He answered this, as usual, with utter silence.

4.   With the same idea of a universal application of the sabbath, I asked him, since God sent the Jews to Babylon for failing to keep it; why did God not send the Babylonians into Judean captivity for the same reason? His only answer was: They had not become Jews and God didn't expect the Gentiles to keep it. So that brought forward the following question:

5.   If God gave the sabbath to the Gentiles, why didn't he expect them to keep it? I begged him to answer, but predicted that he would not, and that the reader would see he was afraid of it. He never said a single word in answer to it. He was afraid of it; he knew he couldn't answer it and hold to his position; and the readers are able to see his predicament.

6.   This question also was totally ignored: Does "the law" always mean the ten commandments? It wasn't an oversight. He had my copy right in front of him, and the question was strongly emphasized. Why didn't he answer? If he said "yes," he feared the passages that show "the law" was done away. If he said "no," he would have no way to get the sabbath into his arguments where only "the law" was mentioned. So he said **nothing.**

7. How could the sabbath, according to Ex. 31:17, be a sign between God and Israel if all other nations were included too? He finished his part of this proposition with no answer ever being attempted. More silence. Silence is a very effective way to answer questions, if your opponent will keep still; but I haven't kept still, and the effect was lost.

8. If the ten commandments constitute the "complete relationship between man and man," as you have contended, is it wrong for a man to bear false witness for his neighbor? or to bear false witness against his enemy? Neither of these is covered in the ten commandments. But no answer ever came.

9. If the restrictions concerning the sabbath have been removed, how should the sabbath be kept today? We were never told.

OTHER POINTS PROVEN

1. I showed that the sabbath law was given, made known in the wilderness in the region of Sinai (Ezek 20:10-12; Neh. 9:13, 14). This shows that it was not given at the creation of man, nor was it known prior to the wilderness journey of Israel. Although I gave this as a major argument, my friend never offered any discussion of the passages. They stand unnoticed and untouched.

2. I proved that expressions regarding the sabbath showed it to be limited to the Jewish age. It was ordered to be kept "throughout their generations" (Ex. 31:16). It was a temporary commandment; it would pass away. You never read: "Thou shalt not kill throughout your generations." God did not say: "Thou shalt not commit adultery, covet or steal throughout your generations." But the sabbath, like the passover, burnt-offerings, circumcision, the Levitical priesthood, etc., was to be kept "throughout their generations." I was never able to draw any comment from my opponent on this. It was unanswerable.

3. I showed that the sabbath was also limited in its scope, for it was given to Israel only. This is definitely shown in Ex. 31:13, 16, 17. No Gentile was ever included.

No Gentile as such was ever commanded to keep the sabbath.

4.   From 2 Cor. 3:7-11 it was shown that the ministration of death, written and engraven in stones was done away. The ten commandments were written and engraven in stones (Ex. 31:18; 32:16). Dugger applied this to the writing of the law on the stones of the altar by Joshua in Joshua 8:30-32, and claimed that was what was done away. But I showed him that Paul referred to the stones associated with the shining of the face of Moses and the veil over his face. Did this occur when Joshua wrote on the stones of the altar? Moses was dead when that event occurred. But Ex. 34:29-35 shows that the face of Moses shone when he came down from Sinai with the two tables of stone containing the ten commandments. That is the writing that Paul says was done away (2 Cor. 3:7-11). Dugger saw his blunder in applying this to the stones of the altar on which Joshua wrote and never again mentioned the matter.

5.   I proved by Rom. 6:14 and many other passages that Christians "are not under the law." Other references were Gal. 5:18; Rom. 7:4, 6; 10:4; Gal. 3:24, 25. To be under the law means to be under its province or dominion (Rom. 3:19). Hence, Christians are no longer subject to the law of which the sabbath was a part.

6.   From Amos 8:5, 9, I showed that God declared the sabbath would be gone when the sun went down at noon and God darkened the earth in a clear day. This occurred at the crucifixion of Jesus (Mark 15:33). There the sabbath ended.

7.   And Paul declared the sabbath was blotted out at the cross (Col. 2:14-16). The handwriting that concerned meat and drink, the new moons, holy days and the sabbath days was blotted out. Hence, to "let no man judge you" in respect to these things. My friend has claimed that the "sabbath days" blotted out as here mentioned were the "yearly sabbaths." But I showed the set order of feasts that were here enumerated—daily, weekly, monthly and yearly—prove the sabbath days were the weekly sabbaths. In 1 Chron. 23:30, 31; 2 Chron. 2:4; 8:13; 31:3; Neh. 10:33 we have the set order of feasts given as kept by the Jews. In these refer-

ences we have their services specified as **morning and evening** (that was their **daily** service), in **the sabbath** (their **weekly** services), in the **new moons** (their **monthly** feasts), and their **solemn feasts**, or **set feasts** (which referred to their **annual feasts, or yearly sabbaths** as outlined in Lev. 23). In Col. 2:16 Paul refers to the same order. He said: "Let no man therefore judge you in meat, or in drink (this was their **daily** service), or in respect of an **holy day** (Revised Version says "feast day." So here are the **yearly sabbaths** or **annual feasts),** or of the **new moon** (their **monthly** feasts), or of the **sabbath days** (their **weekly** sabbaths)." So the yearly sabbaths that Dugger talks about are mentioned as **holy days, or feast days.** When Paul, therefore, referred to the sabbath days he did not refer to yearly sabbaths but to weekly sabbaths. Consequently, he declares that the handwriting of ordinances concerning their daily offerings, their yearly feasts, their monthly feasts and their weekly sabbaths has all been blotted out and nailed to the cross. And that today no man is to be allowed to judge you in respect to any of these things. In the early part of the discussion I called my opponent's attention to this set order of feasts, but, like so many other things, he passed it by in silence. He cannot make "the sabbath days" mean the yearly sabbaths, for they were already mentioned as "holydays." And the only thing to which they can refer is the weekly sabbath. So the handwriting concerning weekly sabbaths has been blotted out at the cross of Christ. It has never been re-enacted in the gospel of Christ.

This will do for my summary. My work on this proposition in this debate is done. I am willing to meet God in the judgment with respect to the things I have taught thus far. I have been conscious of no other purpose but to please him and to get the truth concerning this subject before the reader. So read your Bible carefully in connection with these things; don't let any man deceive you by teaching things not found in the gospel of Christ; don't bring yourself under condemnation by turning to an abrogated law; but strive to keep the requirements found in "the perfect law of liberty."

THE FIRST DAY QUESTION

PROPOSITION

The Scriptures teach that the first day of the week as a day of worship is enjoined upon God's people in this age of the world.

PORTER'S FIRST AFFIRMATIVE

The proposition which I am to affirm at this time reads this way: "The Scriptures teach that the first day of the week as a day of worship is enjoined upon God's people in this age of the world." The fact that I am affirming this proposition is evidence that I believe it; friend Dugger denies it because he does not believe it. One of us, of course, must be wrong; and it is the purpose of this discussion to get before the public the truth on the question. But first, I wish to define the terms of the proposition. By the term "Scriptures" I mean the Bible, the Old and New Testaments, the word of God. There will be no disagreement between us as to the meaning of this term. By "teach" I mean the word of God either says so in so many words, or that such statements are made regarding it as to make necessary that conclusion. By "the first day of the week," I mean the day that is commonly called Sunday. The word "Sunday" nowhere occurs in the Bible; the Bible calls it "the first day of the week" and "the Lord's day." This last expression will be discussed at the proper time. But I am under no obligation to defend the name "Sunday" or any idea or condition that gave origin to that name. All the days of the week have names by which they are commonly called—Sunday, Monday, Tuesday, Wednesday, Thursday, Friday and Saturday —none of which occurs in the Bible. And I am no more obligated to defend anything associated with the name "Sunday" than my friend is obligated to defend what may be associated with the name "Saturday." If he makes any effort along this line, it will be taken care of when he does so.

By "a day of worship" I mean that a certain worship has
been ordained for that day. In other words, I am not affirming that the first day of the week is a sabbath, or a Christian sabbath, or anything like that. The first day of the
week has never been called "the sabbath." Denominational
preachers who make that claim are as far wrong as is my
opponent in the position which he occupies. By "enjoined"
I mean commanded, required, or in some way made binding.
By "God's people" I mean Christians, those who have met
the requirements that make people children of God. We
might not agree as to what those requirements are, but we
are not discussing that point. By "this age of the world"
I mean what we commonly call the Christian age. I do not
mean that this was binding upon men in the Patriarchal
age or the Jewish age, but in this age—the age, or dispensation, that began with the reign of Christ on the first Pentecost after his resurrection.

I believe I have defined the terms of the proposition in
such way that there can be no misunderstanding as to the
issue of debate. I am contending that God requires Christians to worship him on the first day of the week; that he
has specified a worship for that day and expects his people
to honor him in meeting his requirements. And now I in-
vite your attention to a consideration of some things relative thereto.

I. **Events that make the first day of the week important.**
A number of things I wish to notice here, which do not within themselves give a requirement for worship on the first
day of the week, but which serve as a background for the institution of such a worship. God saw fit to show us the importance of the first day of the week in this age by showing
us some things accomplished on that day. 1. Jesus arose
from the dead on the first day of the week. In Mark 16:9
we read this statement: "Now when Jesus was risen early
the first day of the week, he appeared first to Mary Magdalene." This states plainly that Jesus "was risen early the
first day of the week." No greater event than the resurrection of Christ ever occurred on any day, but this happened
on the first day of the week. This will be discussed more

fully in connection with another argument to be given la'er. Elder Dugger will disagree with this, of course, but I shall take care of him when he does. 2. Regeneration was completed on the first day of the week. In 1 Pet. 1:3 Peter tells us that God "hath begotten us again" (or regenerated us) "unto a lively hope by the resurrection of Jesus Christ from the dead." Since Jesus arose from the dead on the first day of the week, this regeneration was completed on that day. 3. Jesus was acknowledged the begotten Son of God on the first day of the week. In Psa. 2:7 we have the statement: "Thou art my Son; this day have I begotten thee." In Acts 13:32, 33 we learn that this was fulfilled in the resurrection of Jesus. 4. Many notable and important events occurred on the first Pentecost after the resurrection of Jesus. All of these add importance to the first day of the week as Pentecost always came on the first day of the week (Lev. 23:11, 15). Among the events that occurred on the first day—the first Pentecost after the Lord's resurrection—are these: the Holy Spirit was given in fulfillment of Joel's prophecy (Joel 2:28; Acts 2:1-4, 16, 17); the church—the mountain of the Lord's house—was established on that day (Isa. 2:2, 3; Acts 2:17); Christ was crowned king on his throne on that day (Zech. 6:13; Acts 2:29-36); and the new law went into effect as the word of the Lord went forth from Jerusalem on that day (Isa. 2:3; Luke 24:47, 49; Acts 2). All of these events show that God honored the first day of the week as the day for the accomplishment of so great things.

II. **The first day of the week begins to come into prominence after the Lord's resurrection.** This is shown by the number of appearances that Jesus made to his disciples on that day. His first appearance was to Mary Magdalene, and that occurred on the first day of the week (Mark 16:9). In Matt. 28:9, 10 Matthew tells us that on that same day Jesus appeared to Mary Magdalene and to another. "And they came and held him by the feet, and worshiped him." The first time the risen Savior was ever worshiped was on the first day of the week. It would have been a good time for Jesus to point out to them that such action placed upon them "the mark of the beast," if so it did. On "that same day"—the first day of the week—two of his disciples were on their way to Emmaus when Jesus appeared to them (Luke 24:13-15). Immediately they returned to Jerusalem and found the eleven gathered together, and as they discussed these things, Jesus appeared to them (Luke 24:33-36). And we read in John 20:19: "Then the same day at evening, being the first day of the week, when the doors were shut where the disciples were assembled for fear of the Jews, came Jesus and stood in the midst, and saith unto them, Peace be unto you." And in John 20:26 we learn that "after eight days," which would be on the next first day of the week, Jesus appeared to them again as they were assembled. These appearances of the Lord to his disciples following his resurrection begin to give prominence to the first day of the week.

III. **The Lord's supper and the assembly.** There are a number of things I wish to present regarding this. 1. I want you to notice the fact that **Jesus commanded his disciples to partake of the supper.** In Matt. 26:26-28 he said to them concerning the bread, "Take, eat; this is my body." And referring to the fruit of the vine, he said: "Drink ye all of it." Luke records him as saying: "This do in remembrance of me" (Luke 22:19). Paul mentions the same thing in 1 Cor. 11:24, 25. So it is definitiely revealed that the Lord has commanded his people to eat of his supper. But that is not all. 2. **The Lord's people are commanded to assemble.** "Not forsaking the assembling of ourselves together, as the manner of some is; but exhorting one another: and so much the more, as ye see the day approaching" (Heb. 10:25). Here an assembling is commanded. It doesn't say the first day of the week. In fact, it doesn't say what day is the day of the assembly. That must be learned from some other passage. But it does imply that some day is necessary—there could not be an assembly without some time for the assembling. So the Lord commands an assembly on some day. Well, we have two things thus far established: the disciples are commanded to eat the Lord's supper; and they are commanded to assemble. But is there any connection between the eating of the supper and the assembly? That brings us to the next point. 3. The disciples ate the Lord's supper **when they assembled.** This is shown in 1 Cor. 11:20-33. They were perverting the institution by making a full meal out of it, and thus they received condemnation on that occasion. But the passage does reveal what was God's will in the matter. This was not an eating at home, but when they came together in the church—into one place (Verse 20). 4. Christians came together for the purpose of eating the Lord's supper. Read 1 Cor. 11:33: "Wherefore, my brethren, when ye come together to eat, tarry one for another." What did they come together to do? Paul said they came "together to eat." That was the purpose of their assembling. Thus we see that their eating the Lord's supper and their assembling were closely related. Jesus commanded both of them; and when they ate the Lord's supper, they did it in an assembly; and they assembled for the specific purpose of eating. And bear in mind this fact: the Lord's supper is the only thing God has ever required Christians to eat in an assembly. Or God has never required Christians to assemble to eat anything else but the Lord's supper. 5. Now, if we can find when Christians assembled—or came together—to eat, we will know when they partook of the Lord's supper in remembrance of Jesus. We have the record in Acts 20:7: "And upon the first day of the week, when the disciples came together to break bread, Paul preached unto them." Here is an assembly—they "came together." And the Lord commanded an assembly (Heb. 10:25). They broke bread. And the Lord commanded Christians to do that (1 Cor. 11:24-26; 1 Cor. 10:16). Furthermore, they came together **to break bread**—for the specific purpose of eating. And since the Lord has never required his people to come together to eat anything else but the Lord's supper, this is the Lord's supper. And when was it done? "On the first day of the week." So here is a worship God has ordained for the first day of the week. I challenge Elder Dugger to take up this argument point by point and show it to be falla- cious. I have numbered the points so as to make it easy for him to get at them. Now, let him try his hand on them.

IV. The meeting at Troas. The last point of the preceding argument introduced the statement regarding the meet·
ing in Troas as recorded in Acts 20:7. I wish now to use
this as a separate, distinct argument to prove that the first
day of the week is a day of worship enjoined upon Christians. It was the custom of Paul and his companions, as
they journeyed here and there, to spend a week at a place.
Such practice we find revealed in Acts 21:3, 4: "Now when
we had discovered Cyprus, we left it on the left hand, and
sailed into Syria, and landed at Tyre: for there the ship was
to unlade her burden. And finding disciples, we tarried
there seven days." Just what was their purpose in remaining at Tyre for seven days is not revealed. The ship unload-
ed her cargo there, and Paul and his companions took advantage of the opportunity to find disciples of the Lord; and
having found such, they tarried seven days. If nothing
were revealed elsewhere of such practice, we would at least
conclude from this that they took advantage of the occasion
to spend some time with the disciples, and, in all probability,
the opportunity to worship with them. But we do have similar history revealed elsewhere. In Acts 28:13, 14 we read
this: "And from thence we fetched a compass, and came to
Rhegium: and after one day the south wind blew, and we
came the next day to Puteoli: where we found brethren, and
were desired to tarry with them seven days." This occurred
while Paul was on his way to Rome as a prisoner. At Puetoli
they found brethren, or disciples of the Lord, and those
Christians desired Paul and others to "tarry with them
seven days." Why would they specify seven days? Why
not tarry five days, six days, or eight days? Evidently
seven days would bring them to the time of their regular
worship, and they wished Paul to be with them at that time.

It is unnecessary for the word "custom" to be used in order to mark a certain custom. When we find a certain practice being followed by a number of men on a number of occasions, we are certain that they were doing what was their
custom to do. And here are two instances where they tarried seven days in order to be with the Lord's people. But an-

other remarkable instance we have in the meeting at Troas. The history of such meeting is found in Acts 20:6, 7: "And we sailed away from Philippi after the days of unleavened bread, and came unto them to Troas in five days; where we abode seven days. And upon the first day of the week, when the disciples came together to break bread, Paul preached unto them, ready to depart on the morrow; and continued his speech until midnight." Again we note that they abode at Troas **seven days.** And, furthermore, this text gives us a reason for the custom of waiting seven days, for upon the first day of the week they met with the disciples for worship.

My opponent will have a hard time facing this Scripture. Although Paul and his companions were there for seven days —a full week—the only assembly of the disciples mentioned is a first-day meeting. There is not even a hint of a sabbath day, nor of a meeting on the sabbath day. Can it be possible that Christians there were sabbath keepers who did not believe in first-day worship? If so, is it not strange that a first-day meeting is mentioned with no reference to a sabbath service? If Sabbatarians had been writing this history, they certainly would never have mentioned a meeting on the first day of the week. They would have told about their meeting on the sabbath day according to the law. But Luke did not even hint at such a thing. If the sabbath day had been observed by Christians at Troas, surely some mention of their service on the day would have been mentioned **instead of a service on the first day of the week.** Yet the only assembly during that whole week mentioned by the inspired writer was a meeting on the first day of the week. Could it be possible that my opponent, if he were recording the assemblies of his people for any particular week, would mention an assembly on the first day of the week and pass in utter silence their sabbath day service? Such is not in harmony with the Sabbatarian attitude.

But why did they assemble on the first day of the week? Luke is very specific about it. He did not say they came together to hear Paul preach. If my friend could find in the divine record where any band of Christians met on the sabbath day, exclusive of Jewish worship and influence, **to hear** one of their number preach, he would at once seize on it as proof of sabbath keeping. He found a number of occasions in the book of Acts, in connection with Jewish worship or influence, on which Paul preached. These he introduced to prove that Paul **kept the sabbath.** But Acts 20:7 tells us that Paul **preached on the first day of the week.** If his preaching on the sabbath day proves he kept the sabbath, I would like to know why his preaching on the first day of the week does not prove that he kept the first day. Elder Dugger, please tell us why the rule won't work both ways. Certainly preaching on a day does not prove the preacher is keeping that day; but if it proves it in one case, it proves it in the other. My friend will never be able to explain this. Paul preached on that first day of the week in Troas, but that was not the thing that occasioned the assembly—they did not come together to hear Paul preach. Luke says they "came together to break bread." Jesus had instructed his disciples to break bread in remembrance of him (Lk. 22:19, 20). Paul taught that when they did this they were showing the Lord's death (1 Cor. 11:26). Also that the breaking of bread was the communion of that body of Christ (1 Cor. 10:16). So when the disciples at Troas met to break bread, they did it in memory of Christ, to show his death, or as a communion of the body of Christ. In other words, it was religious worship. So when they came together on the first day of the week, they came together to worship God. **It was a day of religious worship.** No such meeting by Christians on the sabbath day is ever recorded in the word of the Lord. My opponent and his people would rejoice to find in the Bible a statement that Christians came together on the sabbath day for such a service. It would be abundant proof that they were keeping the sabbath. We are, therefore, following a good example when we meet on the first day of the week for worship, for such worship is backed by the inspiration of the Almighty and recorded under the direction of the Holy Spirit. My friend may oppose it, but it will read the same way when he has finished his opposition.

V. **The time and frequency of the Lord's supper.** This argument will be very closely related to the preceding one, but from a slightly different angle. The Lord's supper was placed in his kingdom. Jesus said: "And I appoint unto you a kingdom, as my Father hath appointed me; that ye may eat and drink at my table in my kingdom, and sit on thrones judging the twelve tribes of Israel" (Luke 22:29, 30). So the Lord placed his table in his kingdom that his disciples—citizens of that kingdom—might eat and drink in his kingdom. I do not anticipate any discussion with my friend as to whether the "Lord's table" means the "Lord's supper." In 1 Cor. 10:16 Paul said: "The cup of blessing which we bless, is it not the communion of the blood of Christ? The bread which we break, is it not the communion of the body of Christ?" And just following that he declared: "Ye cannot drink the cup of the Lord, and the cup of devils: ye cannot be partakers of the Lord's table, and of the table of devils" (verse 21). So what he calls "the communion of the blood and body of the Lord" in one verse he calls "the Lord's table" in the other. Consequently, reference is made to the Lord's supper. That table, or supper, was to be placed in the kingdom of Christ that his disciples might eat and drink at that table. But eating and drinking at the Lord's table involve the two things that follow. 1. There must be a time for the observance of that service. 2. Unless it is to be observed but once in life, there must be the recurrence, or frequency, of it. You cannot eat the Lord's supper without eating it at some particular time, on some particular day. And the question naturally arises: Does the New Testament inform us of the time of the Lord's supper? Does it specify a day for its observance? If no day is mentioned, then the time element is unimportant, and we might partake of it any time that is convenient for us. But if a day is specified, that day must be regarded by those who would partake acceptably before the Lord. If it is a yearly service, we will have a certain day of a certain month mentioned. In that case, it could come but once a year. This was true of the passover of the Old Testament which was to be observed on the fourteenth day of the first month. It was an annual service. If it is to be a monthly service, we will have a certain day of **the month**—not of any certain month —mentioned. But a certain day of the month would make it come on that day of every month; hence, a monthly service. But if it is to be a weekly service, we will have a certain day of the week mentioned. In that case, it would come once a week. But what do we find with respect to eating at the Lord's table in his kingdom? A certain day of a certain month is never mentioned in connection with it. So it cannot be a yearly service. Neither is a certain day of the month mentioned. It cannot, therefore, be a monthly service. But what is the statement with respect to time? The only statement in all the New Testament that points out the time is the statement found in Acts 20:7. Let us read it again: "And upon the first day of the week, when the disciples came together to break bread, Paul preached unto them." Here is the time for the Lord's supper—they came together to break bread "on the first day of the week." This cannot mean a yearly service or a monthly service. We never refer to an event that recurs annually as coming on a certain day of the week. We say Christmas comes on the 25th day of December, or Independence Day comes on the fourth day of July. We never say these come on the first day of the week, although they may sometimes fall on that day. But they come regularly on a certain day of a certain month. So it was with the passover of the Old Testament. It came on the 14th day of the first month, and that day was set apart for that religious service. Just so with respect to the Lord's supper. The New Testament specifies "the first day of the week." As the 14th day of the first month would designate an annual service, and as the 10th day of the month would point out a monthly service, so the first day of the week specifies a weekly service. I ask my opponent the following questions: 1. Do you partake of the Lord's supper? 2. At what time do you partake of it? 3. Upon what scripture do you base your practice? Please don't forget to answer these questions.

That the early church partook frequently of the Lord's supper is shown in Acts 2:42. The passage reads like this:

"And they continued steadfastly in the apostle's doctrine and fellowship, and in the breaking of bread, and in prayers." This was said of them during the period that immediately followed the establishment of the church in Jerusalem and the addition of 3000 souls to it. As they **continued** in a number of things, those things recurred frequently. If they had prayed but one time and would pray no more for another year, it could not be said they "continued in prayer." And if they had broken bread but one time and would break it no more until another year, it could not be said they "continued in breaking of bread." But they did continue in it. Hence, it was a duty that occurred frequently, which would agree perfectly with the idea of a weekly service. But it can never be made to agree with my opponent's idea of the Lord's supper. Watch for his position when he answers my preceding questions.

VI.   The Corinthian contribution.   The record of this contribution gives us adequate proof in favor of a religious service for the first day of the week and, therefore, substantiates my proposition. The Jerusalem church had been impoverished by persecution and famine, and it became necessary for other churches to send it relief. The apostle Paul, while endeavoring to arouse churches to this duty, wrote the Corinthian church in this language: "Now concerning the collection for the saints, as I have given order to the churches of Galatia, even so do ye. Upon the first day of the week let every one of you lay by him in store, as God hath prospered him, that there be no gatherings when I come" (1 Cor. 16:1, 2).

In this statement a number of things of interest is revealed to us. Beyond doubt this is instruction in the matter of religious service. Such giving to the saints of God and to his cause could not be thought of as less than a religious service. And not only was it a religious service, but it was **a religious service enjoined for a particular day.** Giving of our means to the cause of the Lord upon any day of the week would be a religious service; but when such service is commanded for a particular day, it makes it all the more significant, for it not only teaches the service to be religious, but also makes the day a day for that service. And that would exalt the day to the position of a "religious day." Notice that Paul says, "Upon the first day of the week" perform this service. What reason could there be for giving such instruction unless the first day of the week was a day to be devoted to religious service? It would be a fine thing if Dugger will answer this question for us. But watch him and see if he does. If the sabbath had yet been binding on the people of God, then that day would have been the logical one for such contribution to be made. But Sabbatarians claim that the Corinthian contribution was but a home duty. That will doubtless be my friend's claim. If he so contends, I want him to tell us why Paul specified the first day of the week as the day for it to be performed. What reason could there be for performing any home duty on any particular day? Why would not the second day or the third day of the week serve just as well for a home duty? My friend will be helpless when he undertakes to explain why the "first day of the week" is mentioned for a home duty. Home duties are never enjoined for a particular day of the week. But this duty was, and there is no reason for its performance on the first day of the week, except that that day was their day of religious worship.

Furthermore, the apostle did not limit the matter to one week; but, as the original language clearly states, it was to be done on the first day of every week. That makes it a religious service to be repeated. It is a service for every week. Why specify the first day of every week unless that day was a day of worship and assembly? Certainly any day of the week would be appropriate for a home service—the middle of the week, or even the last. But Paul did not say, "Sometime during every week perform this service"; but he said to do it on "the first day of the (every) week." The first day of the week, then, is a day particularly enjoined upon Christians as a day for religious service. If friend Dugger denies this, then let him answer these questions: 1. Was this service a religious service? 2. Could

it be performed just as well on any other day of the week?
3. If so, then why did Paul specify the first day? I predict
that he will pass these questions by in complete silence.
His position will not allow him to answer them. If he
thinks it will, I am begging for the answers; so let us have
them.

Another interesting thing about this is the fact that
Paul gave an order for this to be performed: "As I have
given order to the churches of Galatia, even so do ye."
Webster says that an order is "a rule or regulation; also,
a command; direction." Hence, the apostle gave a commandment for a first-day religious service. This commandment (order) had also been given to the churches
of Galatia. And through the Corinthian letter it is given
to churches of the Lord everywhere (1 Cor. 1:2). Can
my friend find where any apostle ever gave a commandment to any Christian to perform any particular religious
service on "the seventh day of the week"? No such record
can be found in the New Testament. Suppose Elder Dugger
could find in the New Testament a passage like this: "Upon
the seventh day of the week let every one of you lay by
him in store, as God has prospered him, that there be no
gatherings when I come." He would present that as abundant proof in favor of sabbath observance. And he would
be right about it. Then when Paul commands a particular
service to be done on the first day of the week, why does
not that prove the first day as a day for religious service?
It does, and my opponent will never be able to set it aside.
Preaching, or many other religious services, might be done
on any day of the week; but the apostle in this text commands a particular religious service for a particular day
of the week—"upon the first day of the week." It is the
only day of the week for which a specific, definite service
is commanded in all the New Testament. This is significant, and silence on the part of my friend will not
answer the argument. But what is involved in this commandment? Paul answers: "If any man think himself
to be a prophet, or spiritual, let him acknowledge that the

things that I write unto you are the commandments of the Lord" (1 Cor. 14:37). So we have a "commandment of the Lord" for first-day religious service. Does my friend claim to be spiritual? Will he acknowledge that this is a commandment of the Lord? Furthermore, I should like to know, and our readers have a right to know, if my friend and his people obey this commandment. So tell us this, Elder Dugger: Do you lay by in store on the first day of the week? Don't evade the question, but give us an answer. Let us know whether you do what Paul ordered in 1 Cor. 16:1, 2.

This text tells Christians to lay by "in store." This is from an original word that means "in the treasury," or "treasuring up." It simply means "putting it into the treasury." This excludes the idea of a home duty. This laying by in store, or putting into the treasury, was to be done on the first day of every week, Paul said, "that there be no gatherings when I come," or as the Revised Version reads, "that no collections be made when I come." If they did this as a home duty, each one putting aside his contribution at home, then when Paul came this would all have to be collected—there would have to be a gathering of it. But this very thing Paul wished to prevent. And if they carried out his "order" in this matter, no such gathering would be necessary—it would already be placed in the treasury. This is unmistakable evidence that they were to "lay by in store" in their assembly, not at home; for how would their contributing at home prevent the gathering of it when Paul arrived? Perhaps it would be a good idea for friend Dugger to answer that question. I wonder if he will even try. His past silence on so many questions leads me to wonder. It is easy to see why such contribution would be required on the first day of the week. Christians met on the first day of the week to "break bread" (Acts 20:7). The church at Corinth engaged in the breaking of bread (1 Cor. 10:16). Inasmuch as they met on the first day of the week to break bread, there could be no better time to make their contribution. Therefore, Paul ordered them to lay by in store on this day. It is a divine commandment that cannot be set aside by human authority.

DUGGER'S FIRST NEGATIVE

As we enter upon the friendly discussion of this second proposition we deem it of much importance to stay with the divine Word of God as outlined by Elder Porter. God's word is the standard, and by it we will be judged in the last day. Therefore it will take more than mere supposition or man-made-assumptions to establish another day of worship in the gospel age from the day blessed by our creator and used by whatever people were his chosen people in every age down through the gospel age. We shall expect to find some strong texts of scripture supporting this important change in the day of rest, if there was a change made. If Elder Porter can find some plain commands to worship God on the first day of the week, or even just one command, then we will be glad to join in with him in serving God on this popular worldly day, which the whole world reverences by frolic and amusement.

In the first affirmative of Elder Porter he has simply given texts that command certain things to be done on the first day of the week but in no case are the people commanded to assemble on this day as the Lord's day, or to meet on it instead of the ancient sabbath. Perhaps in his next affirmative he will give such texts. We know he will if they are to be found, but let us watch closely and see. Surely there will be very strong evidence, and very plainly set forth, that a new day has been given to take the place of the sabbath of God blessed at the creation of the world, if such a change has been made as he affirms.

All the texts thus far given in his affirmative, are of breaking bread on the first day of the week, and making a special collection of fruit and provisions for the poor saints at Jerusalem on that day which required labor to perform. He says Jesus was resurrected on the first day of the week, hence there was a change made, but surely we would be informed, that because of his resurrection,

Christians were to use this day instead of the ancient sabbath day, if God really desired the change to be made. God commenced his work of creation on the first day of the week but that did not make it a sabbath. Jesus walked eight miles with his apostles to Emmaeus on that day, and met with them in the evening where they were assembled for fear of the Jews, and had the doors all locked so no one could get in. This surely would have been an opportune time for Jesus to have told them to continue to meet on that day for other purposes than the one occasioning this meeting—"For fear of the Jews." Then after eight days they met again and Elder Porter says this was also on the first day of the week. Surely his mathematics slipped a cog here. Let him calculate again and see if he could start on any first day and get another first day, after eight days. After one day, could not be before the same time on Monday: after two days the same time on Tues.: after three days the same time Wed.: after four days the same time Thur.: after five days the same time Fri.: after six days the same time Sat.: after seven days the same time Sunday, and after eight days the same time Monday. This is surely very careless mathematics, as well as argument. He surely needs evidence very badly to use such a text in such a careless manner as this, and say this next meeting was on the first day. It says after eight days, and it might have been several days after for that matter.

Now we come to his next argument of Paul's command to the churches of Galatia to lay by in store on the first day of the week. He says if I had such a text as this in support of the ancient sabbath I would have something indeed. If there was such a text as this in the Bible, it would prove to me that God's ancient sabbath had truly lost its place among Christians, for this was a command to gather fruit and provisions on the first day of the week and not a command to assemble for worship. It was a command to work on the first day, as you will clearly see, if you will follow me with subsequent texts. This same commandment is mentioned in 2 Cor. 9th chapter, and

Romans 15th, as well as in the text Elder Porter calls attention to. Now let us see just what the nature of this commandment was and if it required labor on the first day to carry it out. In Romans 15:25 to 28 we read, "But now I go to Jerusalem to minister to the poor saints there. For it hath pleased them of Macedonia and Achaia to make a certain contribution for the poor saints which are at Jerusalem. . . . . When therefore I have performed this and have sealed to them this **fruit** I will come by you into Spain" (Rom. 15:25, 26, 28). This is exactly the same collection and for the precise purpose. There was a drought in the land and great want among the poor saints at Jerusalem, and it says this was **a certain contribution,** and it was **fruit.** The text in question (1 Cor. 16:1-5) plainly confirms that it was the same collection. It says: "Let every one of you lay by **him in store.**" It was a personal matter. It does not say one word about assembling together but let every one of you lay by **him** in store. Paul says, "I will come by you when I shall pass through Macedonia" (verse 5). Here he speaks of others going with him to bring your liberalities to Jerusalem (verse 3). It shows the collection was not coins or money but liberalities which required assistance to carry. In these parts they raised figs, raisins, dates, etc. and this was the fruit Paul mentions, that embraced this collection, for the poor saints at Jerusalem (Rom. 15: 25, 26, 28), and it required labor to gather it together. In 2 Cor. 9:1 to 6 it is called bounty, and the reason for the command is set forth there, that Paul wanted the churches to be ready. It is a command to labor on the first day of the week at home, and not a command to assemble at church. Elder Porter asks me if we take up a collection every first day of the week, and if not, why not? I ask him if he takes up a collection every first day for the poor saints at Jerusalem? If not why not? Is it not true that your people take up a collection for the preachers on Sunday, and not one penny of it goes to Jerusalem? Read your Bible and you will see that this was "A certain contribution," and for a certain purpose. It teaches the people Christian benevolence, and also that

the first day of the week is the day to labor on and has
no other significance in the gospel age more than it ever had.

Now our readers would like to know, Elder Porter, if
you gather up provisions for the poor saints at Jerusalem
every first day.

Now don't evade the question like you did so many of
my questions in the previous debate. I lived at Jerusalem
over six months and never heard of any of your substance
going there to the poor. Why do you not obey the command of Paul if this is yet to be practiced, and why do not
the many poor saints at Jerusalem receive any of your
bounty?

"If any man think himself to be a prophet or spiritual,
let him acknowledge that the things that I wrote unto you
are the commandments of the Lord" (1 Cor. 14:37). You
affirm that this commandment extends to us in this age,
and there are many poor saints at Jerusalem, then why
not obey the command?

You say this is from an original word meaning the treasury. I deny this assertion and demand the proof. I have
studied the Greek, and lived in Missouri over twenty years,
so come across and show us the goods. The scripture
reads, "Let every man lay by **him** in store." Paul says
it was fruit, and if it was placed in a general storehouse,
it required work to put it there on the first day of the
week, and that is exactly what I earnestly contend that
the first day of the week is a day designed for this work,
and any other legitimate work for a Christian to perform
on any of the other five laboring days.

He says it is legitimate and easy to see why Christians
were required to make a collection for the saints on the
first day of the week because it was the day set apart for
them to use in breaking bread (Acts 20:7). Where is the
command to take the communion service every first day
of the week? If this was the communion service (Acts
20:7) then why is not the wine also mentioned? Paul says
the 'days of unleavened bread" were passed before they
left Philippi (verse 6). When the apostles met every day
to break bread (Acts 2:46) why not also assume that they

took the Lord's supper every day? The writer lived in Egypt and Palestine for about seven months, and it is still a common expression there to break bread when the people eat their common meals. Bread is made in long twists, some of which are from a foot to about two feet in length, and they always break them in eating. This gives place to the expression all over that country "Breaking bread" when eating the common meal. If this was a solemn and important event such as the Lord's supper, why did not the other ministers remain and break bread with Paul? We notice that they set sail and went on to Assos which was by ship route about seventy-five miles around the bay from Troas. Paul by remaining at Troas and preaching through the night could walk across the cape (about 19 miles) the next morning and meet the brethren there. This he did, note verse 13. This was a farewell meeting of Paul with these brethren, and he chose to stay with them all night after the others had departed, and to walk the next morning across the cape and join them there. The scriptures tell us that they gathered together on the first day of the week to break bread, and that there were many lights in the upper chambers (verse 8), hence this meeting was a Saturday night meeting, for the first day of the week commences at sundown Saturday, (Bible time), and what right have we to use any other time. When God made the world, darkness covered the face of the deep, and the Lord said let there be light and there was light, and the darkness and the light he called the first day. Darkness always comes first and then the light. The sun was made to rule the day, and the moon the seasons. This is why the scriptural day commences at sundown, and always did until Rome changed it to midnight. Now people use a machine man has made (a clock or watch) to mark off the day, but God's clock is still running, and has never been rewound or set over. It still marks off God's day, or the Lord's day, on the seventh day of the week and not the first day. The Lord says: "From evening to evening shall you celebrate the sabbath" (Leviticus 23:32). The first day of the week, therefore in question here began at sundown Saturday. The Jews to this day have the same custom of gathering together as soon as the sabbath is past and having a common meal which many of them call "breaking bread in Palestine." This is exactly what they had in Paul's time for it was a night meeting, and many lights were in the upper chambers, and they broke bread after midnight. Read verses 7 to 11 inclusive. Look up your maps on Paul's journeys and you will see clearly that he chose to preach all night and then to walk across the cape which you will see was about 19 miles and join the brethren there, which was the light part of the first day of the week. It was generally practiced by the apostles to remain in one place about a week, and to spend the sabbath with the church and then to go on as in this case. You will notice here that after the brethren had observed the sabbath at Troas, they set sail. Paul remained until the morning preaching through the night and they did not break bread according to the record until after midnight. If you believe, Elder Porter, that this is a command of the Lord, for the communion service, why don't you obey it, and take your communion service at night? The New Testament calls it the Lord's supper, then why take it at noon? Are you obeying the command of the Lord in this? Now do not evade the issue, but please answer the question. The readers have a right to know, and we will wait for your answer.

The apostles in the New Testament, and for over 300 years their followers kept the ordinance of the Lord's supper at the proper time for supper, and kept it once a year on the very day Jesus shed his blood. It was, and is, a yearly ordinance, as the following furnishes abundance of proof. Paul delivered the ordinance to the church at Corinth as he received it of the Lord. This scripture reads, "For I have received of the Lord that which also I delivered unto you, that the Lord Jesus the same night in which he was betrayed took bread." Paul delivered it to the church on the same night Jesus was betrayed, and tells us plainly that the ordinance is to show forth the "Lord's death until he comes." How can you show forth the Lord's death just any time you choose? It has always been the custom to celebrate important events on the very day they occurred, and that would have to be once a year. Could you celebrate your birthday every week, or just any time? No. You show forth your birth with your friends on the same day you were born. The world accepts the 25th of December as the day to commemorate the birth of Jesus, and they do it once a year, but the day he actually died, and shed his blood which is of far more importance, they forget. We could not celebrate the declaration of independence on the 4th of August, or once a week or just any time. Our independence is celebrated once a year on the proper day, viz. the 4th of July. The death of Jesus on the cross, and the day he shed his blood was the 14th day of the month Abib as God named the months, and not as the heathens named them which names the world today follows. The month Abib was to be the first month of the year, and it corresponds about to our April. It was the 14th day of this moon or month that Israel always killed the lamb which typified Christ, and Jesus was crucified also on this same day. In Exodus we read: "This month shall be the beginning of months: it shall be the first month of the year unto you" (Exodus 12:2), also 13:5, and the Lord said to Israel: "They shall take to them every man a lamb, according to the house of their fathers, every man a lamb. . . . Your lamb shall be without blemish, a male of the first year . . . and ye shall keep it up until the 14th day of the same month and the whole assembly of the congregation of Israel shall kill it in the evening" Verses 3-6. This lamb was a type of Christ, and its blood was a type of his blood. We read further, "And this blood shall be to you for a token upon the house where you are, and when I see the blood I will pass over you, and the plague shall not be upon you to destroy you when I smite the land of Egypt." Verse 13. This was the beginning of the passover, or Lord's supper, and note carefully what the Lord says further in the next verse, "And this day shall be unto you for a memorial, and ye shall keep it a feast unto the Lord throughout your generations: Ye shall keep it a feast by an ordinance forever." Notice particularly the two phases in which this sacred ordinance was to be kept. It is clearly separated here, and in a number of other places. It was to be kept as a feast throughout the generations of Israel, but a feast by an **ordinance forever.** This last phase is the ordinance of Jesus Christ, as he introduced it. The first phase was observed as one of the feasts of Israel throughout their generations just as the Lord said it would be, and before Jesus died on the cross he introduced the ordinance supper to be perpetuated **forever,** also as the Lord had herein plainly set forth. This is why the church of the New Testament kept it in its season once a year as we are going to show. It was not an ordinance to be kept just any time people chose to do so, but at the proper time specified by the Lord.

We read further, "Thou shsalt therefore keep this ordinance in his season from year to year" (Exodus 13:10). Israel obeyed and kept this ordinance as a feast of seven days throughout her generations. This is why Joseph and Mary came to Jerusalem every year, as it says, "Now his parents went up to Jerusalem every year at the feast of the passover." This proves conclusively that Israel kept this ordinance as a feast throughout their generations. It is here called the **feast** of the passover. It is called the passover because the destroying angel passed over Egypt that night, and where the blood of the lamb was not found it smote the house with death (Exodus 12:29, 30), hence it is called the passover. As the Lord said the 14th of Abib was to be kept as a feast throughout the generations of Israel, he also said it was to be kept by an ordinance forever. We have proven the first phase to be true, for Joseph and Mary were observing it as the feast of the passover, but just before Jesus died and shed his blood he introduced the ordinance service with the unleavened bread and the fruit of the vine which stood for his body and his blood.

Now we shall come to Luke 22nd chapter and see what we find. Here we read as follows, "Now the feast of un-leavened bread drew nigh, which is called the passover and the chief priests and scribes sought how they might kill him (Jesus) for they feared the people." Verses 1, 2. "Then came the day of unleavened bread when the passover must

be killed." Verse 7. This shows that Jesus was killed on
the very day the passover lamb was slain. The next verse
reads, "And he sent Peter and John, saying, Go and pre-
pare us the passover that we may eat." (Verse 8). "And
when the hour was come he sat down and the twelve apostles with him. And he said unto them, With desire I have
desired to eat this passover with you before I suffer. For
I say unto you, I will not any more eat thereof until it be
fulfilled in the kingdom of God. And he took the cup and
gave thanks and said take this and divide it among yourselves, for I say unto you I will not drink of the fruit of the
vine until the kingdom of God be come. And he took bread
and gave thanks and brake it, and gave unto them saying:
this is my body which was broken for you: this do in remembrance of me." Here we find Jesus telling his apostles
that he would not eat of this bread again or drink of the cup
with them until it was fulfilled in the kingdom of God. Hence
the same ordinance of the passover took on the second
phase of its significance and was to be continued as an ordinance forever. It was to last down through the Gentile
dispensation and on into the kingdom of God when Jesus
would take it again with his apostles. This is why the apostles of Jesus observed the Lord's supper, which is the passover ordinance once a year in the proper season, and on the
same day that Jesus died.

In the previous chapter of Luke viz. the 21st, Jesus is
giving the apostles special instructions regarding when the
kingdom of God was to come, in which he would partake of
the passover ordinance in the second phase of its significance.
Notice verse 21 of this previous chapter where he says:
"And they shall fall by the edge of the sword, and be led
away captive into all nations, and Jerusalem shall be trod-
den down by the Gentiles until the times of the Gentiles
be fulfilled. And there shall be signs in the sun, and in the
moon, and in the stars: and upon earth distress of nations
with perplexity; the sea and the waves roaring. Men's hearts
failing them for fear, and for looking after those things
which are coming on the earth, for the powers of the heavens shall be shaken, and then shall they see the Son of man

coming in the clouds of heaven with power and great glory. And when these things begin to come to pass, look up and lift up your heads for your redemption draweth nigh. And he spake a parable, Behold the fig tree and all the trees. When they now shoot forth ye see and know of your own selves that summer is nigh at hand. So likewise ye when ye see these things come to pass know ye that the kingdom of God is nigh at hand" (Luke 21:24 to 31). Hence the kingdom of God of which Jesus was here speaking, was not to come until after Gentile times were past, which is yet future, and then he will sit and partake of the same yearly passover in the ordinance form as he introduced it with the unleavened bread and fruit of the vine.

In the 11th chapter of 1 Corinthians we find Paul the apostle giving the emblems of the Lord's broken body, and his spilled blood to the Corinthian brethren, and he says, "I have received of the Lord that which I also delivered unto you, that the Lord Jesus the same night in which he was betrayed took bread" etc. Paul introduces it the same night, and not in the day time at noon. Elder Porter, why do you not follow Paul, and Jesus? You do not eat your supper at noon, then why try to eat the Lord's supper at noon? Paul says further, "As often as ye eat this bread and drink this cup ye do shew forth the Lord's death until he comes" (Verse 26.). As the church was dispersed and driven out into the mountains and scattered by persecution it would not be possible for them to keep the passover ordinance even once a year. Many times they would not be able to observe it and this was true after the persecution commenced when they were driven hundreds of miles into the forests and mountains, but as often as they were able to keep the passover, in its ordinance form, as Jesus gave it to them, they would show forth his death until he came. They could not properly commemorate his death on any other day than the 14th of Abib on which day he died, any more than you could celebrate your birthday just any time. The Lord knew that the church would be persecuted and driven out into the forests and mountains, which did happen, and for more than a thousand years they were so scattered. It would not therefore be possible for them to keep the passover in its "ordinance" form every year, and that is why he said, "As oft as ye do this ye show forth the Lord's death until he comes." The church thus scattered, lived on fish, venison, and wild game, and could not have celebrated the passover, in its ordinance form, because of a lack of the necessary provisions, the grain for bread and the grapes for the fruit of the vine. Consequently the expression, "As oft as ye do this," did not mean that this event would be, or even could be celebrated any other time besides the month and the day of the month it occurred. This is why the apostles kept the feast once a year which the following scriptures clearly show. We read as follows, "Christ our passover is sacrificed for us, therefore let us keep the feast, not with the old leaven, neither with the leaven of malice, and wickedness, but with the unleavened bread of sincerity and truth" (1 Cor. 5:7, 8). This is very clear that the feast which the Lord had declared would be kept in its season from year to year, forever, was still being kept by Paul. It was not being kept as the Jews had kept it, for they were to keep it as a **feast** throughout their generation, (Exodus 12:14), but it was to be kept in the second phase **forever.** Paul said Christ our passover was sacrificed for us, therefore let us keep the feast." Here is a command to keep it, and whatsoever Paul commands us to do are the commandments of the Lord. Now why not keep this feast as Paul says, "Not with the old leaven," but as Jesus gave it to us, and Paul says plainly he delivered it "the same night he was betrayed." Again we find Paul refusing to remain longer at Ephesus because he was bound for Jerusalem to keep this feast. He says: "But bade them farewell saying, I must by all means **keep this feast** that cometh in Jerusalem but I will return again unto you if God will, and he sailed from Ephesus." For further evidence that Paul was teaching the churches to keep his commandment about the passover (1 Cor. 5:7, 8), by keeping it himself, we read, "And we sailed away from Philippi **after** the days of unleavened bread and came to them at Troas in five days, where we abode seven days, and when the disciples came together to break bread Paul preached unto them, ready to depart on the morrow, and continued his speech until midnight." The Lord's supper had passed before they left Philippi. It was a yearly **ordinance** and was to be kept "in its season from year to year, forever." Therefore it was only a common meal the disciples partook of at Troas. It says they came together **to break bread,** and that was and still is the common expression used in that country for eating what we call a meal. No wine is mentioned in the meeting at Troas, and furthermore no command is given to break bread every first day, but we are told that they had things common among them and **broke bread daily** (Acts 2:46), which was a common meal, and is so conceded. They would therefore meet on the first day to break bread, for they did it every day, and it was for this occasion the disciples met at Troas, for it plainly says so. It does not say they came together to worship God, or came together for preaching, but the purpose of the gathering was to break bread, which was their regular way of speaking of eating their meals. Why jump at conclusions and claim this was a religious meeting scheduled to take place every first day of the week, when the scriptures no where say so. You are assuming this. It is a jump into the dark, and it only provides you with a flimsy straw to hold to a popular worldly practice of keeping Sunday. You know the keeping of the sabbath separates you from the world, and makes you so different you do not want to deny yourself this much, or bear this cross, therefore like a drowning man you grasp at a straw to support this pagan institution christened by the Roman Catholic church, and forced upon the world to take the place of the ancient sabbath. The Catholics themselves clearly state in their own books that they instituted the Sunday because they did not want a day of rest in common with the Jews. The Jews were at one time God's chosen people, and therefore they observed God's chosen day. Just because the Jews turned away from God and forgot him, is no reason that God changed and accepted another day besides the one he had chosen and blessed at creation. He says, "I am the Lord, I change not" (Malachi 3:6). He did not therefore change, but whoever have become his chosen people, now in this Gentile age, will observe God's sabbath instead of the Pope's counterfeit Sunday.

We shall expect you, Elder Porter, to show a command in the New Testament to meet every first day, or to keep the first day of the week. Or at least give a scripture where the church made it their custom to assemble to worship God on the first day, and this does not mean a command to gather raisins, figs and dates on that day, either. Surely when an old institution like the ancient sabbath was to be changed, and another day take its place, there will be something explicit and definite about it. He says that the day of Pentecost was the beginning of the new order, and the establishment of Christian church which he assumes took place on Sunday, but which we shall later also prove absolutely false. How does he know Pentecost fell on Sunday? By a misunderstanding of the Jewish customs, and confusing the yearly sabbaths with the weekly sabbath he says Pentecost fell on the first day of the week, but I shall show by his own church authority that it did not fall on the first day of the week. He places great stress on Pentecost being the time when the Christian church was launched, but there is not a word said about the change from keeping the ancient sabbath to another day, but we do find the Lord telling us that "They continued steadfastly in the apostles doctrine" (Acts 2:42). They did not institute anything new, but "Continued in the apostles doctrine." Pentecost surely would have been an opportune time to have given wide birth to the new order of first day observance, if such a thing was to be introduced then, as Elder Porter assumes was introduced, but where is the evidence? Where is his scripture that the early church was to keep another day? What is said about this important change from Jewish worship, as he says was made? We want the scripture, and have a right to demand it.

I have given a direct command by Paul to keep the Lord's supper at passover season by Paul, and I wonder if the elder will keep it. Paul says: "Christ our passover was sacrificed for us, therefore let us keep the feast" (1 Cor. 5:7, 8). Let us keep the feast is surely a command. Now, Elder

Porter, you find where Paul or any of the apostles says, "Let us observe the first day of the week," or let us rest on that day. Paul in discussing this matter says, "If Jesus had given them rest, then would he not afterwards have spoken of another day" (Heb. 4:8). This does not say Joshua either as Elder Porter will try to make you believe. Get your Bible and see what it says. Paul is here discussing the day of rest, and says "If Jesus had given them rest, then would he not afterwards have spoken of another day. There remaineth therefore a rest for the people of God, and he that has entered into his rest hath ceased from his own work as God did from his" (Heb. 4:8-10). Paul is here speaking of a day of rest, and not a dispensation. The expression, "Would he not afterwards have spoken of another day," is sufficient evidence to the searcher for truth, that Paul is here discussing a day. Jesus did not give them another day, therefore Paul tells us to enter into our rest as **God did his**, and tells us in verse 4 that God rested on the seventh day. Surely this is sufficient evidence to show that God did not substitute the first day of the week for the ancient sabbath.

If Elder Porter could give such evidence as this in support of Sunday he would be right there with it. Paul in speaking of his work among both the Jews and Gentiles says: "And Paul, as his manner was, went in unto them, and three sabbath days reasoned with them out of the scriptures." (Acts 17:2-4). If Elder Porter could find where "As his manner was" Paul taught the scriptures on the first day of the week, he would sure make a big display of such a scripture. Furthermore it says: "The next sabbath day came almost the whole city (of Gentiles) together to hear the word of God" (Acts 13:42, 44). How he would like to find such a scripture in support of his argument. Let us watch closely and see if he can produce just one such scripture in support of Sunday. We find another scripture speaking of Paul which says, "And he reasoned in the synagogue every sabbath, and persuaded the Jews and **the Greeks**" (Acts 18:4), and in verse eleven it says he continued there a year and six months. During the other days of the week he made tents (verse 3), and not one word is said about him having special meetings with the Gentiles on the first day of the week. Yet he taught the Gentiles every sabbath. How well Elder Porter would like to get such a text in support of Sunday, but thank God there is no such texts found in the New Testament, hence we do not have the confusion they would bring on this sabbath question. The Holy Spirit in giving us the New Testament says, "In the end of the sabbath as it began to dawn toward the first day of the week" (Matt. 28:1). Hence the first day of the week, is just the first day of the week, while the day before is still the sabbath in this age.

PORTER'S SECOND AFFIRMATIVE

Before replying to my friend's negative I wish to present another major affirmative argument, in order to complete my major affirmatives, and then I shall give attention to the things which he has said and will devote the remainder of the discussion to an elaboration of the points introduced and to a discussion of all those things that may be presented in connection with them.

VII. The Lord's day. In Rev. 1:10 we read this statement from the pen of the apostle John: "I was in the Spirit on the Lord's day, and heard behind me a great voice, as of a trumpet." I maintain that the Lord's day mentioned by John was the first day of the week, the day of worship for the Lord's disciples in this age of the world. This will be proven by various points that follow.

My friend will claim, of course, that the Lord's day was the sabbath day. Application of the expression "the sabbath" to the seventh day of the week was a well-established practice, dating back to Sinai. Many times in his writings John referred to that day, but he always called it "the sabbath," never did he call it "the Lord's day." Note the following references in proof of this. "The same day was the sabbath" (John 5:9). "It is the sabbath day" (John 5:10). "He had done these things on the sabbath day" (John 5:16). "Had broken the sabbath" (John 5:18). "On the sabbath day circumcise a man" (John 7:22). "I have made a man every whit whole on the sabbath day" (John 7:23). "It was the sabbath day when Jesus made the clay" (John 9:14). "He keepeth not the sabbath day" (John 9:16). "That sabbath day was a high day" (John 19:31). In these references John referred to the seventh day of the week, and in every one of them he called it the sabbath day. The custom of calling the seventh day of the week "the sabbath" was so well established and so generally known that John, if he had been referring to the seventh day of the week in Rev. 1:10, would have said: "I was in the spirit on the sabbath day." Then there would never have been any misunderstanding or discussion as to what day he meant. But he used a term that had never been used with reference to the sabbath, saying: "I was in the spirit on the Lord's day." It was a new term that described a new institution.

In Jer. 31:31-34 God promised to make "a new covenant with the house of Israel." It was not to be according to the covenant that he made with them when he brought them out of the land of Egypt. But when did God make the former covenant? In 1 Kings 8:9 we read: "There was nothing in the ark save the two tables of stone, which Moses put there at Horeb, when the Lord made a covenant with the children of Israel, when they came out of the land of Egypt." So the old covenant was made at Horeb, or Sinai, when the ten commandments were delivered to Moses. But what was that covenant? Read 1 Kings 8:21: "And I have set there a place for the ark, wherein is the covenant of the Lord, which he made with our fathers, when he brought them out of the land of Egypt." The covenant of the Lord was placed in the ark, but the thing placed in the ark was the two tables of stone containing the ten commandments. God calls this the covenant he made with them when he brought them out of Egypt. But he promised a new covenant. The old covenant contained the sabbath day, but the new covenant contains a new day, called the Lord's day.

New institutions require new names. And we have a new name for the day of worship—it is the Lord's day. The word "Lord's" in this passage comes from a word that was coined by the apostles. It is the Greek word "kuriakos." It is used two times in the New Testament. While the word "Lord" sometimes refers to God the Father, it is here used concerning Jesus Christ. The word used by the apostles points out something that belongs to Jesus, something that has a direct connection with him. In 1 Cor. 11:20 we find this language: "When ye come together therefore into one place, this is not to eat the Lord's supper." "The Lord's supper" is from the Greek "kuriakon deipnon," which means the supper belonging to the Lord Jesus Christ. It cannot refer to any other person. The passover of the Old Testament is called "the Lord's passover" (Ex. 12:11). And in John 13:2 it is called "supper." So the Lord's passover may be called the Lord's supper. But the Lord's supper of 1 Cor. 11:20 has no reference to the Old Testament supper, but to the supper which Jesus instituted that is in memory of him. And while God called the sabbath "the sabbath of the Lord thy God" (Ex. 20:10), or the Lord's sabbath, this cannot be "the Lord's day" of Rev. 1:10. The Lord's day of Rev. 1:10 is no more the sabbath of the Old Testament than the Lord's supper of 1 Cor. 11:20 is the passover supper of the Old Testament. In both these passages "Lord's" comes from the word that points out something that belongs especially to Christ.

We also have the word "Lord's" used a number of times in the New Testament when it comes from the Greek word "kurios." In 1 Cor. 10:21 we read of "the Lord's table (trapedzes kuriou)." The expression is given in the Greek genitive case—the table of the Lord. Whom can this point out but Jesus himself? The altar of the Old Testament is called "the table that is before the Lord" (Ezek. 41:22) and "the table of the Lord" (Mal. 1:7). Hence, it was the Lord's table. But the Lord's table of 1 Cor. 10:21 has no reference to that altar, but it refers to a table directly associated with Christ. We likewise read of "the Lord's death" in 1 Cor. 11:26. This refers to the death of Jesus and to no other. Then "the Lord's body" is mentioned in 1 Cor. 11:29. To no other body but the body of Jesus can this refer. In all of these references the term "Lord's," whether from kuriakos or kurios, means no other being but the Christ. Consequently, "the Lord's day" points out a day that has a special reference to Jesus Christ. And what could that day be? Certainly the day on which he arose from the grave, the first day of the week. It was on that day that Jesus arose (Mark 16:7). No other day has so great an association with Christ and Christianity as the day of his recurrection. The Lord's table does not mean the altar of the Old Testament, but it is a new table introduced in the new covenant; the Lord's supper does not mean the supper of the Old Testament, but it points out a new supper in the new covenant; and the Lord's day has no reference to the day of the Old Testament, but to a new day required in the new covenant.

Furthermore, the first day of the week was a day of gladness and rejoicing among the Lord's people. In Psa. 118:22-24 David prophetically declared: "The stone which the builders refused is become the head stone of the corner. This is the Lord's doing; it is marvelous in our eyes. This is the day which the Lord hath made; we will rejoice and be glad in it."

The language of this Scripture evidently points to the same day to which John referred when he said: "I was in the Spirit on the Lord's day" (Rev. 1:10). Surely "the day which the Lord hath made" is the Lord's day. I know, of course, that in a general sense the Lord made all days, and in that sense all days are his; but there is a particular sense in which he made one day, and that day, therefore, is the Lord's day in a way that the other days are not. "This is the day which the Lord hath made," said David.

The day mentioned by David is a day that would become for the followers of the Lord a day of gladness and rejoicing—"we will rejoice and be glad in it." What day could be such a day? Think of all the days of the week, and which of them could be an especial day of gladness and rejoicing for the Lord's people? On Monday, Tuesday and Wednesday we find nothing in all divine history that would designate them as days of gladness above other days. Many things have doubtless occurred to the people of the Lord on those days for which they should rejoice, but no more so than on other days. On Thursday the Lord was betrayed into the hands of sinners. That incident was one of sadness to the Lord's people. On Friday the Lord was crucified. While by his death he purchased our redemption and made possible our rejoicing over sins forgiven, yet to the Lord's disciples it became a day of gloom and despondency. They had trusted him as their redeemer, they had looked to him as their great leader and coming king; but on that day he was put to death by wicked men. Their hope was blasted, and they were a despondent group. That day would not be associated in divine history with gladness and rejoicing. Then on Saturday the Lord's body lay in the tomb, guarded by Roman soldiers (Matt. 27:62-66). Reflection upon that day by the Lord's people would always bring to their minds the sorrow of his disciples. It could not be the day of gladness to which David referred. During these days sorrow clouded their hearts. Even on the night in which Jesus was betrayed, "Peter went out and **wept** bitterly" (Luke 22:62). On the way to the place of crucifixion a great company followed Jesus "which also **bewailed** and **lamented** him" (Luke 23:27). Such sadness and sorrow remained even till the first day of the week, and on that day we read that "Mary **stood** without at the sepulchre **weeping**: and as she wept, she stooped down, and looked into the sepulchre, and seeth two angels in white sitting, the one at the head, and the other at the feet, where the body of Jesus had lain. And they say unto her, Woman, why **weepest** thou?" (John 20:11-13). To two of the disciples on the way to Emmaus who did not recognize him, "because their eyes were holden," Jesus said: "What manner of communications are these that ye have one to another, as ye walk, and **are sad?**" (Luke 24:17).

On that first day of the week their sorrow was turned into joy. It became a day of gladness to them and to all the children of God till time shall end, for on that day Jesus arose from the dead (Mark 16:9). It was the crowning event of it all, without which even his death would have been of no avail. When once more his disciples came to a realization that their Lord lived again, they were filled with joy. In Matt. 28:8 we learn that certain ones had come to the tomb of the Lord and found his body gone, and they were told by the angel that he had arisen and they should go and report to his disciples. The record states: "They departed quickly from the sepulchre with fear and **great joy**: and did run to bring his disciples word." The glorious appearance of the angel filled them with fear, and the angel's announcement filled them with great joy. It was a day of rejoicing to them. In another Scripture we read of an occurrence on this same resurrection day: "Then the same day at evening, being the first day of the week, when the doors were shut where the disciples were assembled for fear of the Jews, came Jesus and stood in the midst, and saith unto them, Peace be unto you. And when he had so said, he showed unto them his hands and his side. **Then were the disciples glad,** when they saw the Lord" (John 20:19, 20). They were in sorrow before they saw the Lord, but when they saw him their sorrow was turned into joy—then were they glad. Often we hear news that seems to us too good to believe. Such was the case with some of the Lord's people then. Whether it was the same appearance as the foregoing, or whether it was another appearance, it matters not. The Lord stood in their midst, showed them his hands and his feet, explaining that it was not just a spirit, but that it was he himself; and so we are told that "while they yet believed not for joy, and wondered, he said unto them, Have ye here any meat?" (Luke 24:41). They were so filled with joy at the thought of a risen Lord that they could scarcely believe; it seemed too joyful to think it could be true.

With all these facts before us, how can we reach any other conclusion but that the first day of the week was a day of great rejoicing to the Lord's people? To this day the prophet evidently pointed as "the day which the Lord hath made; we will rejoice and be glad in it." It is the Lord's resurrection day. It is the Lord's day, a day that has a peculiar reference to him as no other day has, thus fulfilling the meaning of the expression "kuriake hemera" (the Lord's day) of

Rev. 1:10, which points out a day that belongs to Christ
The day, therefore, has been set aside as a day of worship
in this dispensation (Acts 20:7; 1 Cor. 16:1, 2).

I shall now notice Elder Dugger's first negative. I shall
have to be brief, but the points can be enlarged upon later
if necessary. All that he said concerning a new day of rest,
a new sabbath, and so on, was wasted effort. I am making
no effort to prove that Sunday is a sabbath. Although my
arguments were all numbered, he paid but little attention to
any of them except two. I would be willing to risk the whole
issue on these two, however. I thought he would deny that
Jesus arose on the first day of the week, but he made no
denial of it. Perhaps he will later. John 20:19 does not
state the disciples met on this first day of the week "for
fear of the Jews." But the **doors were shut** where they
were assembled **for fear of the Jews."** Whoever heard of a
group of men meeting in public assembly because they were
afraid of somebody? Verse 26 tells of another meeting
"after eight days." Dugger says my "mathematics slipped
a cog" when I said this was the eighth day, the next first
day of the week. Then I suppose the "mathematics of Jesus
slipped a cog" when he said he would arise "after three
days" (Mark 8:31) but also said it would be "the third day"
(Matt. 16:21). According to Dugger, if he arose "after
three days" it would have to be on "the fourth day," and it
might be several days later. But according to Jesus, "after
three days" meant "the third day." So I have pretty good
company when I say "after eight days" meant "the eighth
day."

Now to a further study of the Corinthian contribution (1
Cor. 16:1, 2). My friends says this contribution was a collection of figs, raisins and dates. Suppose it was. They
would still have to lay it by in store on the first day of the
week. But how does he prove his contention? He refers to
2 Cor. 9 and Rom. 15. In Rom. 15:28 he found this statement: "When therefore I have performed this, and have
sealed to them this **fruit,** I will come by you into Spain." The
word "fruit," he thinks, indicates it was figs, raisins and
dates. My! My! What an argument! I suppose, then,

when he "sealed this fruit" to them, that he canned it for them when he got there. Certainly it was their "fruit," for it was the product, or effect, of their love and liberality. I wonder if Dugger never heard of such use of the word "fruit." Otherwise, when John told the Jews to "bring forth fruits meet for repentance" (Matt. 3:8), he meant for them to bring a basket of grapes. And when Paul wished to "have some fruit among" the Romans (Rom. 1:13), he wished to raise a fig tree. Or when he desired fruit to the account of the Philippian church (Phil. 4:17), he, of course, was looking for a shipment of dates. This argument of Dugger's is about as sensible as one made to me by one of his brethren once. He said that this contribution was "meat" of some kind, for in 1 Cor. 16:4 Paul said: "And if it be meet that I go also, they shall go with me." But others had to help him carry it, according to verse 3, and Dugger thinks that proves it was not money. Well, I wonder how many bushels of figs, raisins and dates a few brethren could carry from Corinth to Jerusalem. Could they carry enough that it would be called a liberal contribution for a whole church, or for a number of churches as in this case? (1 Cor. 16:3; 2 Cor. 9:13; Rom. 15:26).

Dugger refused to answer my question as to whether his brethren take up a collection on the first day of the week, but he asks me if we take up one for the poor saints in Jerusalem. The residence of the saints is an incidental matter. If we thus obtain funds for the saints in Tulsa, in Washington, or anywhere else, we are carrying out the principle of the commandment. Dugger, do your brethren take up a collection the first day of every week for anybody anywhere? Please give me an answer. His reference to our previous debate, in which he says I evaded his questions, will produce a laugh for those who heard that debate; and it will doubtless cause those who have read the first proposition of this one to smile. I have no reputation for evading questions; and he can rest assured that his questions will be answered, although he has definitely refused to answer mine. He tells us that this collection was a home duty. Then why did Paul say "that no collections be made when I come"? According to Dugger, collections would have to be made after Paul arrived. Furthermore, why require a home duty to be done "on the first day of the week"? Why wouldn't some other day do just as well? Why didn't Dugger answer these questions? Then the expression, "in store," is from the Greek "thesauridzon," from the verb "thesauridzo," which means, according to Liddell and Scott: "to store or treasure up, lay by." The noun form, "thesauros," is defined by the same authority: "a store or treasure house: any receptacle for values, a chest, casket." So it does refer to the treasury, not to a home duty, and a man from Missouri who has studied Greek has been shown.

Let us now notice his argument about the meeting in Troas (Acts 20:7). He says this could not refer to the Lord's supper, for there is no mention of the wine. Well, he claims 1 Cor. 5:8 refers to the Lord's supper, but no wine is mentioned in that verse either. To be consistent, Dugger, you will have to give up your argument on 1 Cor. 5:8. The fruit of the vine is not mentioned in Acts 2:42, but it certainly refers to the Lord's supper. Acts 2:46 does not say "the apostles **met** every day to break bread." This breaking of bread was "from house to house," or "at home," as the margin says. Certainly it was not the Lord's supper. I know that "breaking bread" often refers to a common meal; and I know that it also refers to the Lord's supper (1 Cor. 10:16). Dugger will not deny this. So what does it mean in Acts 20:7? Dugger says they came together to eat a common meal, but Paul, writing to Christians on another occasion, said: "Wherefore, my brethren, **when ye come together to eat,** tarry one for another. And if any man hunger, let him eat at home" (1 Cor. 11:33, 34). Christians did not come together in public assembly to eat common meals—they ate such meals at home—but in Troas "the disciples came together to break bread" on the first day of the week. This breaking of bread was therefore not a common meal. The bread which Christians broke when they came together was the Lord's supper (1 Cor. 11:20). This point my friend will never be able to touch. The argument stands as an impregnable wall against all the assaults of Sabbatarians.

But Dugger wants to know why the other preachers did not stay for this meeting if it was the Lord's supper? I suppose they could break bread wherever they were, as the service is not limited to any locality. But the record does not say they left before this meeting. In verse 6 Luke says: "We abode seven days" in Troas. So that would embrace the meeting here. Dugger says this was a farewell meeting; however, the record does not say, "they came together to bid Paul farewell," but "they came together to break bread."

My friend informs us that this was a Saturday night meeting. Suppose they did begin their count at sundown Saturday, would that change it? It would still be "the first day of the week," and that is all I am contending for. But why don't I take the supper at night, since it is the Lord's **supper**? The time of the day is not specified in God's requirements—any time on the first day of the week—in daylight or in dark—is still the first day of the week. And the word "supper" in the expression, "the Lord's supper," does not necessarily mean a night meal. It is from the Greek "deipnon" which may refer to the early meal, the late meal, or the chief meal. So his contention fails here. Dugger says: "You will notice here that after the brethren had observed the sabbath at Troas, they set sail." I wonder where he "noticed" that. Not a word is said about it in the divine record. The fact still stands that the only meeting mentioned was a first day meeting—not a word is said about a sabbath meeting. Isn't that strange if they were so strict in observing the sabbath? Why does not my friend clear up this matter? He has made no effort to do so. His silence emphasizes his inability to do it.

Next he informs us that the apostles, throughout the New Testament, observed the Lord's supper once each year, on the 14th day of the first month. Let us have one verse of Scripture that says so. There is only one passage in all the New Testament that gives the time when they observed it, and that is Acts 20:7, which says "on the first day of the week." I challenge him to produce a passage anywhere that says they did it on the 14th day of the first month. 1 Cor. 11:23 does not say that Paul delivered the supper to the

Corinthians **on the same night that Jesus was betrayed.**
But it states that Jesus instituted the supper the same night
that he was betrayed. I sometimes wonder if my friend
can read simple English. It is contended that we could
not show forth the death of Jesus unless we eat the supper
on the day of the month on which he died. I wonder! Baptism, then, could not picture his burial and resurrection
(Rom. 6:3, 4) unless the person baptized is put under the
water on the day of the month on which Jesus was buried
and brought out of the water on the day of the month on
which he was resurrected. That, according to Dugger,
would require every man to stay under the water a full 72
hours.

But he endeavors to prove his position by going back to
the passover of the Old Testament which was observed annually on the 14th day of the first month (Ex. 12:2; 13:3).
In Ex. 12:14 he finds "two phases" of it. 1. To be kept a
feast throughout their generations. 2. To be kept "as an
ordinance forever." He says the Jews observed the first
phase of it, and the second phase began when Jesus instituted
the supper. I am beginning to think that no absurdity can
faze my opponent. Let me ask him this question: If the
"ordinance phase" did not begin till Jesus instituted the supper, how did the Jews keep it as an ordinance for 1500 years
before it began? Moses said to the Jews in the very text
he gave: "Ye shall keep it a feast by an ordinance forever."
So the Jews were told thus to keep it **from its very beginning**
in the days of Moses. The command is repeated in Ex. 13:10,
which you introduce. Even the stranger that sojourned
among them could keep it in that "phase" (Num. 9:14). An
ordinance is simply something that is ordained, an established rule or law. And the passover existed in "ordinance
form" from the time it was first commanded. His claim that
it began in "ordinance form" when Jesus instituted the supper is the height of absurdity. Let him tell us how the Jews
kept it that way for 1500 years prior to Jesus. I predict he
will keep silent. A little later he argues that the Jews kept
it **as a feast** throughout their generations, but the apostles
did not keep it that way. But he introduced 1 Cor. 5:7, 8

and Acts 18:21. The first passage says: "Let us keep the feast." The other says: "I must by all means keep this feast." If these passages refer to what Dugger claims, they contradict his argument. Christians did not keep it as a **feast,** my opponent says, but the Jews kept it that way. But both Scriptures refer to "feast." So his texts contradict his argument, and he has lost again.

There is no discussion between us as to whether Joseph and Mary, Jesus and his disciples kept the passover till Jesus died. The New Testament references that he gave to show this I gladly accept. But I deny that it was continued in the Christian dispensation and call for the proof.

He introduces Luke 22 relative to the institution of the supper. Attention is called to the statement of Jesus that he would not eat any more till it was fulfilled in the kingdom of God. Then he connects with this Luke 21:21-31 to show the kingdom of God would not come till Jesus comes. Then he will eat again the passover annually, according to Dugger. Well, Jesus in Luke 22:29, 30 told his disciples they would eat at his table in his kingdom. So if his kingdom has not come as yet, neither Jesus nor his disciples can eat of it in this age, and if his disciples ate of it throughout the New Testament period and in all their wilderness wanderings that Dugger described, they did so in rebellion to the Lord. Where were they to eat it? Jesus said "in the kingdom." Dugger says that is still future. So if Dugger eats of it on the 14th day of the first month now, he has started too soon. Dugger, please explain this to us.

We have abundant proof in Acts 20:6, 7 that the Lord's supper was not taken during passover week once a year. Luke says: "And we sailed away from Philippi after the days of unleavened bread, and came unto them to Troas in five days; where we abode seven days. And upon the first day of the week when the disciples came together to break bread, Paul preached unto them, ready to depart on the morrow: and continued his speech until midnight." I have already shown that this breaking of bread was not a common meal, for Christians did not assemble for common meals on that day. It is the Lord's supper. And it was celebrated

after the days of unleavened bread. Hence, it was not taken
un the 14th day of the first month. Dugger says they met
every day to break bread, and of course, did the same on the
first day of the week. I challenge him for the text that
says they met every day to break bread. His assertions are
not sufficient; let us have some Scripture for it.

But Dugger says: "The Catholics themselves clearly
state in their own books that they instituted the Sunday
because they did not want a day of rest in common with the
Jews." But does this Catholic claim prove anything? They
also claim the Catholic Church is the true church, that Peter
was the first pope and has had successors all down the line,
that popes are infallible and that priests should not marry.
Will Dugger swallow all of this because the Catholics claim
it? If the fact that the Lord does not change (Mal. 3:6)
proves the sabbath must still be observed, it also proves
animal sacrifice must still be offered. Why does my friend
refuse to notice this point?

I have shown both a command for a first day meeting (1
Cor. 16:1, 2) and a Scripture that shows it was their custom
to assemble for worship on that day (Acts 20:7). The sabbath was not changed, but it was abrogated, done away, and
there is "something explicit and definite about it" in Col.
2:14-17.

My opponent promises to prove that Pentecost did not
fall on Sunday. I will be looking for the proof. He says
nothing new was instituted that day, but "they continued
in the apostles' doctrine" (Acts 2:42). But don't forget
that a first day assembly is part of the apostles' doctrine
(1 Cor. 16:1, 2; Acts 20:7). He contends that he has "a
right to demand" the Scripture that shows "this important
change from Jewish worship." Let him read Col. 2:14-17
and he will find the Scripture he demands. But he thinks
it should be revealed in the record at Pentecost. I wonder
if he thinks that all the differences between the Jewish religion and Christianity are revealed in the second chapter
of Acts. Why that chapter doesn't even say anything about
Christians observing the passover in its "ordinance phase."

Neither does any other chapter. Yet that is what my friend needs to find somewhere.

He returns to 1 Cor. 5:7, 8 and claims Paul gives a direct command to observe the Lord's supper on the 14th day of the first month. If I should grant that this text refers to the Lord's supper, there is not a word in it that tells anything about when it was to be. The only passage that does tell when they observed it is Acts 20:7, and it says the first day of the week. Reference is again made to Heb. 4:8, and the expression, "Would he not afterward have spoken of another day," is used to prove he did not speak of another day. But it shows the very reverse. Verse 7 says he did speak of another day through David a long time after they had received the sabbath. But he would not have done so if the Canaan rest or the seventh day rest had been the rest Paul says remains for the people of God. Whether it was Jesus or Joshua does not change the meaning. The marginal reading of the King James Version says Joshua; so does the the reading in the Revised Version. Check it for yourself.

His return to the references in Acts gives him no help. I fully blasted him from his position on this in the first proposition. He found where Paul on the sabbath day "reasoned with them out of the Scriptures as his manner was." But he needs to find a text that says "his manner was" to "observe the sabbath." This he has signally failed to do. No, if I couldn't find better proof in favor of first day worship than that, I would make no display of it. All of these references merely state that Paul preached on the sabbath. Does that mean he kept the sabbath? If so, then when the record says he preached on the first day of the week, why does not that mean he kept the first day? I insisted that Dugger tell us about this, but he passed it by in complete silence. If it proves it in one case, it proves it in the other. But preaching on a day does not prove the day is being religiously kept. I have preached on every day of the week. So has my friend. Please tell us, Dugger, if you keep the first day of the week when you preach on that day. Don't dodge, nor evade, but face the point with courage and tell us about it. Watch and see if he does.

I do wish my friend would go back and deal with my other arguments that he passed by silently. And especially my fifth argument concerning the time and frequency of the Lord's supper. Luke tells us the church in Jerusalem "continued steadfastly in the apostles' doctrine and fellowship, and in the breaking of bread, and in prayers (Acts 2:42). This was said of those who were baptized on the day of Pentecost. It points out their practice within the first year of their service. It shows a frequency of breaking bread, for they continued in it. But the passover of that year had already passed, and it was not time for another, and according to Dugger, they **had not broken bread at all.** I challenge my friend to deal with the statement of Acts 2:42 in the light of his position on the Lord's supper. He will probably answer with silence.

DUGGER'S SECOND NEGATIVE

My friend seems to think I have slighted his most important arguments in favor of Sunday observance, but the readers will be the judge of this. No argument in favor of first day observance by the apostolic church has been slighted, or intentionally overlooked. There are no scriptures whatever that furnish arguments in favor of first day observance that we need to fear, or that anyone else has any difficulty in answering. He again refers to Acts 2:42 where they broke bread daily. Now if the breaking of bread on a day makes it holy, and proves it to be, a day of rest, then **every** day is holy. It does not make a day holy or confirm it as a day of rest just because anyone makes it their custom to preach on that day, but when I have positively proven that Saturday was the Holy Day of the Bible, and our friend willingly admits this, then when I show positive proof that Paul, an apostle to the Gentiles, made it his custom to observe it all through his ministry, and have shown 84 sabbath days he used in preaching the gospel, surely this adds weight to our argument that the seventh day sabbath not only was, but still is, **God's Holy Day.** Then when the Holy Spirit has called this day upon which Paul preached "the sabbath day" surely this proves my argument true. My friend says it makes no difference whether the word in Heb. 4:8 is Jesus or Joshua, then he goes ahead to try and prove it is Joshua, saying the revised version gives it that way. The same word is used in the Greek where it says Jesus was baptized, where he was crucified, where he was buried and where he was resurrected. Therefore if it means Joshua in one place, why not in the other places also? This attempt to dodge the force of this text, by saying it is a wrong translation and should be Joshua will not take well with honest readers. Your Bible says: "If Jesus had given them rest, then would he not afterwards have spoken of another day" (Heb. 4:8). It makes no difference how much comment is made on these verses, they read just the same, and they surely mean what they say. God here says a "sabbath remains for the people of God," and tells us to enter into our rest as God did his, and plainly says he rested on the seventh day (Heb. 4:4). Now why not turn your back on the old world, with all of her false worship, and worship the true God, in the true acceptable way. Nothing else will be accepted by him, and no one will be saved besides those who "keep the commandments of God, and the testimonies of Jesus" (Rev. 12:17 and 14:12, also 22:14).

I wish Elder Porter would quote all of certain verses he has given on the sabbath question and not stop the quotation just at the right point to throw a false light on the practice of our Saviour. We appreciate his frank admission that when John spoke of the seventh day he always called it "the sabbath," and never called it the Lord's day, but he quotes as follows: "It was the sabbath day when Jesus made the clay" (John 9:14) and "He kept not the sabbath day" (John 7:23). It looks like our friend purposely just quoted enough of this scripture to make it appear that Jesus did not keep the sabbath, when if he had given the full quotation, the readers would see clearly that Jesus made the clay on the sabbath to heal the blind man, and then the evil men said he broke the sabbath. Surely our opponent did not intend to place himself with these accusers of our Lord, when Jesus in defense of the sabbath said, "It was lawful to do good on the sabbath," and not once did he ever tell anyone not to honor it or to keep it. It was his accusors who said: "He kept not the sabbath."

Our friend assumes that the text in Rev. 1:10, "I was in the Spirit on the Lord's day," refers to the first day of the week, but there is not a word said about which day it refers to. If we go by the Bible and the Bible only, then if this expression referred to any particular day of the week, it would refer to God's sabbath day because we read, "The seventh day is the sabbath of the Lord" (Exodus 20:8), and Jesus says in speaking of the seventh day, "I am Lord even of the sabbath day" (Mark 2:28). Therefore if we settle this point according to the scriptures, and the scriptures only as our proposition is affirmed, then the seventh day of the week is the day the apostle refers to, and not to the first day of the week. Our friend again assumes that Jesus was resurrected from the dead on the first day of the week, hence it became the "Lord's day," but again we appeal to the Bible. What does the Lord say?

We ask our readers to prayerfully consider this important matter, and ask God to give wisdom, and guidance in its consideration, because Good Friday as the crucifixion day, and Easter Sunday as the resurrection must be established by the word of God, if God's people accept them as true. How in the name of reason can anyone get three days and three nights between Friday evening and Sunday morning? The only sign Jesus gave that he was the Son of God was that he would be in the grave "three days and three nights." He said to the doubters, "There shall be no sign given but the sign of the prophet Jonah. As Jonah was three days and three nights in the whale's belly so shall the son of man be three days and three nights in the heart of the earth" (Matt. 12:40). Now if Jesus was not in the earth three days and three nights then he is not the Christ. If buried, as my friend says he was, on Friday and resurrected on Sunday, then he has failed, for it is a mathematical impossibility to get three days and three nights from Friday to Sunday. By calling a part of a day one day, and if the resurrection did occur on Sunday morning, then we might get the days in, but what about the nights? This is impossible. Furthermore, there is not a text of scripture showing the resurrection to have occurred Sunday morning. Let us examine every one. Mark in 16:2 says: "Very early in the morning the first day of the week they came unto the sepulcher, at the rising of the sun. And they said among themselves, who shall roll us away the stone, from the door of the sepulchre. And when they looked they saw that the stone was rolled away." Then we find the angel saying to them, "He is not here, he is risen, behold the place where they laid him." This text tells of a visit to the tomb, early in the morning of the first day, but Jesus was gone. Not a word is said about when he arose, but we will give you the scripture soon that tells the full account. Luke 24:1-3 says: "Now upon the first day of the week very early in the morning they came to the sepulcher, bringing the spices which they had prepared, and certain others with them and they found the stone rolled away from the sepulcher, and they entered in and found not the body of the Lord Jesus." Again we see that he was gone when the visitors came, and nothing said about when he was resurrected. John 20:1-8 also tells of a visit early the first day of the week when it was yet dark, but they found not the body of the Lord Jesus. He was gone. Not one of these witnesses tell us when he was resurrected. But we have still another witness left to testify, and that is Matthew. We therefore go to the last chaper of this book viz.: Matt. 28:1-6 which reads, **"In the end of the sabbath,** as it began to dawn toward the first day of the week, came Mary Magdalene, and the other Mary to see the sepulcher. And behold there was a great earthquake, for the angel of the Lord descended from heaven and came and rolled back the stone from the door of the sepulcher." Here we are told just when these events did take place, and the Lord say it was "In the end of the sabbath." From creation when the Lord said darkness was upon the face of the deep, and the Lord said "let there be light and there was light," and when he said, "the evening and the morning was the first day," this has been the divine order. The dark part of the day always comes first. Man has commenced the day at midnight. It was the Roman power that did this. God says "From even until even shall you celebrate your sabbaths" (Lev. 23:32). All Bible dictionaries and Bible scholars know that the original day ended with sundown, therefore, the days met each other, at sundown when Jesus was resurrected, and not at midnight. In the end of the sabbath, was just before sundown on Saturday, as it was drawing near to the first day of the week. If anyone wishes to believe that the days met at midnight, then the visitors would have to come to the tomb just before midnight when it was getting light toward the first day of the week, if the word "Dawn" meant getting light in the morning, as is often contended. The Greek word from which "dawn" is here translated means drawing on towards, and not getting light in the morning. Consequently the earthquake occurred in the end of the sabbath, just as it says, and the angels descended in the end of the sabbath, and they rolled away the stone in the end of the sabbath. They also told the visitors "he is not here for he is risen as he said" (Verse 6). My friend has already admitted that when the word sabbath occurred, it referred to the 7th day, or Saturday, therefore Jesus was resurrected on Saturday and not on the first day. He lay in the tomb through the sabbath day resting as God did at creation, and "In the end of the sabbath," the angels came delivering him from the powers of darkness. Now if as our friend argues, the resurrection of Jesus on the first day makes it "The Lord's day," then Saturday is sure enough the Lord's day. We have the scripture on our side, and he has no argument whatever for assuming that the resurrection occurred on the first day. He gives Mark 16:9 as evidence of the crucifixion on Sunday, but let us examine the text, which reads, "Now when Jesus was risen early the first day of the week, he appeared first to Mary Magdalene." As punctuation was placed in these texts by the translator, we must seek the true meaning, that will harmonize with other scripture, regardless of punctuation, which is not inspired. The fact that the word "Risen" is used here, is evidence that the act did not occur on the first day of the week, but at some time indefinite. All grammarians know, that "risen" is the past perfect tense of the verb "rise." This verb is conjugated "rise, rose, risen." "Risen" is past perfect tense, showing the act was at sometime previous but indefinite. Consequently there is nothing in this text to show that Jesus arose early the first day of the week, and as other texts clearly teach us that the resurrection occurred the night before or "In the end of the sabbath," this text must show when Jesus appeared to Mary rather than when he was resurrected from the dead, and in John 20:14, 15 we find that he did appear first to Mary Magdalene, and this appearance was on the first day of the week. Jesus commenced his work on the first day of the week the same as God did in the beginning of creation, and he walked with the apostles to Emmaus a distance of eight miles that day (Luke 24:13-19).

Now as we have shown clearly that Jesus was resurrected in the end of Saturday, the crucifixion must have taken place, and the burial just three days and three nights before. This would bring us to Wednesday as the day of crucifixion, and not Good Friday, as the world claims. Daniel 9:26 and 27 says the Messiah would be cut off, and that the sacrifice would cease "in the midst of the week." The Jewish animal sacrifice and blood offerings ceased in having any more virtue, the very moment the blood of Jesus was shed upon the cross. Daniel said the offering was to cease in the midst of the week. Consequently Jesus was crucified on Wednesday. As Jesus was placed in the tomb in the end of the day (Matt. 27:57-62), hence he would have to be resurrected in the end of the third day from the time he was buried. This would be Saturday, and it perfectly harmonizes with all accounts of the crucifixion and resurrection. The prophecy of Daniel 9:26, 27, evidently has a two-fold meaning as do some other prophecies. We have written to eminent astronomers in both England and the United States to calculate the day of the week the crucifixion of Christ occurred. The scriptures clearly teach that it was on the 14th of the Jewish month Abib, Exodus 12:1-6, and Luke 22:1-7. Their answer has always been Wednesday.

In regard to our opponent's argument that David prophetically declared of the first day of the week, "this is the day which the Lord hath made, and we will rejoice and be glad in it." He assumes this refers ahead to the first day of the week, but it says "This is the day our Lord hath made." He will affirm that Jesus was with God in creating the world, therefore Jesus had a part in making the sabbath day from the seventh day of the first week of time, hence Jesus was with the Father in this work, and the "Lord's day" if referring to any certain day of the week would refer to Saturday and not Sunday. The special form of the Greek word "Kuriakos," which he says has a special meaning, relative to a special day belonging to the Lord Jesus, simply refers to something belonging to Jesus. It is the possessive case of this word. Those who read this work, and who have studied either Latin or Greek, will know that in these languages, there are different words, and different forms of the same word according to their grammatical use in the sentence. All nouns as well as verbs have different endings, when used in the possessive case, as this word is here used. It does refer to something belonging to the Lord for it says "Lord's day." I never did believe that this referred specially to any day of the week, but that it does refer to the "Day of the Lord," or the Lord's day. John was in vision, looking forward to the "Day of the Lord's Wrath," the day of the Lord's jugments upon sin. He was taken ahead to the "Day of the Lord" referring to the judgment day.

If the Lord had of intended to change as important an institution as the sabbath day, and give the followers of Jesus another day, surely he would have made the matter very clear and definite. Our friend would not have been compelled to use the far fetched, assumptive arguments, in his claims for the first day of the week as he has been referring to. For him to try to make so much out of this text "Lord's day" when not a word is said about any day of the week, shows that he lacks good sound definite scriptures in support of his proposition. Not one argument has been presented yet, which proves his proposition, and every scripture he has used will apply more forcefully, and harmoniously with the truth of the same sabbath day being continued in this age, than it will for the establishment of another day of rest.

My friend keeps constantly persisting that I will not answer his arguments, surely he knows better than this. Not one argument have I refused to notice and answer, yet on the sabbath question and also on this question he willingly ignores my arguments, and passes over some of them as if they do not pertain to the question. There is a reason why he thus slips over them. When he assumed that "After eight days" brought them to another first day I challenged his mathematics, and he fails to acknowledge his mistake and frankly admit that "after eight days" beginning with a first day, would not bring us squarely on another first day. Then when he tries to answer another argument that the collection for the saints was fruit, he makes light of this scripture. Romans 15:28 is speaking of the very same collection for the same saints as 1 Cor. 16, and I challenge him to prove otherwise, and the Lord says it was fruit. They raised and dried fruit in the territory of that church, and the Lord says it was fruit they were sealing or sending to the poor saints at Jerusalem. The very reason why Paul said "There be no collection when I come" proves again that it was not money, for they could have easily taken that up after he came, as is usually the case now. It being fruit and provisions, he wanted it gathered and prepared and ready. 1 Cor. 16:3 again shows the liberalities to be burdensome as others would have to go with Paul to bring them to Jersualem.

He says a man from Missouri who has studied Greek has been shown that the Greek word "thesauridzon" means "in store," which means to store or to treasure up, suggesting a store house or treasure house. Our friend from Missouri, is happy indeed that his opponent has made this discovery for himself, as it is exactly what I have been trying to show him from the text in question (1 Cor. 16:2), that this was a laying by in store at home, in a store-house, and not at church. It required labor to store away these provisions in a store-house, and they were consequently commanded to labor on the first day of the week (1 Cor. 16) in order to do this.

My friend, there is no meeting mentioned in 1 Cor. 5:8.
Paul is not speaking of a certain meeting held there, as
you certainly know. Therefore neither bread, or wine are
mentioned. The Lord simply tells us here that the old
institution was to be carried over into the New Testament
church. That the passover was to be kept, but in a different
way. My reason for using this text was to prove that they
did not take the Lord's supper just any time, or every
week, but it was a definite institution, to be observed once
a year, just as it had been in the Old Testament order.
But here it was to commemorate the death of Jesus on the
cross, and you have not answered this argument and cannot
do so. It is the word of God, and is irrefutable. You say
"Christians did not come together in public assemblies to eat
a common meal." But the Lord says they had all things in
common, and they went from house to house, and did break
their bread daily. This was of course at home, and it was
at one of these home gatherings when it says they came
together "to break bread." that Paul preached unto them.
Why does it not say they came together to take the Lord's
supper. What right have you to assume this, when the
Lord does not say so? The Lord tells us just why they
came together at this night meeting, and it says it was
"to break bread." It does not say it was to worship God,
to hold a public meeting, or even to take the Lord's supper.
If it said this then we would have to believe it, but why
try to read something else into this text that is not there?
Why not leave it just as it is. It was a farewell meeting
of the brethren with Paul as the context shows, and held
after sundown Saturday for it was "the first day of the
week and dark." Therefore it was the dark part of the first
day, and the light part of the day was spent by Paul
walking across the cape to Assos, while the other brethren
were sailing around the cape, after having kept the sabbath at Troas. My friend says "the bread which Christians
broke when they came together was the Lord's supper,"
and he refers to 1 Cor. 11:20. It was the Lord's supper
referred to in this particular text, but if the bread Christians broke whenever they came together was the Lord's

supper, then they ate the Lord's supper daily, for they
broke bread daily, when they came together, in one another's home, (Acts 2:46) having all things common. He
says, it was Dugger who said the other brethren sailed
away before the Troas night meeting of Paul's when they
broke bread, but he failed to notice verse 13 where the
author of Acts 20:13 says: "We went before to ship, and
sailed unto Assos there intending to take in Paul for so
he had minded to go on foot." So it was not my statement
but that of the Lord's, although my friend said not a word
was found that told us this in the divine record. He better
read his Bible a little more closely hereafter. No wonder
my friend hangs so hard to Acts 20:7 for it is the only
place in the entire New Testament where a religious service
is recorded as taking place on the first day of the week,
and it happened to be in the night where Paul preached
until morning, to a company of disciples who came together
to eat their common meal as was always their custom
following the sabbath. He has admitted that the day before
the first day of the week was, and still is the sabbath day,
consequently he must agree that this Troas meeting where
they met to eat their common meal on the dark part of
the first day of the week, was following the sabbath. It
is not necessary for this to be stated in that particular
text, neither is it necessary for the Lord to mention every
meeting occurring on the 7th day as having occurred on
the sabbath. We have over fifty such texts in the New
Testament however.

He makes another wild assertion, as follows, "There is
only one passage in all the New Testament that gives the
time when they observed the Lord's supper, and that is
Acts 20:7." Please read the text. Not one word is said
about it. The word "Lord's supper" is not there, or even
hinted at being there. What right has anyone to try to
read such things into the Bible when anyone can see that
it is no where to be found? There are several texts in the
New Testament that tells us when they observed the
Lord's supper, as previously given. One of these is in
Luke 22:1-7 where it says Jesus introduced the supper

on the very day the passover lamb was killed, and this was
on the 14th of the month Abib. It was not confined to
any certain day of the week, for it came on different days
each year the same as your birthday, or any other fixed
date. The noted historians, Mosheim, and Eusebius speak
of Constantine about the year 321 placing the passover or
Easter on a fixed Sunday, stating that before this time
it occurred on different days of the week, falling on the
14th of the Jewish month Nisan or Abib. Jesus tells us
in Luke 22:7 to 20 when it took place then, and Paul speaks
of another Lord's supper (1 Cor. 11:23-26), where he
plainly says he gave it to the church **"As he received it
from the Lord,** the same night he was betrayed." This
does not say he gave it to the church for every first day
of the week. No, it is indeed far from that. He again
says, "Christ our passover was sacrificed for us therefore
let us keep the feast." He was speaking of the passover
feast, and tells them how to keep it, with the unleavened
bread, and the fruit of the vine. Now I have accepted
your challenge, friend Porter, and given you the texts, and
I can give you plenty more if this is not enough. Paul
says "He received of the Lord that which he delivered unto
the church, that the Lord Jesus the same night he was betrayed took bread" (1 Cor. 11:23-26). I ask my friend if
this was on the first day of the week, Jesus was betrayed?
You are not keeping the Lord's supper as commanded by
Paul when you try to observe it the first day of the week.
You have no scriptural authority. Paul says "the same
night he was betrayed," and not the day after he was
resurrected. His comparison to baptism, misses the mark
a long ways, for it does not in any way compare to this
truth. God has given us special instructions concerning
both of these ordinances, and not left us to guess at their
application.

He asks why Paul mentions keeping "this feast," when
it was only to be kept a feast by Israel, and then kept as
an ordinance forever. I see this truth is new to my opponent, and he has several things to learn yet. I am glad to
answer every question concerning this matter. Moses said

it would be kept "A feast to the Lord throughout your generations, ye shall keep it a feast by an ordinance forever" (Exodus 12:14). Now you see it is to be kept a feast in both dispensations. The word "feast" is mentioned in both phases, therefore Paul speaks of keeping the feast of the passover, but he kept it as we all know, and as the Lord plainly tells us, by using the unleavened bread, and the fruit of the vine, and just observed it at one service, and not for a whole week as Israel did under the first phase of this ordinance. It was of course an ordinance, as far as the word "ordinance" applies, but under the second phase when it was to be kept **forever,** there was to be a change, and the New Testament makes this change clear.

My friend seems to think that the disciples have already eaten the Lord's supper with Jesus in his kingdom, according to his promise in Luke 22:29, 30. I would like for him to give the text when this occurred. Surely if it happened the Bible must record it. Elder Porter does not believe the kingdom is yet future, hence he must think it is already set up here on earth. Surely it has utterly failed in its intended mission if this is true, in such a world filled with sin, sorrow, misery, death, war and destruction. The kingdom was to grow and fill the whole earth with peace, and not with war. See Isaiah 2:1-5, also 11:1 to 9, and 9:6, 7. Then Daniel 2:44, 45, and Psalms 110. The kingdom was to grow and fill the earth, and surely there has been but little progress during these 1900 years since Christ was here. The kingdom is future, and the apostles are going to sit with Jesus and eat the Lord's supper in his kingdom here on earth. This is not what Dugger thinks either, but it is exactly what the Lord says. Note this **"when** the Son of man shall come in his glory with all the holy angels with him **then,** shall he sit upon the throne of his glory. . . . . Then shall the king say unto those on his right hand, Come ye blessed of my Father inherit the kingdom prepared for you from the foundation of the world" (Matt. 25:31, 34). This is when the Lord's supper is to continue **forever,** and when Jesus will eat it anew with his disciples.

See Matt. 5:5, also Matt. 6:9, 10, Rev. 11:15, 18, and Rev. 21 where the holy city comes down from God upon this earth.

In my previous negative, the facts were brought out that the Roman Catholic church changed the law of God, when it changed the sabbath from Saturday to Sunday, and I gave some statements in proof of this. Now my friend asks me why I accept their teaching about this when I will not accept it on other matters? Here is the reason why, Elder Porter. The prophet Daniel would be a false prophet, if the Roman power did not change the law of God, for he told us plainly in chapter 7:25, that the little horn of the 4th beast was going to change times and laws. No one acquainted with history will dare to deny that Rome, and the church of Rome fulfill this prophecy. Hence this power must be found to do the things Daniel said they would, or Daniel has prophesied falsely. Many histories tell us that Rome changed the sabbath, through a long series of civil edicts, the first of which was by Constantine, 321 A.D., and then later the popes placed their supposed divine approval upon it, and it became the general practice of the church, and of the world.

While the names we have for all the days of the week, are of heathen origin, the same as Sunday, yet this day, having been named after the sun, "sun-day," became the greatest of days to the heathens. Most of them worshiped the sun because it was the greatest body of light in the heavens. Some worshiped the moon also, and called the next day, Moon-day, or Monday. When the Roman emperor Constantine embraced Christianity, he desired to make a law pleasing to the religion of the heathen, and especially to many who claimed to have embraced Christianity, but wanted to hold on to many of their pagan rites and festivals. See book called "Library of Universal Knowledge," article Sabbath. Or any history of Constantine. The Catholic book called Catholic Christian Instructed says, Question.— "What warrant have you for keeping the Sunday in preference to the ancient sabbath which was Saturday?" Answer. —"We have for it the authority of the Catholic

church, and apostolic tradition." Question.—"Have you
any way of proving that the church has power to institute
festivals and precepts?" Answer.—"Had she not such power
she could not have done that which all modern religionists
agree with her. She could not have substituted the observance of Sunday, for the observance of Saturday the
seventh day, a change for which there is no scriptural
authority." These and many more could be taken from
her works, to prove that she pleads guilty of the charge.
That she makes a self confession of being the very power,
Daniel prophesied would come and would change the law of
God. Hence the keeping of Sunday, instead of the true sabbath, is "worshiping the beast," the same as is sprinkling
for baptism, instead of immersion, for sprinkling came from
the same source. God made the heavens and the earth in
six days, and gave the sabbath to commemorate his power,
and also as an everlasting sign of his greatness. Now the
fourth beast (Daniel 7th, and Rev. 13th chapter), comes
along and gives Sunday as a sign of it's power. Which
are you going to believe and follow? Are you going to
receive the mark of the beast in your forehead, which is
the seat of your intelligence, and thinking power, or in
your hands with which you perform labor? This is the
closing message of the age, (Rev. 14:9, 10), and the seven
last plagues will visit those who fail God and worship
another in his place. Reader, you better take this matter
seriously, and ask God earnestly in prayer, to lead you and
guide you in its decision. Everything popular with the
world is wrong in religious matters, because the Holy Spirit
has largely been withdrawn from mankind because of their
wickedness and rebellious hearts. Prayer and much prayer,
for God's help, and presence, is all that will avail in studying
your Bible, amidst the confusion of this time.

Pentecost did not fall on Sunday the year of the crucifixion. My friend says it did, but he also said Jesus was
crucified on Friday, but as he was not, then Pentecost
could not come on Sunday either. Pentecost was always
calculated from the yearly sabbath which came the next
day after the Jews killed the passover lamb, the day of the

week it came each year would of course depend on the day of the week the Jewish passover fell upon. Jesus was killed on the same day they killed the lamb (Luke 22:1-7). As Jesus was crucified on Wednesday as we have shown, and not on Friday, hence Pentecost did not fall, and could not have fallen on Sunday that year. We take the following from Millennial Harbinger, Vol. 7, page 555, and Alexander Campbell says:

"The Hebrews, as you are aware, observed with great solemnity the seventh day, which they called 'Sabat'— rest, cessation from labor, because on this day God rested from the work of creation. From this word is derived the Greek and the English "Sabbath.' They used the word Sabat, however, to denote any cessation from work, whether that of the seventh day, Exod 16:23, 25, 26, 29, etc.; or of the tenth day of the month, Lev. 23:32 (comp. Lev. 22:39) or of the feast of trumpets on the first day of the seventh month (Lev. 24); or that of the seventh year (Lev. 25:2, 4, 6, 8).

"From the great respect paid to the 'sabbaths' they were accustomed also to reckon by them. Thus in Lev. 25:8: 'Thou shalt number seven sabbaths of years unto thee, seven times seven years; and the space of the seven sabbaths of years shall be unto thee forty and nine years.' Here we have the 'sabbath of years,' or the period of seven years. **And in the computation for** the day of Pentecost, (Lev. 23:15, 16.): 'And ye shall count unto you from the morrow after the sabbath, from the day that ye brought the sheaf of the wave-offering; seven sabbaths shall be complete; even unto the morrow after the seventh sabbath shall ye number fifty days.' **Here we have the sabbath of days, or the period of seven days.** In this way sabbath came to signify, both among the Greeks and Hebrews, not merely the principal day of the week, but the week itself."

The above evidence is conclusive, and exactly agrees with all Hebrew works, and Bible dictionaries, regarding the calculation of Pentecost. My friend will not discredit this eminent scholar of his own church and its founder. I have this old book before me on my desk as I write, and it is open for the inspection of anyone visiting my home.

My friend has failed so far to bring up any substantial evidence from the sacred writings for the observance of Sunday. Every argument, like this one relative to Pentecost, has fallen down. Even his assertion that Jesus was resurrected on Sunday, has proven false, by Jesus' own words, that he would be in the earth three days and three nights. I want him to bring up some evidence. He only has one more affirmative to do it. Let him show where it was the custom of the apostles to gather together for prayer and for preaching the gospel on the first day. Let him give one text where Jesus or the apostles told any one not to work on that day, or where it is called a holy day, a day of rest, or even a day of worship.

As he has failed so far, remember reader, that the seventh day is still God's day. It belongs to him, and none of us have any right to use it for ourselves. It is for God's work, and God's worship, and our rest spiritually and physicially, and is so set forth in both the Old and the New Testament.

PORTER'S THIRD AFFIRMATIVE

I need only to keep emphasizing my major affirmatives, discuss the points that come up in relation to them and keep my opponent's covering thrown back. Dugger refers to Acts 2:42, "Where they broke bread daily," and says, according to me, this makes every day holy. But Acts 2:42 does not say they "broke bread daily." I challenge him to find that statement in the text. This text tells us "they continued steadfasly in the apostles' docrine and fellowship, and in breaking bread, and in prayers." I predicted he would make no reply to my argument, and he did not. This passage shows frequency—they **continued** in breaking of bread. According to Dugger they had not broke bread at all at that time and would not till the 14th day of the first month of the next year. The daily breaking of bread is mentioned in verse 46 as another thing altogether and was done "from house to house," or at home, as the margin reads.

My friend keeps going back to the sabbath question, trying to establish that which he failed to establish in the first proposition. He tells us, however, that "it does not make a day holy * * * just because any one makes it their custom to preach on that day." Fine! I thank you for that admission. But he says he has found "84 sabbath days" which Paul "used in preaching the gospel," and he thinks this proves the sabbath holy. Suppose he had found a thousand sabbaths which Paul "used in preaching the gospel." He has already said that such a custom would not prove the day holy. So all that he has said on that point during this discussion has been surrendered by this admission. Yes, your Bible says "Jesus" in Heb. 4:8 if you read the King James Version, and it says "Joshua" if you read the Revised Version. I have made no effort to correct the translation but merely gave two translations already made. But read it either way, and it does not affect the argument. The fact remains that the rest that remained for the people of God had not been entered (verse 6) and a long time after they had received the sabbath God spoke of another day in David (verse 7). Furthermore, this rest was a promise (verse 1), but the sabbath rest was a commandment (Luke 23:56). I wonder if my friend doesn't know the difference between a promise and a commandment.

He complains because I did not quote all of the verses that mentioned the sabbath in the book of John. I was merely showing that he referred to the seventh day as the sabbath, and that had he meant the sabbath in Rev. 1:10 he would have used that term instead of "the Lord's day." So I just quoted enough of the passages to show that point. I didn't think any one would fail to see that, and certainly I didn't think Dugger would miss the point. Yes, I know it was the enemies of Christ who said "he kept not the sabbath" and did not intend to suggest anything else. I have said all the time that Jesus kept the sabbath because he lived "under the law" (Gal. 4:4). But Christians are "not under the law" (Rom. 6:14). That shows the difference.

My argument relative to "the Lord's day" in Rev. 1:10 still stands. I said the verse itself does not tell what day

was meant, but that related texts do show. And he has
miserably failed in his effort to overthrow the argument.
He thinks it might refer to the seventh day, if it refers to
a day of the week at all, for Jesus said: "I am Lord also
of the sabbath" (Mark 2:28). But note the word "also"—
Lord **also** of the sabbath. That shows he was Lord of the
other days too, and that would prove all days are the Lord's
day. But the truth is that Jesus was showing them he was
Master even of the sabbath and could do with it as he pleased.
He did and took it away, according to Col. 2:14-16. Later in
my friend's argument he says "the Lord's day" of Rev.
1:10 refers to the day of judgment. If so, John was already
there, for he said: "I was in the Spirit **on** the Lord's day."
He did not say: "I saw a vision of the Lord's day." But it
was "on the Lord's day" that he was "in the Spirit" and had
the vision. The day of judgment was far in the future to
John, and he could not be any where **on** it. He refers to the
past—"I **was** in the Spirit." When were you in the Spirit,
John? **"On** the Lords' day." The day was **present** when
John was in the Spirit; it was **past** when he told about it. If
I should say: "I was in my car on Independence Day," I
wonder if Dugger would think that Independence Day could
be in the future. It would have to be **present** at that particular time that I was in my car; and it would be **past** when I
told him about it. Now, you watch how my friend clears
up this matter about "the Lord's day" being the judgment
day. I predict he will pass it in complete silence. He is making a reputation for silence when he gets into a predicament.

I showed from Mark 16:9 that Jesus arose on the first
day of the week. But my friend denies this and tries to
prove he was crucified on Wednesday and arose on Saturday.
I shall notice his effort and then show that he was crucified
on Friday and arose on Sunday. Other Scriptures besides
Mark 16:9 show this to be true. Matt. 12:40 is introduced
to prove Wednesday crucifixion, as it states that Jesus would
be "three days and three nights in the heart of the earth."
If Jesus was not in the grave full 72 hours, my friend thinks,
the sign of his Messiahship fails. He wonders how "three

days and three nights" can be found from Friday to Sunday. It is easy enough when you consider the Jewish method of counting. There are three expressions which they used interchangeably—three days and three nights, after three days, and the third day. I might ask my friend if Jesus was in the grave full 72 hours, how he could get out "on the third day"? The Bible says he would arise "the third day" (Matt. 16:21). But according to Dugger, it would have to be "the fourth day." Don't expect him to clear this up, for if you do, you will likely be disappointed. But these expressions are used interchangeably. Matthew says "three days and three nights" (Matt. 12:40). Mark says "after three days" he would rise again (Mark 8:31). And Matthew, quoting the very same statement of the Lord, says he would be raised again "the third day" (Matt. 16:21). Why these different expressions? Simply because they counted any part of a day a whole day. So any part of three days could be called "three days and three nights," for the word "day" often included the night. Esther said: "Fast ye for me, and neither eat nor drink three days, night or day" (Esther 4:15). At the end of that time she promised to appear before the king. This involves "three days and three nights," for it says: "three days, night or day." But Esther 5:1 says: "Now it came to pass **on the third day**, that Esther put on her royal apparel, and stood in the inner court of the king's house." So the three days and nights simply reach to the third day. That is also true of the statement of the Lord about his burial and resurrection. "After three days" and "the third day" are also used to mean the same thing in Matt. 27:63, 64. Consequently, the sign of the Messiah does not fail if Jesus was crucified on Friday and arose on Sunday. We have one full day and parts of two others. With these parts counted as days, as the Jewish method was, it takes care of the "three days and three nights."

He introduces also Dan. 9:26, 27, which speaks of the Messiah being cut off "in the midst of the week," to prove Wednesday crucifixion. Sunday, Monday and Tuesday were on one side of it, and Thursday, Friday and Saturday on the other side. So Wednesday was the midst of the week. But the fallacy of Dugger is easily seen here. Begin reading at verse 24 and you will find "seventy weeks determined" upon God's people. These are divided into groups of seven weeks, sixty-two weeks and one week. In the last week, in the midst of it, the Messiah is cut off. So Dugger makes this a literal week of seven days. If that is so, then the other 69 weeks are literal weeks also. But Daniel says: "Know therefore and understand, that from the going forth of the commandment to restore and to build Jerusalem unto the Messiah the Prince shall be seven weeks and three score and two weeks." (verse 25). Here we are told there would be 69 weeks from the command to rebuild Jerusalem to the Messiah. If these are literal weeks, and they must be if the 70th week is, then it was only 483 literal days from the command to restore Jerusalem to the Christ. But we know it was that many years. Hence, in this prophecy a day is to be taken for a year, as Ezekiel on one occasion gave instruction to do (Ezek. 4:6). So the week, in the midst of which Jesus was cut off, was a week of seven years and not seven literal days. A man is hard pressed for an argument who will so misapply Scripture in order to prove a theory.

But what does the Bible say about when Jesus was crucified? Referring to the day of the Lord's death, Mark says: "And now when the even was come, because it was the preparation, that is, the day before the sabbath" (Mark 15:42). This writer says Jesus died the day before the sabbath. The sabbath came on Saturday; and the day before the sabbath was Friday. Let my friend's astronomers deny it, if they will; I would rather take Mark's statement for it. But what sabbath was this? The one which was immediately followed by the first day of the week. Read Mark 15:42 to 16:2 and you can see for yourself. Jesus died the day before the sabbath and "when the sabbath was past" (Mark 16:1) certain ones came "very early in the morning the first day of the week" (Mark 16:2). This was the same sabbath that followed the death of Jesus, and it was followed by the first day of the week. Read the whole account, Mark 15:42 to 16:2, forgetting about the chapter division, for it was not divided into chapters when Mark wrote it, and you can't fail to see that it was the weekly sabbath that immediately followed the crucifixion of Jesus.

Let us now look at his proof of Saturday resurrection. He introduces the records of Mark (16:1, 2), Luke (24:1-3) and John (20:1-8), which state that certain ones came to the tomb "early in the morning the first day of the week." But my friend thinks these give no idea as to when he arose, for his body was gone when they got there. Then Matthew's record is given to prove when he arose, but according to Matthew's record Jesus was gone when they got there. So that would not prove anything, according to Dugger. Yet Matthew said: "In the end of the sabbath, as it began to dawn toward the first of the week." I am not contending that they followed the Roman division of days; certainly they began their count at sundown. My opponent wastes a lot of effort along that line. Nor does the passage indicate that they came at the time the days met. My friend's position on this reduces the records to an absurdity. He claims that Matthew records a visit that took place on Saturday, and the others a visit that occurred on Sunday. But Matthew and Mark name the same persons who came. So I want Dugger to tell me why these women came on Sunday morning with spices to anoint the body of Jesus when they had been there on Saturday and knew his body was already gone. Dugger, please explain this in the light of your position. Then, why did the women, according to Mark's record, wonder who would roll away the stone, when they had been there the day before and knew the stone was already rolled away? I wonder if he thinks these women had no more sense than that. Yet that is the way it was if Dugger's position be true. Watch and see if he makes any effort to explain this absurdity. I predict he will answer with his usual silence. But there is perfect harmony between the records—all record the same visit. "In the end of the sabbath" of Matthew's record is from the Greek "Opse de sabbaton." The word "opse," according to Greek scholars, may be translated "after." Defining this word Thayer's Greek-

English Lexicon says: "With a genitive—opse de sabbaton, the sabbath having just passed, after the sabbath, i. e. at the early dawn of the first day of the week." So "in the end of the sabbath, as it began to dawn toward the first day of the week" simply means "when the sabbath had ended, as the first day of the week began to dawn." And many translations so give it. Note the following. C. B. Williams' translation: "After the sabbath, as the first day of the week was dawning." Twentieth Century Translation: "After the sabbath, as the first day of the week began to dawn." Weymouth's Translation: "After the sabbath, in the early dawn of the first day of the week." Wesley's Translation: "Now after the sabbath, as it began to dawn toward the first day of the week." Goodspeed's Translation: "After the sabbath, as the first day of the week was dawning." Wilson's Emphatic Diaglott: "Now after the sabbath, as it was dawning to the first day of the week." These translations are in perfect harmony with the meaning of the Greek, and they make perfect harmony between the four records of the event; but if we accept Dugger's application, we have intelligent women coming to anoint the body of Jesus, knowing his body was not there, and wondering who would roll away the stone, knowing it was already rolled away. I still say he will make no effort to clear up this absurdity in his position. But I am willing to be surprised if he wants to undertake it. This, too, agrees with the meaning of the word "dawn"—"as it began to **dawn** toward the first day of the week." The other writers say it was "early in the morning" of the first day. But my opponent says the Greek word from which "dawn" comes does not mean "getting light in the morning." That is what he says. What do the Greek scholars say? The word is "epiphoskouse" from the word "epiphosko." Thayer's Lexicon, recognized as one of the greatest in all the English-speaking world, defines this word like this: "To grow light, to dawn." And Liddell & Scott's Greek-English Lexicon says: "To grow towards daylight." But Dugger denies these great Greek scholars and says the word never means what they say it means. So take your choice. If you think he knows more about it than they do, then take what he says. But I believe I'll accept the Lexicons. So Jesus did not arise on Saturday, and my friend's argument fails.

But when did he arise? Mark says: "Now when Jesus **was risen early the first day of the week,** he appeared first to Mary Magdalene" (Mark 16:9). No one would ever have thought this meant anything but that Jesus arose the first day of the week if he had not been looking for proof of a false theory. But "was risen," my friend says, "is past perfect tense." So he thinks Jesus arose before the first day of the week. Yes, it was "past perfect tense" when Mark wrote about it, but remember that he wrote about thirty years after the incident occurred. So he said he "was risen." But "appeared" is also past tense, and I suppose that means he appeared to Mary before the first day of the week. If it works in one case, it works in the other. What straits false teachers are driven to as they try to defend their theories! But let us look at some other texts that show Jesus arose on Sunday. In Matt. 16:21 Jesus said he would "be killed and be raised again the third day." Note that. He would be raised "the third day" from the time he was killed. Now turn to Luke 24. Verse 1 tells of certain disciples who came to the tomb "upon the first day of the week." Then verse 13 says "that same day" two of them went to Emmaus. That was still the first day of the week. While on their way to this village they were discussing the death of the Lord and were sad. Jesus appeared to them in such way that they did not recognize him and asked them why they were sad. One of them asked him if he was a stranger and did not know the things that had come to pass. Jesus asked, "What things?" They told him about the death of Jesus. (Verses 14-20). Then they said: "But we trusted that it had been he which should have redeemed Israel: and beside all this, **today is the third day** since these things were done." (Verse 21). What "today"? That **same first day of the week** on which some had been to the tomb and on which these went to Emmaus. So they said: **"Today** (this first day of the week, Sunday) **is the third day"** since Jesus died. But Jesus said he would be raised "the third day" from his death.

If a man is able to put two and two together and get four, he should be able to see that if Jesus would arise "the third day" from his death, and Sunday was "the third day" from his death, then Sunday was the day of his resurrection. At least, that is what these disciples thought, for they said "certain women" of their company "were early at the sepulchre" and found the body of Jesus gone. (Verses 22 and 23). I wonder why they did not say "They found his body gone late yesterday afternoon."

Dugger thinks David's statement, "This is the day which the Lord hath made" (Psa. 118:24), could not refer to the future, for it said "hath made." I wonder if he doesn't know that prophecy is often spoken in past tense. Verse 22 says: "The stone which the builders **refused** is become the head stone of the corner." Does he think this means Jesus was already rejected and had become the chief corner stone before David wrote? I have before shown that "this day which the Lord hath made" is the same as "the Lord's day" in Rev. 1:10. It was a day of gladness and rejoicing because Jesus arose on that day. The effort to set aside the argument on the Greek word "kuriakos" by calling it the possessive is very weak. Certainly there is a way to express the possessive in the Greek. But the word "kurios," generally translated "Lord," has its possesive; and the word "kuriakos" has its possessive. They are not the same word —kuriakos is found only twice in the New Testament (1 Cor. 11:20; Rev. 1:10) and refers to Christ. The Lord's day (kuriake hemera) is a day especially associated with Christ, and no other day is as the day of his resurrection. Of course the possessive in the Greek is expressed by the Genitive case. But the day·is the Lord's, the one he made, a day of gladness and rejoicing, the day of his resurrection, the first day of the week.

Dugger says he has not refused to notice even one argument, but I "willingly ignore" his. Turn back to those questions in the first proposition that I begged so hard for him to answer; then see if you can find where he said anything about them. I even enumerated them for him, but not a word did he say. Now let him point out the ones I have ignored of his. I challenge him to do it. Watch and see if he does.

As to the Corinthian contribution he says I made light of Rom. 15:28. Oh no, I merely showed the absurdity of his application of it. He claimed it was literal fruit—figs, dates and raisins—and I showed him some other Scriptures containing the same use of the word "fruit." Although Dugger says he has answered every argument, I am unable to find where he even mentioned these Scriptures. He thinks the collection could not have been money, for if so, it could have been collected after Paul arrived. Well, Dugger, if it was what you say it was, a collection would have to be made after Paul arrived, for you say each man put it in his own storehouse at home. There would have to be a collection of it after Paul got there. But Paul said: "That there be no gatherings (collection) when I come" (1 Cor. 16:2). Please explain how there would be no gatherings after Paul came, if your position is true. I haven't been able to get you to say anything about this, although "you have answered all my arguments." And tell us, too, why Paul specified "the first day of the week." Why would not the second day or the fourth day of the week do just as well? What reason could there be for specifying the first day, if your position is true? I have begged you to answer this, but not a word have you said; although you have "not refused to **answer any argument.**" Perhaps I don't know what it means to refuse; but if I do, you have done it. And still he thinks it had to be literal fruit, for he had to have brethren to help him take it to Jerusalem (1 Cor. 16:3). I asked him if this little band of brethren could carry enough bushels of figs, dates and raisins to be called a "liberal contribution" from all the churches concerned. He says he has answered everything, but reader, see if you can find where he said anything about this. I just can't find it. Since my friend does not seem to know why other brethren went with Paul to take this offering to Jerusalem, if he will read 2 Cor. 8:19-21, he will find this precaution was taken to prevent any blame, or suspicion, being placed upon Paul in the matter—not to carry a heavy load of figs.

The man from Missouri still thinks this offering was laid by at home, and he denied that the Greek word "thesauridzo" ever means treasury. Certainly it sometimes means storehouse, but Dugger denied that it ever meant treasury and called for the proof. I gave it, but he ignored it. I'll give him some more. The noun form of this word is "thesauros." Thayer's Lexicon says it means: "The place in which goods and precious things are collected and laid up; a. A casket, coffer, or other receptacle, in which valuables are kept. b. A treasury. c. A storehouse, repository, magazine." Dugger, can you see those two words, a treasury? You say it never means that; Thayer says it does. Which shall we take? Liddell & Scott's Greek-English Lexicon, in defining the word, gives as an example, "the treasury of a temple." Dugger, can you read that? Then don't say it never means that. The reader is going to be able to see your blunder here whether you can see it or not. And in 1 Cor. 16:1, 2 it cannot be a store-house at home, for then there would have to be a gathering after Paul arrived. The fact remains that Paul ordered Christians to perform this religious service on the first day of the week, and the argument stands as an impregnable fortress against the attacks of Sabbatarians.

And the argument on Acts 20:7 still stands. The disciples "came together on the first day of the week to break bread." Dugger says this was not the Lord's supper but a common meal. I showed from 1 Cor. 11:34 that Christians did not **come together** to eat common meals—they did that at home. But Dugger says it was the custom of Christians to "come together to eat their common meals" following the sabbath. Show us some passage that mentions any such custom. Your word is not sufficient. Paul said: "If any man hunger, let him eat at home" (1 Cor. 11:34). Dugger says: "You are wrong Paul. It was always their custom to assemble following the sabbath for such meals. And you did it yourself at Troas." The "Lord's supper" is not mentioned in Acts 20:7. No, those words are not, and there are many expressions concerning that institution in which those words are not used. It is often called "breaking bread." And the bread which Christians broke when "they came together" was the Lord's supper (1 Cor. 11:20, 33). And the bread broken in Acts 20:7 was the bread broken when "they came together." It was the Lord's supper. Dugger says: "They broke bread daily, when they came together" (Acts 2:46). The passage says they broke bread daily "from house to house," or at home; **not when they came together.** Read the passage for yourself. I can't understand a man's heart who will add things like that to a passage. He thinks I made a wild assertion when I said Acts 20:7 is the only passage that tells when Christians observed the supper. Certainly I knew it was instituted the night Jesus was betrayed, but he said he would place it in his kingdom (Luke 22:29, 30), and the only passage that tells when they did it in that kingdom is Acts 20:7. The statement still stands. He thinks Acts 20:13 which says "we went before to ship, and sailed unto Assos" proves they left before the meeting at Troas in verse 7. Oh no, it merely shows they left before Paul did. But verse 7 says they stayed at Troas seven days. I called his attention to this before, but he silently passed it by. So I had already read the Bible a little more closely than he thought. I take no issue with my opponent about the Old Testament passover being observed on the 14th day of the month Abib, but we are not discussing the Old Testament passover; we are discussing the Lord's supper of the New Testament. It was observed on the first day of the week after the days of unleavened bread had passed (Acts 20: 6, 7).

My friend quotes 1 Cor. 11:23-26 as saying Paul says he gave it to the church "as he received it from the Lord, the same night Jesus was betrayed." But the passage says no such thing. Dugger even emphasized "as he received it from the Lord," but that is not even in the passage. But Paul said: "I have received from the Lord **that which** I delivered unto you." Nor does he tell them to take it "the same night Jesus was betrayed." I am astonished at my friend's not being able to read simple English. Even a sixth grade pupil would be ashamed of him. Paul said:

"Jesus the same night in which he was betrayed took bread." He instituted the supper "the same night in which he was betrayed." But Dugger says Paul told them to partake of it "the same night in which Jesus was betrayed." I would not want to impugn any man's motives, but this looks to me like a wilful wresting of the scripture to sustain a theory. I don't see how any man otherwise could get such an idea of it.

Dugger thinks he presented to me a new truth from Ex. 12:14 about his two phases of the passover. No, no. It was just a new form of error. Truth is consistent, but Dugger's position is not. Note his contradictions. In his first negative referring to the practice of Paul he said: "It was not being kept as the Jews had kept it, for they were to keep it as a **feast** throughout their generations." In his second negative he says: "Now you see it is to be kept as a feast in both dispensations." That is a clear-cut contradiction and cannot be truth. Concerning the "ordinance phase" he said in his first negative: "This last phase is the ordinance of Jesus Christ, as he introduced it." In his second negative he says concerning the Jews before Jesus **introduced it**: "It was of course an ordinance, as far as the word 'ordinance' applies." That's another plain contradiction. Do you call that truth? Truth does not contradict itself. But it was to be for "an **ordinance forever.**" I see. But I note that the blowing of trumpets was given "for an **ordinance for ever**" (Num. 10:8). Is Dugger keeping this ordinance?

A full discussion of whether the kingdom is future cannot be had here—only as it pertains to this question. Not one of the references given by Dugger, Isa. 2:1-5; 11:1-9; 9:6, 7; Dan. 2:44, 45; Psa. 110, even intimate the kingdom to be future. They are all contrary to that idea. And his reference to Matt. 25:31-34 is unfortunate for him. This points out the judgment scene, not the beginning of the kingdom. Any one can read Matt. 25:31-46 and see for himself. The Lord said he would place his table in his kingdom (Luke 22:29, 30). Did the apostles eat of it where Jesus placed it or did they eat of it elsewhere? (1 Cor. 11).

I challenge Dugger to answer this. Jesus said he would "drink it new" in his Father's kingdom. This simply refers to a new method—to a communion with his disciples as they partake of it—hence not the old literal form of drinking. Paul said he and the Colossian brethren were in the kingdom (Col. 1:13). John said he was in the kingdom (Rev. 1:9). But Dugger says it is still future. Yes, I know that in the regeneration the apostles were to sit on thrones (Matt. 19: 28), but they were to do that the same time they would eat at the Lord's table (Luke 22:30). But they were to eat at the Lord's table **before** Jesus comes—"till he comes" (1 Cor. 11:26)—not after he comes. Why don't you notice this, Dugger? I called your attention to it before, but you said not a word about it, although you claim you have answered everything. The reader will see your failure in this. You put it "after he comes"; Paul put it "till he comes."

I know that the Roman power, according to Dan. 7:25, would seek to change times and laws. But I deny that they abolished the sabbath and substituted Sunday, regardless of their claim. If so, then Paul was a worshiper of the beast when he said to let no man judge you in respect to the sabbath (Col. 2:14-16) and when he ordered a first day service (1 Cor. 16:1, 2). And the brethren who met at Troas in Acts 20:7 were all worshiping the beast. Furthermore, early writers spoke of first day observance a long time before Constantine made his edict in 321 A.D. Daniel did not prophesy falsely, but my friend made his prophecy sustain a false idea. Remember that the Catholics claim their church is the true church, Peter was the first Pope and that popes are infallible; but that doesn't make it so. And the same is true with their claim concerning Sunday. And let Dugger remember there is a vast difference between worshiping the sun on Sunday and worshiping God on Sunday.

I showed the importance of Sunday by the many things that occurred on the day of Pentecost in Acts 2. My friend denies that this Pentecost fell on Sunday. I am amused at his statement relative to the quotation he gives from Alexander Campbell. He said his opponent "will not discredit

this eminent scholar of his own church and its founder."
I inform my friend that I have no church. Also that Campbell did not found the one to which I belong, nor any other.
I no more accept Campbell as authority than I do Dugger.
The Bible is our authority—nothing else. But the quotation from Campbell does not even intimate that Pentecost
did not fall on Sunday. He might have said it somewhere
else, but he **did not say it** in the quotation Dugger gives.
Let us see, however, if Pentecost that year fell on Sunday.
The rule given in Lev. 23:15, 16 says: "Ye shall count unto
you from the morrow after the sabbath, from the day that
ye brought the sheaf of the wave offering; **seven sabbaths
shall be complete:** even unto **the morrow after the seventh
sabbath** shall ye number **fifty days."** Pentecost means
fiftieth. So fifty days must be counted in reckoning it.
And within that fifty days there must be "seven sabbaths
complete." And it follows "the morrow after the seventh
sabbath." Let us try the rule on Dugger's position. He
says Jesus was crucified on Wednesday, the 14th of the
month; that the yearly sabbath came on Thursday, the 15th;
and that the count for Pentecost began the next day—
Friday, the 16th. So let us begin our count that way—on
Friday—and count fifty days. I shall number each day
and emphasize each 7th day to mark the sabbaths and see
the results. So here we go. Friday, of course, is the sixth
day of the week. So we will begin with the sixth day.

   67 — 1234567 — 1234567 — 1234567 — 1234567 —
1234567 — 1234567 — 123456

Note that we have seven sabbaths. That is what the law
said. Also we have 50 days. That is right too. But where
does the 50th day fall? On Friday, the sixth day of the
week. And that is what Dugger wants. But what did the
law say? "On the morrow after the seventh sabbath." But
Dugger's count makes it fall on the sixth day after the
seventh sabbath. The law said on the first day—the morrow—after the seventh sabbath; but Dugger makes it on
the sixth day after that sabbath, which would be five days
too late. Check the count and you will see this is true. But
suppose we start counting where he does and stop "on the

morrow after the seventh sabbath." Look at the diagram again. We count to the morrow after the seventh sabbath, and we have only 45 days, but the law said 50 days. So he is wrong either way we take it. Seven sabbaths had to be complete, and these were weekly sabbaths, for you couldn't get seven sabbaths of any other kind within a period of fifty days. The weekly sabbath always came on the seventh day of the week. "The morrow after" any of them would be the first day of the week, and since Pentecost always came "on the morrow after the seventh sabbath," it always came on the first day of the week. That was true the year Jesus died; and Dugger is just wrong as to when to begin the count. I call upon him to take up this argument and deal with it. But I will not be surprised if he ignores it entirely. Such has been his custom in the past. I know that he cannot answer it; and if he does not know it, he will find it out when he tries. But I do beg him to make an effort. We wait to see what he will do about it.

DUGGER'S THIRD NEGATIVE

Elder Porter denies the fact of Alexander Campbell having anything to do with the founding of the church with which he is affiliated. This is no doubt true of that particular off-shoot he holds to, as there are no less than eight different branches coming from the old line church known as the Christian Church of which Alexander Campbell was the founder. This is a fact generally known by old members of all of these different branches. He says he will not take Alexander Campbell's word for anything any more than he will my word, but he wants the Bible. This is fine, but when it comes to an understanding of the Greek language, from which our Bible was translated, this is quite another matter. The Bible itself does not deal with these points. Alexander Campbell was a Greek scholar, and he knew the facts concerning the ancient word for "week" which was "Sabat", and the truth, if you want the truth, hangs on his explanation of these facts. The Lord says, "From the morrow after the sabbath (and this sabbath was a yearly Jewish holy day, and not the weekly sabbath), you shall count seven sabbaths or seven weeks." Hence this does not teach, or even infer, that Pentecost would always fall on a Sunday, as my opponent tries to teach. The work of Josephus, that eminent Jewish scholar and historian agrees with this, and so do all other Jewish Rabbis, teachers and scholars. The Jews never did celebrate Pentecost on a fixed Sunday, as it would be if our opponent's contention were true. Why does he oppose all scholars on this point, and even disregard the clear explanation of Alexander Campbell, the founder of the Christian Church, from which his church sprung, which fact he cannot deny? The only reason is, to try to make a point that Pentecost, in the days of the apostles came on Sunday, which facts will not allow. He claims the crucifixion occurred on Friday, and as already clearly explained, it fell on Wednesday. Pentecost is calculated always from the Jewish passover, hence the day of the week this event fell upon, fixes definitely the day of the week Pentecost fell the year our Lord was crucified. These seven sabbaths, were not weekly sabbaths, but the word "Sabat," as Alexander Campbell clearly explains, set forth fully in the previous negative, means a week, or a period of seven days, counting from the morrow after the yearly high day sabbath, which always fell on the 15th of the Jewish month Abib.

I have in my possession all of the copies of the "Millenial Harbinger," issued for three years under the editorship of Alexander Campbell, and there are many excellent articles by this profound student of the Greek text that would do my opponent good to read. Alexander Campbell understood the correct system used by the Hebrew people in calculating their festivals, and he teaches very plainly that Pentecost did not come on a fixed first day of the week, or Sunday, but that it rotated falling on different days of the week on every year, just as our birthdays and the 4th of July and other events falling on certain days of the month. Our opponent has entirely the wrong slant to these things, and he is in opposition to all scholars who give forth the truth, when they have no ax to grind, or no other prompting motive except the plain facts of truth.

Elder Porter calls Acts 20:7 one of his major affirmatives, when there is absolutely nothing said in this text about keeping the first day of the week, as a holy day, or a sacred day, or of it taking the place of the ancient sabbath, which was the seventh day of the week. The text says nothing about worshiping God, as the purpose of their meeting, but that they came together **to break bread.** We have shown already that following the sabbath the Jews had always made it their practice to meet together and eat, or take refreshments, which they called "breaking bread." Furthermore we lived in that country ourselves, and it is still the custom there of speaking of a common meal as breaking bread. Surely if this is one of his best arguments, he has failed to produce any good reasons for observing Sunday instead of the ancient sabbath of God, in this age. He has but one more affirmative after this one, and it seems from his first statement here, that he is already through bringing forth evidence on the subject, and he says all he needs to do now, is to hold to his major affirmative argument, and keep the covers rolled back from over his opponent. It seems that Elder Porter, has finished his evidence, and no more scripture is forth-coming in proof that the first day of the week was chosen by the apostles as a day of worship in place of the ancient sabbath. Surely he has some definite proof of this change. So far his three affirmatives, which include this one, is void of such proof. Not a text has yet been produced showing that Jesus or the apostles made it their custom to meet with the saints on the first day of the week. He has not given a text where we are told not to work on the first day, or where it is to take the place of the ancient sabbath, or where anyone was told not to work on the first day. When an institution like the sabbath was to be changed, which has been observed for thousands of years, by all people in the world, who were God's people, surely there is something definite about such a change. We urge him in this final thesis to bring forth the evidence. Show where the apostles made it their custom to assemble for worship on the first day of the week, if it is there. Show one text where they ever held a religious meeting on that day. So far he has shown but one religious meeting occurring on that day, and that was after dark on Saturday night, as we have proven. Also it was not called for the purpose of a religious gathering, but they came together to eat a common meal after the sabbath was passed. Then Paul preached to them through the night, and walked about nineteen miles on the light part of the first day to catch the other ministers who did not stay for the night meeting, but who spent the light part of that first day sailing around the cape from Troas to Assos. This day was spent in labor, for sailing in those days, required real work, rowing and manipulating the sails on the ship. Now we urge him to bring forth some concrete evidence. Produce some scripture where they made it their custom to meet on the first day, and where they did hold one religious meeting on that day, or where in the entire Bible God, or Jesus, or any of his apostles or prophets, ever called the first day of the week, a holy day, a sabbath day, or where anyone at any time, was ever told not to work on that day, or where the first day was ever called the sabbath day. We have given you many texts where the seventh day of the week, Saturday, was called the sabbath, in both the Old and the New Testament. One you remember is in Matt. 28:1 where it says "In the end of the sabbath as it began to dawn toward the first day of the week." This is New Testament scripture, and it calls the first day of the week, just the first day of the week, but the Lord calls the day before the first day of the week, the sabbath. Hence it is the sabbath. The word sabbath means rest, hence it is the rest day, just the same as it always was. God says he never changes, (Mal. 3:6), and unless you can give us positive proof, that another day was substituted for the seventh day sabbath, the readers will see your failure.

In verse one of Hebrews 4, the Lord speaks of the promised rest in Eden, this is true, but he has told us how to obtain this eternal rest, and it is through obedience. Obedience to the commandments of God through the indwelling Christ, by the power of the Holy Spirit. Unless we are overcomers of this wicked world, and all of her false ways and doctrines, and keep God's commandments we will not enter that Eden rest. The sabbath day here in the text in question (Heb. 4:4-9) is brought forth as important in our work of preparation. Unless we observe God's sabbath rest, we will not enjoy the promised eternal rest, for we are disobedient. See Rev. 22:14, also 14:12, and 12:17, also 1 John 5:3, 4 and many more.

We have already clearly shown that all who break the law are under it. Just as the man going down the street ignoring the traffic laws, and passing the red lights is overtaken by the police, and given a tag. That man gets under the law, under the power of the law; under the penalties of the law. He remains under it, until he pays his fine, or is pardoned, by the governor or judge. That is exactly where we all were. All were born in sin, under the law, and we must pay the penalty of the wicked, or receive our pardon through the grace of our Lord Jesus. After we have accepted the pardon offered by Christ, and he has set us free we are under his grace, or his favor, and released from the power of the law. Now after we are pardoned, and stand not under law any longer, but under grace, shall we break the law? Does the pardon given by the governor or judge of any court give the offender the right to go and break the speed laws again? No, by no means, does it. Then why try to argue that because we, one time sinners, now stand pardoned through the great favor or grace of Christ, can break the ten commandment law? It is absurd and ridiculous. Such teaching is exactly what the apostle Peter spoke of in 2 Peter 3:15, 16, where he says of Paul's writings, there are things in them hard to understand, which some people wrest (or twist) to their own destruction. That is exactly what our opponent is here doing. He is dealing with Paul's writings, and wresting them in such a way as to teach you that because you are under grace, you do not need to keep the law of God. Paul says "Do we then make void the law through faith? God forbid, yea we establish the law" (Rom. 3:31). He also says the law has dominion over a man as long as he liveth (Rom. 7:1). The Lord also says "Not the hearers of the law shall be justified but the doers of the law" (Rom. 2:13). James says we are to keep the whole law, referring to the ten commandments (James 2:10, 11). Therefore even if we are under grace as I gladly admit we are, we must also keep the law of God, and we can only do so, as the power of the Christ dwells within us, through his Spirit, by daily prayer.

As to the Lord's day, we have previously made a clear scriptural statement about this, and everyone who is praying to God for wisdom, and seeking him daily for the power of the Holy Spirit, will see the truth. God repeats it over and over again, in scriptures already given that the "seventh day of the week is the Lord's day." What right has Elder Porter to contradict God, and declare, the first day of the week to be the Lord's day, when there is not one text to prove it. I said if John was on any certain day of the week, and my opponent affirms he was, then it was on Saturday, and not Sunday, for God plainly says, "The seventh day is the sabbath of the Lord thy God" (Ex. 20:8, 9), and also he says the sabbath day is "my Holy Day" (Isa. 58:13).

I see Elder Porter still vainly endeavors to prove the Lord did not mean what he said, when he gave as the only sign of his messiahship, that he would be in the grave "three days and three nights." It is certainly fine indeed that we have a man with so much profound wisdom, who can now tell us clearly what Jesus meant, in-as-much as Jesus used the wrong words and failed to say what he meant. Through different witnesses the Lord has told us how long he would be in the earth, and "By the mouth of two or three witnesses, let every word be established" (2 Cor. 13:1). One witness says "the third day", another says "after three days," and another makes it specific by saying "As Jonah was three days and three nights in the whale's belly, so shall the Son of man be three days and three nights in the heart of the earth." We get from these three witnesses the truth. It is clear enough, that we need not be confused. The false doctrine from Rome, however, says he was crucified on Good Friday, and resurrected on Easter Sunday. This came from the wine of Babylon, upon which the whole world was made drunk

(Rev. 17:1-4, and 18:1-4). It is time for us to throw off the bondage of Rome, and do away with this wine of Babylon. The only thing that keeps people from believing the truth of all these witnesses, and taking it just as it reads, is the wine of Babylon. False doctrines from Rome. If Jesus had not of said "Three days and also three nights," then our friend's explanation might have done, but when Jesus said three days, and he also said three nights, then just parts of days will not do. He says if my explanation is true then Jesus would have come out of the tomb on the 4th day. Let us see if he would. He was placed in the tomb late on Wednesday, then after one day would be Thursday at the same time, after two days would be Friday at the same time, and after three days would be Saturday at the same time, and the angels came to the tomb "in the end of the sabbath," and our Saviour was resurrected then, for it is said that the angels came at that time, and rolled back the stone from the sepulcher. It does not say they had come, but that they came (present tense), at that time. Then he was not in the tomb on Sunday morning, and everyone who believes the words of God will know that he was not.

Elder Porter says the chapter divisions were made by man, and for us not to pay any attention to them but to read right on from one chapter into the other just as if there was no time elapsed between, and we would see that Jesus was crucified on Friday the day before the weekly sabbath. In the oldest Greek canuscripts, which I have personally seen, in the museums at London, England, and other places, the chapters are divided. Unless we study the word of God, as the Lord tells us, we will be mistaken about many things. He says "by the mouth of two or three witnesses, let every word be established." Then we must take the testimony of Matthew, of Mark, of Luke, and of John, relative to the resurrection of Jesus, for they all speak of it. After we have consulted each one, then we take all the evidence we have gathered together, remembering that it is all true. It all came from God, and must not contradict. John's testimony clearly informs us in chapter 19:14, and 32 that Jesus was crucified on the "preparation for the passover," and that it was the "high day sabbath," that drew on. Read it and see for yourself if you really want the truth. It was not the day before the weekly sabbath which would have been Friday, but the preparation for the big sabbath, that always came the 15th of Abib, the day after the Jews killed the passover lamb. See Leviticus 23rd chapter.

Notice carefully that Elder Porter says, the different writers all record the same visit to the tomb, but he is again wrong, and contradicts the plain testimony of God. Notice the following scripture, "Yes, and certain women also of our company made us astonished which were early at the sepulcher, and when they found not his body, they came saying that they had also seen a vision of angels which said he was alive, and certain of them which were with us, went to the sepulcher, and found it even as he had said, but him they saw not" (Luke 24:22-24). Now I wonder if Porter will acknowledge his mistake, or still contend that there was just one visit made to the tomb. Here we find some went and told others, then they went. While some of the same women were in the companies that made different visits, but it was not the same women who were there the night before that did the talking, when they asked who would roll the stone away, etc. This would be absurd, of course to believe, but this was a time of great excitement. The sepulcher was near Jerusalem, and of course there was a crowd of people there, and others coming and going all day. People were just as curious then as now, and a time like this would arouse the whole population. The place of the tomb of Jesus was evidently the scene of a constant crowd with new people coming and going throughout the day. To show again that it was different visits, we notice that the women coming there in the end of the sabbath which was before sundown Saturday night, did not bring the spices to anoint his body. It says "They came to see the sepulcher." They were keeping the commandment relative to the sabbath, and would not embalm his body, or carry 40 pounds of spices, with which to do

this work out there on the sabbath, but early in the morning of the first day of the week they brought their spices,
and it says "certain others were with them." They came
from different parts of Jerusalem, a city of one hundred
and sixty thousand people, and with no telephones, the
news of the late evening visitors to the tomb had not
reached the others, therefore according to previous arrange-
ments, they kept their appointment and the women who
were not there the night before, and knew not, the startling
events that had occurred naturally brought their spices,
and came in the morning of the first day of the week. It
was these women who raised the question, of who would
roll the stone away, etc.

After our friend gives a number of different translations
which suit him, then he says "But according to Dugger's
explanation," etc.

The common Bible which most everyone has in their
home, is the King James translation. It was translated
from the original Greek by 47 eminent Greek scholars.
These men knew their Greek. The king of England chose
50 Greek professors from among all the professions, and
religious sects known in his day. Forty-seven of them
came, and in the Jerusalem hall, of West Minster Abby in
London where they spent three years translating the Bible.
It was agreed that if any of them mistranslated one sentence, he would lose his head. It was under this drastic
discipline that the work was done. Therefore our holy
scriptures, which Porter says is a wrong translation on
this text, came from unprejudiced, Greek scholars. Many
different churches, today have a translation of their own,
made by some eminent evangelist or scholar, belonging to
that particular church, and therefore giving certain scriptures a rendering that suits their doctrine. This results in
the worst of confusion. Why do these men put themselves
up against 47 eminent Greek scholars, and say they are all
wrong, but this one man is right? What folly, and how
ridiculous it is. Porter has to condemn our Bible to establish his point. He says it is wrong, that others have discovered this error, and they now correct the mistake made

by all of these 47 men. Yet these men did the translating in the fear of death, if they made one crooked move. They had no motive for mistranslating Matt. 28:1. They were not trying to hold up error and propagate a false day of worship because it is popular, as many men to-day are endeavoring to do. These eminent Greek scholars he refers to, such as Liddell and Scott, Thayer, etc., do not dare say that the Greek word in this text "epiphosko," with its special grammatical context and construction means "after," or "past," or "getting light towards." Neither do they give it this meaning with the construction it has in this text in question.

I have taken the Greek text just as it reads, copying it word for word from my Greek New Testament, and presented it to the professor of Greek at the following state universities: Alabama, West Virginia, Iowa, Missouri, Michigan, Oklahoma, and California, and every one of these men translated it "late on the sabbath," or "after the sabbath." They translated the Greek sentence just as any student would in class, and any other professor of Greek will translate it the same way who wants to hold his reputation as a Greek scholar. The sabbath question is now a live issue between many people all over the world. We are in a fight over error that has crept into religious practice, such as Good Friday, Easter Sunday, etc., which came from Rome, and many people have been taught these things until they actually believe them to be true, and try to make the Bible read their way by getting out a late translation correcting errors as they call it. You have quoted from some of these translations trying to prove them right and our common version of the Bible wrong. Why inject such needless confusion into the minds of people, causing them to doubt the truth of any translation? I admonish you, Elder Porter to take our common Bible, translated by able and learned men, who were much more familiar with the Greek language than most people are today. It is time to throw off the traditions, dogmas, and teachings from Rome.

It is amusing how the Elder tries to get around the grammatical construction of Mark 16:9 viz. "When Jesus was risen," which we showed was past perfect tense, therefore it did not say he arose that day but at a time previous and indefinite. He said it was written this way because Mark wrote it several years after it happened. How cunning and deceptive is his dodge of the real issue. So was Matthew 28:1 written several years after Jesus arose from the dead, but the Holy Spirit narrated that event as present tense. Why? This is not hard to answer. It was because Jesus arose that day, "In the end of the sabbath," which the Holy Spirit said preceded the first day of the week. Here the Lord told us that the stone was rolled away then, present tense, that the angels also descended then, present tense, etc., although this was written years after he arose, and it was past tense when it was written. All we need to do, dear reader, is to believe the Lord, and we will not get confused.

Porter misleads us again by stating that the women talked together on the road to Emmaus, on the first day of the week, saying that "To-day is the third day," since Jesus died. They do not say any such thing. Read just what they do say (Luke 24:14-20). They say "Besides this today is the third day since these **things were done.** The question followed, "What things" (verse 19). Here is the answer "The things concerning Jesus of Nazareth." It is true that this was the first day of the week, and it was also the third day since **these things** were done. The things concerning Jesus of Nazareth, pertaining to his crucifixion and burial were not done, or finished, until Thursday morning. He was crucified in the midst of the week, just 72 hours before his resurrection. His resurrection was "In the end of the sabbath"? (Matt. 28:1), hence he was crucified just 72 hours, "three days and three nights" before. This brings us to Wednesday. He was buried in the even (Matt. 27:57-60). Then verse 62 says, "Now the next day that followed" . . . . certain ones came to Pilate and said they would take his body away and say he had risen from the dead, so Pilate told them to go and make the sepulcher as sure as they could, and they sealed the stone and set the Roman watch (see verses 62-66). The

Roman watch consisted of 60 soldiers, twenty of whom watched 8 hours at a time. This was done on Thursday morning, and it finished the "things **concerning Jesus of Nazareth.**" Therefore Sunday would be the third day "since **these things** were done." They were not all done until the important event of the sealing of the stone with the Roman seal, and the placing of these 60 men guard over the tomb. This makes perfect harmony out of the whole scripture narrative, and Jesus was in the grave just three days and three nights, or 72 hours as he said, and he arose on the sabbath day, not the first day.

Porter comes back again with Psalms 118:24, "This is the day which the Lord hath made," and still claims it is Sunday, because some prophecies are given as if they were passed when they are future. This is true, for prophets often narrated visions they saw in the past relative to future things. If we had some other scripture showing that God or Jesus had ever made but one day holy, then we might think this possibly referred to the future, but not a word is said in the New Testament about the first day being a holy day, or made by the Lord Jesus, or even chosen by him in any way whatsoever. We still maintain, and so will any other person who has studied either Greek or Latin, that the arrangement of words in the sentence determines their endings. This is true of "kuriakos," and simply shows it to be in the possessive case.

The Elder tries to make it appear that his arguments previously set forth in the other proposition were so difficult that I purposely ignored them. Let him bring forth some of these profound and difficult questions that we could not handle. I challenge him to even show one. He wants me to show some scripture that he failed to answer. I guess he has run out of anything further to present on this proposition and wants me to introduce something from the previous one, in order for him to fill in his space, and have something to talk about. So far he has just rehashed the same old arguments which at first seemed to contain evidence in favor of the first day of the week, but since I have explained them and shown positively that they contained no command whatever for first day worship, he is at sea, like a rudderless ship dodging here and there. If he has any real argument for Sunday observance, showing that Sunday is the sabbath or the Lord's day I want him to bring it out and stop vizzeling around. I have given substantial scripture showing that the 7th day is still the sabbath in the New Testament, such scripture as Matt. 28:1, "In the end of the sabbath as it began to dawn toward the first day of the week," etc., which no one can get around. The first day of the week is just the first day of the week, and the day before it is the sabbath. Anyway this is what the Holy Spirit called it down in the gospel age, and it must be so.

He insists that it was not fruit they gathered on the first day of the week in 1 Cor. 16:1, but I gave Paul's words in Rom. 15:28 that the gathering was fruit. It must have been the kind of fruit they raised at those places, and it required others to go along with Paul to carry whatever it was to Jerusalem (1 Cor. 16:3). The reason he did not want them to gather it when he came, he wanted them to have this prepared, and be ready to attend his meetings. Let me ask him a question. If it was money, then why did he not want them to gather it when he came? Most preachers take up the money when they call around. You ask why Paul does not tell them to gather this on the second day of the week, or the third day? And why did he specify the first day? If you want to be critical, Paul did not specify the first day, for the word "day" is in italics. This shows it is not in the original Greek. The text really reads "On the first of the week," not on the first day of the week. Furthermore if the churches were meeting on the first day of the week, why did not Paul say, "When you come together on the first day of the week, bring your collection for the poor saints at Jerusalem"? Why is there not some text similar to this found in all the New Testament, if the church was meeting on that day, and if it was to take the place of such an important practice as keeping the seventh day, over as long a period of time as they had kept the seventh day? Why is there not something more in the New Testament than simply an order to take up a special collection of provisions, on the first day of the week, and another where they just came together to "break bread on that day." You claim the breaking of bread on the first day of the week mentioned here, was the Lord's supper, and that it was taken on the first day of the week always. The Lord tells me that the taking of the unleavened bread and the cup, was to "show forth his death" until he came. Where do you find the scripture that they were to show forth his death, on the day you say he was resurrected? Why take the bread at noon, as you do when Jesus called it a supper, and Paul gave it at night? You have refused to answer these questions, and now you have but one more affirmative. Are you going to continue to ignore them? Let us wait and see.

Elder Porter is sure fond of misquoting me, and thus making the readers believe I have had to re-trace my steps. He says "the man from Missouri denies that the Greek word "thesauridzo, ever means "treasury." Now please go back and read the other pages and see just what the man from Missouri did say. I said I was happy indeed that my opponent had made the discovery of just what the Greek word did mean, and I agreed with just what he said it means, and I still agree. What is the sense of spending so much time rehashing over this? Is it all he has? Is there nothing in the New Testament telling us to worship on the first day, or to not work on that day, or that the early church met on that day to worship God? We admit that the Lord commanded them to use it as a day of business, collecting for the saints, and have shown that this was fruit they collected on that day in Romans 15th chapter, and thus required labor, and not rest on that day.

The Elder thinks that a sixth grader would do better than his opponent in understanding his arguments, and it is indeed unfortunate that he happened to get tangled up with such an ignorant man. It would be fine indeed to have much learning, like Elder Porter, and be able to see that "Three days and three nights" can intervene between Friday evening and Sunday morning: also that beginning to count on the first day of the week the phrase, **"after eight days"** brings us square on another first day of the week: that when it says "the apostles came together **to break bread,"** on the first day of the week, sure means they came together to hold a religious service every first day; that when the scripture speaks of "the Lord's day," it means Sunday when not one word is said about what day of the week it refers to: also when the Lord calls the day before the first day of the week the sabbath in the New Testament, that he did not mean what he said. It is too bad Elder Porter that I am so ignorant I cannot see these things. You know the Lord speaks of people in the last days who he says, "will be ever learning, and not able to come to a knowledge of the truth" (2 Tim. 3:7 also 4:3, 4). Do you suppose I am really one of these? What would you advise me to do with myself, so I could see that from Friday evening until Sunday morning, just one day and two nights, made "three days and three nights," etc.?

He claims the Lord established the table in the kingdom while he was here and quotes the scripture that they were to eat of the bread "till he comes," and not after he comes, and gives Luke 22:30. This reads, "And I appoint unto you a kingdom, as my Father hath appointed unto me. That ye may eat and drink at my table in my kingdom, and sit on thrones judging the 12 tribes of Israel." Again I find my thinking powers lacking, that which it takes to see, where the apostles sat on 12 thrones **then,** judging the twelve tribes of Israel. There may be some sixth graders who could see this, by the evidence you have given, but I will confess, that my mentality is not sufficient to be able to do so.

You have surely disjointed scriptural connections here again, dear Elder, and I adjure you to look once more. You will see that in 1 Cor. 11:26 it says the bread and the cup, or "the sacrament" show forth his death till he comes, but after he comes then he partakes of these emblems again with them in his father's kingdom. It will also be at that time, the 12 apostles will sit with him, and judge the 12 tribes of Israel. This is made even plainer in Matt. 19:28 where it says "When the Son of man shall sit in the throne of his glory, ye shall sit with me on 12 thrones, etc." In Rev. 3:21 Jesus also says, "He that overcometh will I grant to sit with me on my throne, even as I also overcame and am sat down with my father on his throne." There are two thrones you see, and Jesus is not on his throne yet, but he will be when he comes. See Isa. 9:6, 7, and Luke 1:30 to 33, and Matt. 25:31.

He says the following scriptures do not refer to the future kingdom, Dan. 2:44, 45, Isa. 11:1-9, and Isa. 2:1-5, etc. Please read them for yourself and see. If the kingdom referred to here has already come, and we are in it now, then surely it has come far short of what God said it would be, with such violence, war, wickedness and sin, as we have today. He thinks his church is the kingdom of God on earth, set up on the day of Pentecost, and that it is this stone, that was to grow and fill the whole earth. It looks to me like it had made a terrible failure during these 1800 years, when it was to grow and fill the whole earth, with peace and righteousness. Someone is surely seeing things wrong. We will let the readers be the judge.

Will he please give the scripture where Jesus established the table in the kingdom of God, and his followers were to break bread every first day of the week, to commemorate his death on the cross.

PORTER'S FOURTH AFFIRMATIVE

I shall notice some of the statements of my friend when I give my summary. But a few of them I wish to note in advance of that. First, however, I wish to give an additional thought on Heb. 4:8. I have stated that the validity of my argument did not have to depend on whether it was translated Jesus or Joshua. The Authorized Version gives "Jesus"; the Revised Version gives "Joshua." Dugger thinks Joshua would be a mistranslation, for it is the same Greek word that is elsewhere translated Jesus, referring to Christ. I wonder if Dugger did not know that the words are the same, Jesus the Greek form, and Joshua the Hebrew form. Defining the Greek word "Iesous" from which we get the word Jesus, Liddell & Scott say: "Greek form of the Hebrew Joshua." So the word may be translated either Jesus or Joshua, and the word does not always refer to Jesus the Christ. The context of Heb. 4:8 shows reference is made to Joshua and not to the Christ. The same thing is true of the word in Acts 7:45, translated Jesus in the King James version and Joshua in the American Revised. The same word is used in Acts 13:6, Bar-iesous, Bar-Jesus, the son of Jesus, where the word cannot refer to Jesus the Son of God. I do not expect Dugger to make any serious attempt to answer this, but he will just come back and say it refers to Christ, ignoring the fact that "Iesous" is the Greek form of the Hebrew Joshua.

I am astonished at my friend's lack of information about the Church of Christ and the Christian Church. The Church of Christ is not an off-shoot of the Christian Church. We occupy the same ground that was occupied before the division occurred, and the Christian Church is the faction. People who are informed on this will feel sorry for my friend. But Alexander Campbell did not found either body. This is just another of Dugger's blunders.

That fine speech Dugger made about the 47 translators of the King James Version losing their heads if they mistranslated any part of the Bible loses its effect when we note that, just before he made that speech, he corrected those same 47 translators. In Lev. 23:15, 16 they translated: "Seven **sabbaths** shall be complete." But Dugger says it should read: "Seven weeks shall be complete." This he says because the original word "sabat" means week. Well, I wonder why they did not lose their heads over that deal. Perhaps no one discovered their mistake till Sabbatarians began to try to overthrow the arguments in favor of the first day of the week, and then it was too late for them to lose their heads, for they were already dead. But did not Dugger know that in the expression, "from the morrow after the sabbath," the word sabbath is from the very same original word? But he will not let it mean "week" here but says it "was a yearly Jewish holy day." So if this original word means a day in this case,

why must it mean week in the rest of the verse. I suppose
Dugger had overlooked this fact. Furthermore, the Greek
word "sabbaton" from which we get the English word sabbath in the New Testament also means "a week." But
when Dugger reads that Paul at Corinth "reasoned in the
synagogue every sabbath" (Acts 18:4) he would not think
of letting it mean week, as he wants to be sure to have
Paul work on the first day of the week making tents.
According to Moses the count for Pentecost began "on the
morrow after the sabbath" of the passover week and ex-
tended till seven sabbaths were complete, and "on the
morrow after the seventh sabbath" was Pentecost. That
put it on the first day of the week, and I am not in conflict
with all scholars at this point. This is purely an assertion
by Dugger. But suppose we grant his claim that the word
should be translated "week," and that the count began on
the 16th of Nisan, or Abib, we would still have Pentecost
falling on Sunday the year Jesus was crucified. He was
crucified "the day before the sabbath" (Mark 15:42), and
if he died on the 14th day of the month, Friday would be
the 14th. He arose the third day (Matt. 16:21), which
was the first day of the week (Mark 16:9). The first day
of the week, therefore, would be the 16th. So the count,
according to Dugger, began there. When you count seven
weeks from that date and reach the morrow after the
seventh week, it falls on the first day of the week. Thus
my argument still stands that Pentecost fell on Sunday.

The discussion over the day of the Lord's resurrection
is vital to this issue. If Jesus arose on the first day of
the week, it attaches an importance to that day that Dugger
does not wish. So I return to the things that concern this.
As to "the three days and three nights" of Matt. 12:40 I
have already shown the Jewish way of counting clears up
this difficulty, for they counted a part of a day for a whole
24 hour day. This would take care of the night. But if
Dugger is unwilling to take this, I might remind him that,
after all, the text does not say "three days and three nights
in the grave" but in "the heart of the earth." From the
time Jesus was betrayed till he arose he was in the hands

of the ruling power of the earth. That will give him his extra night. So take it either way and Dugger's argument fails. If he replies that Rome, not Jerusalem, was the heart (or center) of the powers of earth, I might remind him that a sepulchre in a rock on the surface of the earth is not the heart (center) of this old earth either. I have shown that Jesus would arise "the third day" (Matt. 16:21). Now, I would like to know how Dugger would get his resurrection on the third day according to his count. He has completely failed at this point. The sabbath before which he was crucified (Mark 15:42) is clearly shown to be the one that preceded the first day of the week, if you will just read the closing of chapter 15 and the opening of chapter 16. But Dugger thinks there was a division of chapters by Mark because he has seen it so in old Greek manuscripts. I wonder if he thinks those manuscripts were the original. My friend insists that the sabbath that followed the crucifixion of Jesus was the yearly passover sabbath, not the seventh day, because John calls it a "high day" (John 19:14, 31). Now, look what my friend has done. He makes the passover sabbath the "great sabbath," or "high sabbath." Thus he exalts the passover sabbath above the weekly sabbath and makes the greatest sabbath commandment in "the law of Moses" instead of in the ten commandments. I thought he wanted the ten commandments to be the greatest of all. He has now ruined his position on that. The fact is, the passover sabbath (the day after the killing of the lamb) and the weekly sabbath (the day before the first day of the week) came on the same day that year. The day, therefore, had the importance of both the passover sabbath and the weekly sabbath attached to it and was called a "high sabbath day."

My opponent admits that it would be absurd to believe the same women came back to the tomb on Sunday morning with spices to anoint the body of Jesus who had been there the day before and found his body gone. The first group, he says, did not come to anoint his body but only "to see the sepulchre" according to Matthew. But Mark tells of a different group of women who came the next day to anoint his body, not having heard of his resurrection. Well, let us see what the record says about it. Who were they who came according to Matthew? He says: "Mary Magdalene and the other Mary" (Matt. 28:1). Get that. Matthew mentions two Marys. But what does Mark say? Does he say the same ones came on Sunday morning, or was it a different group? Here is his statement: "And when the sabbath was past, Mary Magdalene, and Mary the mother of James, and Salome, had bought sweet spices, that **they** might come and anoint him" (Mark 16:1). Who prepared these spices? The same two Marys mentioned by Matthew, and Salome. Did these same Marys come to anoint the body of Jesus? Dugger says they did not. What does Mark say? Read the next verse: "And very early in the morning **they** (They who? The two Marys and Salome who had prepared the spices.) came unto the sepulchre at the rising of the sun." And what else did "they" do? Verse 3 says: **"They** said among **themselves,** Who shall roll away the stone?" Note that is the same "they" who prepared the spices that came to anoint the body of Jesus and wondered who would roll away the stone. And they were Salome and the two Marys who were mentioned by Matthew. So according to Dugger he will have to believe what he says is absurd to believe. Certainly they did not go there on Saturday and then go back on Sunday to anoint the body when they knew it was already gone. Dugger will never get out of this predicament. If it was somebody else who brought the spices, why did not the Marys tell them that Jesus had already arisen, and let them dump their forty pounds of spices and get rid of the load? But Luke reports that some had been to the tomb and said they "had **also** seen a vision of angels" (Luke 24:22-24). Dugger thinks this means some had seen the vision on Saturday, and these also saw it on Sunday. No, not that. They had been to the tomb and they **also** saw the vision; this was in addition to their being to the tomb, not in addition to a vision seen by some one else. Who were these that made this report? Luke says: "It was Mary Magdalene, and Joanna, and Mary the mother of Jesus, and

other women" (Luke 24:10). So he mentions the very ones
mentioned by Matthew. That ruins my friend again. His
argument that the excitement of the hour caused some one
else to make these statements is ridiculous. Matthew, Mark
and Luke name two of the same women. So I am still
insisting that they record the same visit. My friend is
wrong as usual.

I gave a number of translations that give Matthew's
record as saying "after the sabbath." He rejects all of
these and makes his fine speech about the 47 translators
losing their heads. I also showed the Greek word "opse"
may be properly translated "after," and gave Thayer's
definition to prove it. Dugger passed this by. Yet he tells
us he presented this text to Professors of Greek in various
universities "and every one of these men translated it 'late
on the sabbath' or 'after the sabbath.' * * * And any other
professor of Greek will translate it the same way whc
wants to hold his reputation as a Greek scholar." Thank
you, Dugger. The professors of Greek whom you consulted
said it might be translated "after the sabbath." That is
the very thing I affirmed and you denied. So all your Greek
professors agree with me. And every other Greek scholar,
you say, will do the same thing. That's fine. I hardly expected my opponent to admit so much. Thus he admits
that Matthew's language, according to all Greek scholars,
may be translated: "After the sabbath, as it began to
dawn toward the first day of the week, came Mary Magdalene and the other Mary to see the sepulchre." This
makes perfect harmony between his record and that of the
other writers. I am glad to know that my opponent knows
that all Greek scholars will agree with this. This is all I
contended for. I thank you again, my friend. But before
making this admission Dugger says that Liddell & Scott
and Thayer "do not dare say that the Greek word * * *
'epiphosko' * * * means 'getting light towards'." I gave
their definitions in my preceding affirmative. Liddell &
Scott say: "To grow towards daylight." Thayer says:
"To grow light, to dawn." So they do say what Dugger

says they dare not say. Why did he not notice what they said instead of making a reckless assertion?

Mark plainly states that the resurrection of Jesus occurred on the first day of the week (Mark 16:9). Dugger tried his hand on the tense of the verb and got into it. Now, he tries to recover by a reference to Matt. 28:1. He says this was written after it happened too, but Matthew used the present tense in telling it. He tells us that "they came (present tense) * * * the stone was rolled away (present tense), the angels also descended (present tense)." Do you remember his saying something about the sixth grade pupil? Well, if I had a sixth grade child, and he thought that **came, was rolled,** and **descended** were present tense of the verbs, I would want to have his mentality examined. I suggest to Elder Dugger that he make a date with a good English Grammar every night for the next six months and see if he can learn to distinguish between the past tense and present tense of verbs. I wouldn't blame his brethren for being ashamed of him at this point: I am ashamed of him myself. And while I am talking about the tense of verbs I might mention again the words of Mark 16:9: "When Jesus was risen early the first day of the week." Dugger said that all grammarians know that "risen" is the past perfect tense of "rise." So he claimed the statement shows that Jesus arose before the first day of the week. I granted that the incident could be in the "past perfect tense" at the time Mark wrote, for he wrote 30 years later. But strictly speaking "was risen" is not the "past perfect tense"—it is the simple past tense. As to the principal parts of verbs, "risen" is the perfect participle, but it might be used in any of the tenses. "Is risen" is present tense; "was risen" is past tense; "will be risen" is future tense; "have been risen" is present perfect tense; **"had been risen" is past perfect tense;** "will have been risen" is future perfect tense. So Dugger was wrong on this. "Was risen" of Mark 16:9 is the same tense as "was rolled," or rolled, in Matt. 28:2. Dugger says "was risen" is past perfect tense and "was rolled" is present tense.

But he is wrong about both of them; they are both simple past tense.

My friend dies hard on the statement made by the two disciples who went to Emmaus who said: "Today is the third day since these things were done" (Luke 24:21). He was so befuddled that he called them "the women." Well, one of them was named Cleopas (Luke 24:18), and Cleopas was the husband of a wife named Mary (John 19:25). I haven't learned yet how a woman can be a husband. Perhaps Dugger learned that along with his tense of verbs. But how does Dugger fix up their statement? They, speaking of the first day of the week following the Lord's death, said: "Today is the third day since these things were done." That puts the resurrection of Christ on Sunday, for he was to arise the third day, and they said "today is the third day." My friend thinks he has it fixed by asking "What things?" Then he finds the answer: "The things concerning Jesus of Nazareth." So far, so good. But let me ask: "What things concerning Jesus of Nazareth?" Certainly not all things that concerned him. So which of the things? They answer: "How the chief priests and our rulers delivered him to be condemned to death, and have crucified him" (verse 20). So they say: "This is the third day since Jesus was delivered and crucified." Dugger says it is not so, but that it was the third day since the Roman guard was placed at his tomb (Matt. 27:62-66). It so happens, however, that they said not a single word about the guard being placed at the tomb. That is not a part of "these things" which they mentioned. Dugger puts that into their mouths when the divine record does not even mention it. He is certainly hard pressed. He claims "these things" mentioned by these disciples were not done (finished) until the tomb was sealed and the guard was set. Think of that! Jesus was not delivered to be condemned to death till his tomb was sealed and the guard was stationed. He was not crucified till the Roman soldiers were placed at his tomb. That is what Dugger claims. A fellow who thinks that came, rolled and descended are in the present tense is likely to say anything. If he could make the present tense extend over thirty years, he ought to make it extend till the next day, of course. But Jesus was delivered (it was complete, or finished) and crucified (this was finished) the day before the guard was placed at his tomb (Matt. 27:62). Matthew says this guard was placed "the next day." So you can't count from that event; it was not even hinted at in "these things" mentioned by the disciples. It was "the third day" since Jesus was delivered and crucified, not since the guard was placed at his tomb. My friend's cause is hopelessly lost at this point. Jesus arose the third day after his death, and Sunday was the third day.

Dugger professes a dislike for hash, but he goes back to the first proposition and brings up again all those scriptures about "the law," "the commandments," being "under the law," and such like, which have been thoroughly discussed during the first proposition. Whether he has a dislike for hash depends on whose hash is being served.

He claimed I had willingly ignored his arguments. I challenged him to present some of the arguments ignored and predicted he would be silent about it. And sure enough he was—not one word did he say. But his challenge to me to produce some questions in the first proposition that he would not answer is pitiful. In the summary of my final negative I numbered nine distinct "Unanswered Questions." The reader can turn back and read them, and if any reader ever finds Dugger's answer to any of them, I wish to would write me a letter and tell me where he found it. I could not locate such an answer. But he asks me why I take the communion at noon when Jesus called it a supper and Paul gave it at night. He says I have refused to answer this. So I guess this is what I "willingly ignored." But if the reader will turn to the latter half of my second affirmative, he will find where I showed the word "supper" is from the Greek "deipnon" and may refer to any meal of the day. Then if he will turn to the latter part of my third affirmative, he will find my discussion of his claim that Paul gave the supper at night. It was in this connection that I mentioned the sixth grade pupil. Dugger, think hard and see if you can't remember that. Have you completely lost, your memory or forgotten how to read? What will the reader think when he sees my answer in black and white and then reads your statement that I "refused to answer" them. Don't be so reckless with your statements and save yourself some embarrassment.

Yes, I am sure Dugger is among those described by Paul who are "ever learning and never able to come to a knowledge of the truth" (2 Tim. 3:7). Dugger wants to know what I would advise him to do. I recommend that he give up his contention for the Old Testament law, turn to the Lord, and when he does, Paul says: "the veil will be taken away" that is upon his heart or mind (2 Cor. 3:14-16). If the sixth grader can understand that "after three days" (Mark 8:31) would end on "the third day" (Matt. 16:21). then I am not uneasy but that he can also see that "after eight days" (John 20:26) would end on "the eighth day," even though my friend with a veil over his heart is not able to see it.

It is still unnecessary to enter a long discussion about whether the kingdom has been established. I showed that Paul, the Colossian brethren and John were all in it (Col. 1:13; Rev. 1:9). So I suppose it was not to be established thousands of years in the future. Dugger put on his silencer when he reached these passages. It is true that Christ is on his Father's throne now (Rev. 3:21), but he is also on "his throne" (Zech. 6:13). The fact is, the Father's throne and the Son's throne is the same throne (Rev. 22:1). But I asked Dugger the question: "Did the apostles eat at the Lord's table where he placed it, or did they eat it somewhere else?" Jesus said he would put it in his kingdom (Luke 22:29, 30). How did Dugger answer this question? With his usual silence. And the fact remains that they were to eat of it "till he comes" (1 Cor. 11:26), not after he comes. If by eating it they show his death till he comes, what will it show after he comes? Don't look for an answer or you may be disappointed.

A SUMMARY

I shall now give a summary of at least some of the things I have proven. All of his crowing about my not showing the scripture that calls Sunday the sabbath, or that says it took the place of the sabbath, or that says not to work on that day, is misspent exercise. I do not claim it to be the sabbath, or that it took the place of the sabbath, or anything like that at all. So if you want to crow about that, go to it, for you can do a better job crowing about a claim that I do not make than you can in meeting the claim I do make. But the reader will see your failure.

I. I showed that the first day of the week is made important by a number of events. 1. The Lord arose that day. He was to arise "the third day" following his death (Matt. 16:21). But Sunday was "the third day" from that event (Luke 24:21). So Jesus arose that day (Mark 16:9). Dugger has never been able to shake this, although he has tried desperately. His effort to prove Jesus was crucified on Wednesday by the use of Daniel's prophecy in Dan. 9:27 must have burned his hands, for he dropped it like it was hot. Maybe he'll say some more about it now that I'll have no chance to reply. 2. Regeneration was completed on that day, the day of the Lord's resurrection (1 Pet. 1:3). 3. Jesus was acknowledged on that day to be the Son of God (Psa. 2:7; Acts 13:32, 33). 4. A number of events occurred on the first Pentecost after his resurrection, which I have shown to be the first day of the week. These events include the outpouring of the Holy Spirit (Joel 2:28; Acts 2:1-4, 16, 17), the establishment of the church (Isa. 2:2, 3; Acts 2:17), the crowning of Christ as king on his throne (Zech. 6:13; Acts 2:29-36) and the going forth of the word of the Lord from Jerusalem (Isa. 2:1-3; Luke 24:47, 49; Acts 2).

II. I have shown that the first day of the week began to come into prominence after the Lord's resurrection. This is shown by the number of meetings with his disciples on that day (Mark 16:9; Matt: 28:9, 10; Luke 24:13-15, 33-36; John 20:19, 26).

III. The relation between the Lord's supper and the assembly has been shown. 1. Jesus commanded his disciples to partake of the Lord's supper (Matt. 26:26-28; Luke 22:19; 1 Cor. 11:24, 25). 2. The Lord commanded his people to assemble (Heb. 10:25). 3. But they ate the supper **when they assembled** (1 Cor. 11:20-33). 4. Christians **came together for the purpose of eating** the supper (1 Cor. 11:33). This states definitely that they "came together to eat." The Lord's supper is the only thing that God required them to eat in the assembly. 5. But they "came together" to eat —"to break bread" on the first day of the week (Acts 20:7). This argument, presented step by step in my first affirmative, was never referred to by my opponent. The argument proves that the commandment to eat the Lord's supper was obeyed when they assembled—came together—on the first day of the week.

IV. That the first day of the week was a day for religious service or worship has been shown by the meeting at Troas recorded in Acts 20:7. The passage says: "And upon the first day of the week when the disciples came together to break bread, Paul preached unto them." Paul and other disciples had waited at Troas for seven days until this meeting (Acts 20:6). This custom of waiting seven days at a place is also shown in Acts 21:3, 4 and Acts 28:13, 14. Seven days would bring them to the regular worship, as it did at Troas, on the first day of the week. Though Paul and his companions stayed at Troas a full week, not even a hint is made of a sabbath service; the only service mentioned is a first day service. Is it not strange that a first day service is the only one mentioned if the disciples were such devoted keepers of the sabbath as present day Sabbatarians are? But the disciples came together on the first day of the week "to break bread." Sometimes breaking bread refers to a common meal (Acts 2:46). And sometimes it refers to the Lord's supper (1 Cor. 10:16). But which is it in Acts 20:7? I have shown that it could not be a common meal, for Paul tells Christians to "come together to eat" the Lord's supper, but if any man hungered, "to eat at home" (1 Cor. 11:33, 34). So they did not assemble to eat common meals; they did that at home. But when they assembled—came together—to break bread it was to eat the Lord's supper. Therefore the breaking of bread in Acts 20:7, which they "came together" to do, was the Lord's supper. It was a religious service performed on the first day of the week. Dugger has never been able to shake this argument. He merely asserts it was a common meal, but I have never been able to persuade him to notice the language of Paul that they did not come together to eat common meals (1 Cor. 11:33, 34). Why has he not noticed this? Dugger says: "We have shown already that following the sabbath the Jews always made it their practice to meet together and eat, or take refreshments." I know that he **asserted** that, but certainly he has not **shown** it. He has never offered one bit of evidence for this statement; it rests upon his assertion. And that doesn't prove anything—except that Dugger is wrong. So here was a first day religious service, and the very form of expression, "when the disciples came together," indicates their custom on the first day of every week. If I should say, "Upon the fourth day of July when the American people celebrate the declaration of independence," you would understand that the American people celebrate the declaration of independence the fourth day of every July. So "upon the first day of the week when the disciples came together to break bread" indicates a breaking of bread the first day of every week. I have shown also that the Lord's supper was not taken once a year at the time of the Jewish passover, for "the days of unleavened bread" had passed before this meeting at Troas (Acts 20:6).

V. I have shown two things that are involved in the Lord's supper—the **time** of its observance and its **frequency.** It would be impossible to take it without taking it at some time. If it had been a yearly service, the record would have stated a certain day of a certain month; if it had been a monthly service, it would be on a certain day of the month; and if it is a weekly service, it must be on a certain day of the week. And this last is exactly what the New Testament says: "the first day of the week" (Acts 20:7). So it is not

a yearly service, nor a monthly service, but a weekly service. That it had a certain frequency—that it recurred—
I have shown from Acts 2:42. "They continued steadfastly
in * * * the breaking of bread." This was said of the early
church during the first year of its existence. I asked my
friend to tell us how the early church **continued** in this service during that time if it was taken only once a year, as
he claims, and the time for it had not arrived. But he has
never referred to this question. According to him, they
had not even taken it one time, but Luke said they "continued steadfastly" in it. Could it have been true that they
"continued in prayer" if they had prayed but once or had
never prayed at all? This cannot be set aside by an appeal
to verse 46 which speaks of a daily breaking of bread at
home, from house to house, for this in verse 42 is associated
with their other public services—prayer, fellowship and the
apostles' doctrine.

VI. I have shown that Paul, by divine authority, ordered
the Corinthian church and others to lay by in store on the
first day of the week (1 Cor. 16:1, 2). My opponent has
had a hard time dealing with this passage. It was a religious
service. It was ordered for the first day of the week. It
was given as a divine commandment (1 Cor. 14:37). And
they were to lay by in store to prevent any collections being
made when Paul came—"that there be no gathering when
I come." This was not an offering to be laid by at home,
as Dugger claims, for then it would have to be collected
after Paul came. I have asked my friend to tell us how a
collection would be avoided when Paul arrived if his position about this is correct. Although I have challenged and
begged him to give us this information, he has never made
any attempt to do it. I have also begged him to tell us why
Paul specified the first day of the week if this was just
a matter of gathering the goods at home. Why would not
some other day do just as well? I predicted he would be
helpless in answering this question. And he has never
been inclined to answer. His third affirmative said: "Paul
did not specify the first day, for the word 'day' is in italics."
So that is the way he answers it. He says it should read:

"The first of the week." So again he is correcting those 47 translators who were in danger of losing their heads. Dugger, can you not see an inch past your nose? And did you not know that the word "day" is not in the original in Acts 20:7? Neither in Matt. 28:1? Or in Mark 16:9? Yet you claim all of these refer to the first day. And did you not know that the word "day" is not in Acts 18:4 that tells that Paul reasoned in the synagogue every sabbath? And did you not know that it is not in scores of other passages you have used to sustain the "sabbath day"? What is the matter with you, Dugger? You must be in a tight place. You say 1 Cor. 16:1, 2 does not refer to "the first day" of the week, but just the "first of the week." But heretofore you have been using the passage to prove that Paul commanded Christians to work on the first "day" of the week. But, in an effort to get out of one tight, you get into another. After all, what would "the first of the week" be if it is not "the first day of the week"? I won't have any chance to reply to your answer, but I would like to see it anyway. So answer this question, **please.** If this had been a matter of storing goods at home, the third day or the fourth day of the week would serve just as well. I again ask why Paul specified the first day of the week. Dugger will never answer. His doctrine will not allow him to. You watch and see. But he still claims this refers to literal fruit —dates, figs and raisins. I showed the word fruit simply meant the result of their liberality and gave a number of such uses of the term. But I want to ask my friend again, since I have not been able to get him to answer so far, if Paul and his few companions could carry enough bushels of figs, dates and raisins from Rome, Achaia, Macedonia and Galatia all the way to Jerusalem to be called a "liberal contribution" from all these churches? Dugger saw the "handwriting on the wall" and refused to answer. He asks me: "If it was money, why did he not want them to gather it when he came"? Simply because he wanted them to have it ready without further collections. Dugger says he ordered it to be laid by in store so that they would be through with their work and "be ready to attend his meetings."

That isn't what Paul said. He said: "that there be no gathering (collection) when I come." You or Paul, one or the other, is wrong, and I don't believe it is Paul. He now denies that he denied that the Greek word "thesauridzo" means the treasury. This is the word used in 1 Cor. 16:1, 2: "Lay by in store." So it looks like I have misrepresented him. But I turn back to his first negative and here are his exact words: "You say this is from an original word meaning the treasury. **I deny this assertion and demand the proof.** I have studied Greek and lived in Missouri over twenty years, so come across and show us the goods." So I did not misrepresent him; instead I "showed him the goods." And now he says in his third negative: "I agreed with just what he said it means, and I still agree." So he has retraced his steps. I am glad my friend agrees "with just what I said." So the word does mean putting it into the treasury, and that sets aside his contention that it was a home duty. Hence, I don't need any more than this: Dugger has surrendered the whole thing on this passage. I didn't expect him to do so well.

VII. I have shown from Rev. 1:10; Psa. 118:22-24 and other scriptures that the first day of the week is the Lord's day. It is the day on which the Lord arose from the dead and brought untold joy to his disciples, and the day became "a day of gladness and rejoicing among his people." But Dugger said "the Lord's day" of Rev. 1:10 was the judgment day. I took that so completely away from him that he didn't even mention it again. I asked him how John could be anywhere "on a day" that was two thousand years or more in the future. He saw his predicament and said no more about it.

But my work is done. I have enjoyed this discussion and can go before God with a clear conscience in the day of judgment regarding the things I have said. My friend may have much to say in his last about giving the scripture that shows Sunday to be the sabbath, that it took the place of the sabbath, or that says not to work on the day. I did not bind myself to prove any such things about it. It is not the sabbath. It did not take the place of the sabbath. The sabbath was abolished (Col. 2:14-16) and the first day is an entirely different matter. I have proved that God authorized worship for the first day of the week, and that it is therefore a day of worship enjoined upon Christians in this age. That was my proposition and it has been sustained by the scriptures.

DUGGER'S FOURTH NEGATIVE

It was the purpose of our opponent to bring forth conclusive evidence from the scriptures, that the first day of the week was the day ordained of God for worship in this age. He has finished his last and final affirmative, which surely brings disappointment to many honest people who have sincerely believed that the apostles always met on the first day of the week for worship, and that there were many scriptures in the New Testament to sustain this practice. My own father, who was a college man, and a minister for many years, also believed this until he was called upon to make the matter a personal investigation. He was also surprised and disappointed, just as hundreds of others have been. This final affirmative of Elder Porter, is only a repetition of what has gone before, and it sadly lacks real evidence which many earnest people have looked for, and would like to find. My friend has done his best, and not only that, but much better than many could do. It is no fault of Elder Porter, but the trouble is a lack of evidence. When the New Testament is as silent on a subject, as it is on this one, who could do more than he has done? When there is absolutely no command to cease work on the first day, or to worship God on that day, or even where the early church made it their custom to hold meetings on the first day, there is nothing left to do in sustaining such a proposition, but to argue over the technical meaning of Greek words, translations; etc.

If the reader will carefully look back over the evidence given he will see that there is not one thousandth part as much in the Bible in favor of holding religious services on the first day, as there is on the seventh day of the week.

The seventh day is so clearly set forth there is no danger of mistake. My friend admits this by saying "the first day is not the sabbath," and that it did not take the place of the ancient sabbath.

He tries, however, to make you believe I have re-traced my steps, and in trying to dodge the issue have gotten into more difficulty, but you will see that I have not done so. It is the truth we want. He said the Greek word "the-sauridzo," meant **"the** treasury," as if the laying by in store (1 Cor. 16:1, 2), meant a specific treasury like the church treasury. I demanded the proof for this, and I still demand it, for he has not brought forth the goods. Furthermore he fully knows he has not, and that he cannot. He quoted from Thayer the Greek lexicographer, and here is just what he said: "Thayer says it means the place in which goods or precious things are collected and laid up, a casket, coffer or other receptacle in which valuables are kept **a treasury,** a storehouse, repository, magazine." Then he quotes just one illustration of Liddell and Scott, where they say "the treasury of a temple." Here is the goods he says he brought up that made the man from Missouri back-track. Now let us see. I demanded proof that this word always meant **"the treasury."** From his own authorities, and just as he gave them the proof is here that it does not always mean **the** treasury, for Thayer gives as above "a storehouse, or a treasury." Then he only quotes one illustration from Liddell and Scott because it is the one that suits him, but Liddell and Scott also give more examples of the use of this word just as Thayer gives, and they also give "a store-house." Surely this is just a little tricky, to make believe that the word used in 1 Cor. 16:1, 2 always means **"the** treasury, when it does **not,** for these Greek authors say it is also used for "a treasury," or "a storehouse," just as in this text. "Let every one of you lay by **him** in store," and it does not signify a gathering together but simply a store-house at home. This text is not translated "the treasury," but "lay by him in store." So here is proof that the Greek scholars translating the Bible rightly translated it "storehouse." Also with the Greek context of 1 Cor. 16:1 it does signify laying by in store at home.

This text says "Lay by **him**." It does not say lay by at church or even lay by together. I have given plenty of texts that this included provisions. Paul said it was fruit, and he did not mean good works either, for others were to go with him to bring the liberalities to Jerusalem. Note verses 3 and 4. Paul says **"they"** shall go with me. So it would have taken more than one besides Paul to carry the provisions from Corinth, as he says **"they."** This would mean at least two besides Paul, and men with camels could carry more than a bushel or two of this dried fruit that Paul tells of, and I believe Paul knew more about it than our friend. This text is not a command to rest on the first day, or to worship on that day. The word "day" is not included by the translator as belonging to the text, for it is in italic letters. This was so done by the translators that we might know it was not in the original Greek, and of course they would not lose their heads for putting it that way. Yes, the word day is also in italics where it refers to the sabbath, but the Bible sets forth so plainly which day the sabbath is, that when it says "they met every sabbath" we do not need the word day to specify clearly that it was the seventh day of the week, for that is stated many times in the Bible. If it said Paul "met the last of the week" with the brethren and preached, and I would try to make you believe this was on the very last day and therefore the sabbath, my friend would sure go up in the air and tell you I was losing my head. His arguments are very loose, and uncertain when all of these places simply say "the first of the week" in the original. And even allowing him to use the word day, then where is the real substantial evidence he was supposed to present to you? He has failed in presenting one text that even shows where they held just one religious meeting on the light part of the first day of the week. He showed one text where they held a night meeting on the first day, which was a fare-well meeting of Paul as we have shown, and the purpose of their gathering together at that time was "to break bread," or to eat a common meal.

My friend refers again to the ignorance of his opponent. Yes, it is too bad indeed that he happened to get in this discussion with one so ignorant, but it happens that I have held public discussions with just twelve leading ministers of this same church, or at least they called it the church of Christ, and their belief was the same, as near as I could tell. They all denied being followers of Alexander Campbell, but every one failed to give proof of their existence prior to his time, or to name any of their leaders before Alexander Campbell without naming men connected with the Presbyterian church, or some other known denomination. Elder Alexander Campbell, knew why Pentecost never came on a certain fixed day of the week, the same as all Jewish Rabbis know. The "sheaf offering," of the Jews corresponds to Pentecost, or it was always calculated by counting fifty days from the sheaf offering (Lev. 23:14-16), and there it plainly says fifty days. The sheaf offering was always calculated from a certain day of the month as we have previously shown. We are not finding fault with the translator, because as Alexander Campbell says, the Hebrew word "sabat" signified the week itself, so in verse 15 it says to number seven sabbaths complete, but in the next verse it says to number fifty days which would cover the seven weeks. This proves that it refers to weeks, and furthermore the "sheaf offering" was calculated by the season, and the day of the month and not by the day of the week, which was the starting point for Pentecost.

Now we will again notice Heb. 4:4-9. My friend naturally thinks the Greek word here should be translated Joshua because the way it is translated in our common Bible it ruins his theory completely, and does away with the keeping of any other day besides the 7th day. As the Greek word "Iesous," also refers to Joshua, he is sure it should be that way here. Now let us examine the text and see. There is much difference in the position held by Joshua and that of Jesus. By reason of their position and power with the Father, which one of them, would naturally be referred to here? Joshua had no authority to change long established institutions like the sabbath, but Jesus could have had such authority, as he was the Son of God. In this text it plainly says "There remaineth **therefore** (or for this reason) a rest for the people of God, and he that has entered into his rest hath ceased from his own works as God did from his." Because, or for the reason that Jesus did not give them another day, the same day remained. This could not have been said of Joshua for he would not have had such authority, nor would his decisions altered or changed matters whatever with God, as to the sabbath day. The text is consequently rightly translated Jesus, and Jesus did not give them rest, nor speak of another day. And for this reason, we are to enter into our rest **"as God did his."** That is exactly what it says in this text, and verse 4 also tells us that God rested the 7th day from all his works. Those who pray daily for God's presence to guide them, will possess enough of his spirit to find joy in doing his will in every matter, and also in keeping his sabbath day instead of the counterfeit Sunday with only a few texts to furnish them a flimsy excuse, such as the night meeting where it says they came together to break bread. This I have plainly shown was only a common meal, for the Lord's supper comes once a year, to show forth his death (1 Cor. 11), and he did not die on the first day of the week.

Jesus was not resurrected on that day either, as we have abundantly shown. Our friend is certainly very hard pressed, when he has to claim the Bible is wrong and it should have been translated different in so many places. He says the word "Jesus" should be Joshua in Heb. 4:8: that it should read "after the sabbath" instead of **"in the end of the sabbath"** (Matt. 28:1), also that 1 Cor. 16:1, 2 should read "Lay by in the treasury," instead of "Lay by **him** in **store."** It is surely pitiful that a man of his ability will say the Bible, and that others will also join with him in trying to bolster up these feeble props behind a long cherished heathen tradition of Sunday keeping. He accuses me of finding fault with the translators, but not in one

case have I done so. I am standing by our old standard
Bible, and defending the knowledge and integrity of the
47 eminent Greek scholars who translated it from the Greek
into the English. They are attacked by many modern
modernists, and church prelates who want their own erron-
eous creeds supported, and doctrinal errors which crept in
through Catholic propaganda centuries ago, defended. I
simply showed to you people the facts that Hebrew "sabat"
was used interchangeably in ancient times for both sabbath, and week, and I did this by Alexander Campbell the
leading theologian of my friend's church.

The Lord plainly tells us that the earthquake occurred
and that Jesus arose **"in** the end of the sabbath" (Matt.
28:1), but my friend declares it is wrong and vainly tries to
bring evidence forth to prove it. Liddell and Scott nor
Thayer do not as he says confirm his contention. He
makes much over what he says that I said, but go back
and see just what I did say, as it is on record. Here it is,
word for word. I said, "Liddell and Scott nor Thayer do
not dare to say that the Greek word, in this text 'epiphosco'
with its special grammatical context and construction"
means "after," or "past," or "getting light towards." There
is some difference in what I said and what he now tries to
make you think I said. I said with its "special grammatical
context" (the words preceding and following). Surely I
have looked this up, and I know just what they say. The
Greek "opsie" is always rightly translated "late," and not
after, having the setting that it has in this text, and that
is just why 47 eminent Greek scholars put it this way. I
know it does not suit my friend, but it fits the truth, that
Jesus was resurrected from the dead just 72 hours after
he was put in the grave.

Liddell and Scott, Wilson, and also Thayer all give Matt.
28:1, and Luke 23:54 for the use of "epiphosko." In the
former it says, "as it began to dawn towards," and in the
latter "the next day drew on." The word means to draw
on towards, and in Matt. 28:1, with the Greek word "opsie"
preceding it, we have the rendering "In the end of the sabbath as it began to dawn, or draw on towards the first day

of the week." As the two days met at the going down of the sun, the event occurred just before sundown Saturday and just 72 hours after Jesus was placed in the tomb, for he was to be there three days and three nights. My friend now tries to back-track and says the tomb was not the heart of the earth. Since he sees his mathematical blunder of trying to get three days and three nights between Friday evening and Sunday morning as he tried to do at first, he now thinks that the three days and three nights apply to the time Jesus was in the hands of the Roman officers. We will therefore turn the scripture search-light on this false teaching also, and expose another of his errors. If, as Mr. Porter says, Jesus was taken Thursday night after supper (Luke 22) while in the garden, he would be in the hands of the Roman officers just Friday and Saturday, which was only two days, and not three days, as he said. This teaching again throws Jesus in the false light of an imposter because the only sign of being the Son of God has failed.

The expression the heart of the earth means the tomb, from which he was resurrected because he was there just three days and three nights just as Jonah was three days and three nights in the whale's belly (Matt. 12:40).

My friend advises me to take a course in English so my brethren will not be ashamed of me, but dear people it is not English we need it is God's presence through the power of the Spirit. I took a course in English before graduating from Wayne college, and later I took a special course in English and Rhetoric at the University of Chicago, but where I received the greatest benefit in seeing God's word rightly was at the throne of grace in daily prayer for more wisdom and knowledge of God's way, the only way to eternal life. I advise my friend to take a course of prayer three times every day as Daniel, and all other of God's ancient worthies did. "All who hunger and thirst for God's truth and righteousness and seek him for it, will be bountifully rewarded (Matt. 7:7-14). My friend makes much fun of me for mis-speaking myself as he says, and saying the women went with the apostles to Emmaus, but I fail in finding any argument in such ridicule, in establishing his proposition. I will here give his "mis-quotation" of the Bible, and on a very vital point too. He did it because of a lack of knowledge of the scriptures, and such errors when not corrected lead people into serious error, and darkness. Here is just what he said word for word. He said "was risen" in Mark 16:9 is the same tense of the verb as "was rolled," in Matt. 28:1. Dugger said "was risen" is in past perfect tense, and "was rolled," is present tense. He also seasoned his surrounding remarks with much ridicule, and the words **"was rolled"**, are not found in Matt. 28:1, or in the context. This is another of his many mistakes, of what he thought was in the scriptures. Many people believe the New Testament says things it does not say about this sabbath question and are surprised to find that what they thought was there, is not there.

What I said about Matt. 28:1-4 being in the present tense, I still affirm, and so will every other intelligent person who reads it. While this was recorded about 30 years after the events happened just the same as Mark 16:9, yet this is written in the present, while Mark 16:9 is recorded in the past tense. The word "risen" used there is the past perfect tense of the verb "rose," regardless of how much he tries to twist it and pull it around. The events recorded in Matt. 28:1-4 are recorded in the present tense, just as they happened then, while the angels were present, and while the holy women were at the tomb, and it says this was **"in the end of the sabbath,"** and I believe it was still on the sabbath, but in the end of the day, just as the Lord says it was. The event of the resurrection of Jesus is told in Luke 24, John 20, and Mark 16, all of which were recorded 30 years after the event happened, but it is speaking of what the women found the very morning the visitors arrived at the tomb. It makes no difference when the narrative was told whether it was 30 years or a hundred years, the writer told what they found at the tomb when they arrived, and in Matt. 28:1 when they came there in the end of the sabbath they saw the angels roll the stone away, and this happened right then, present tense, which was quite different indeed from what they saw when arriving the next morning.

The Lord plainly tells us that Jesus arose from the dead "in the end of the sabbath," and that the next day that followed was the "first day of the week." He was therefore buried just 72 hours before this, or three days and three nights, and this would bring us back to Wednesday and the end of Wednesday, the midst of the week (Dan. 9:27). It could not have been on Friday, therefore it was not on the preparation day for the weekly sabbath, but the passover sabbath, and this is exactly what the scriptures tell us, as we have previously shown you. In John 19:14, and 31 we are plainly told that it was the preparation for the passover and the day before the **"high day sabbath."** Our friend now says that the high day sabbath was when the weekly sabbath came on the same day the yearly sabbath came on, but you notice that he gives no authority for the statement and he has a good reason, because there is none to give. The Jews always regarded the yearly sabbath which came once a year the special sabbath because it only came yearly, while the sabbath according to God's eternal law came once every week. There is no way that my friend can get the crucifixion on Friday, and the resurrection on Sunday to save his life, without doing violence to the scriptures of truth. We agree with him that some of the same women are mentioned in each narrative by the different writers Mark, Luke and John, as well as Matthew, and that while the same visit is recorded by some of these yet, not by all because Luke 24:22-24 speaks of two visits, and says that some of the same women who were there before went back with others and found it even as the first ones had said. It makes no difference what my friend says, this is God's word, and it is true whether he believes it or not.

The first day of the week being the third day since **these things** were done, has been explained in a way which does not do violence to the other scripture narrative, for this explanation makes harmony. The things mentioned as **"these things"** in Luke 24 certainly did include all things pertaining to the crucifixion and burial of Jesus, as well as sealing the stone and setting the watch, because they were not done until these very important things were **done.**

They were done as we have previously shown you on the morning after Jesus was buried or Thursday morning, making Sunday "the third day since these things were done."

It seems that our friend again tries to mislead you by emphasizing that particular part of the narrative about "a vision of angels." He does not think the women could come to the tomb in the evening and others come the next morning and see the same vision of angels, but it does not say "the vision," as if it was all one vision seen by the visitors on both occasions. It says the other women going to the sepulchre said they also saw "a vision of angels." This is quite different indeed, and it puts a different meaning entirely on the narrative. Let us watch with care, and earnestly pay heed to the word of the Lord, lest we be led off into error, by those who "are ever learning and never able to come to the knowledge of the truth."

He says he gave me nine distinct questions in his final negative on the former proposition which I refused to answer. This absolutely is not true, because I answered every argument he brought forth against the truth of God's holy sabbath day in our former proposition. This, the readers will be able to judge for themselves. Just because he says I have failed to answer his argument, does not make it so. There is no scripture, nor argument to be brought forth against the truth, but what can be answered, and for which God has furnished us abundant evidence. He says he answered all of my argument, but when he referred to the Lord's supper being taken at noon as he practices it in his church, he tried to make you believe that the Greek word "deipnon" used here for supper could refer to any meal of the day. This is some more of his slippery dodges which he says are answers to my argument. He seems to forget that Paul said "I have received of the Lord that which I also delivered unto you that the Lord Jesus the same night in which he was betrayed took bread." Now I wonder if the Greek word here for night, could be craftily handled so it would mean day, and give him an excuse for taking the Lord's supper at noon? After Jesus had been in the grave just 72 hours, or three days and three nights he arose, and it was immediately **after** three days too, or the scriptures would not have been fulfilled. It was within the very next minute after he had been in the grave three days and three nights that he came forth, but immediately "after eight days" from one Sunday would not bring us to another Sunday regardless of his vain juggling of the scriptures. No, not even if it started within a fraction of a second after, for there are just seven days in the week as everyone knows.

He again speaks of the kingdom, and says I answered his question by my usual silence, but we will let the people judge as to this matter. The apostles did eat of the Lord's supper the night he gave it and where he gave it, but this was not in the future kingdom, soon to come. Because as I previously stated, and to which my friend is notably silent, the twelve apostles are to sit there judging the twelve tribes of Israel, and he knows this did not happen then, neither has it since. In Rev. 21:1 this throne being jointly between the Father and the Son, is here on earth, after Jesus returns for it says plainly that the holy city the new Jerusalem **comes down from God out of heaven.** Zechariah 6:13 is also future when Jesus will be both priest and king, and will wound the heads over many countries as we are also told in Psalms 110. The phase of the kingdom of God, known as the kingdom of grace, is here, and has been here since the days of Jesus, and it is this kingdom and phase of the glorious kingdom we have mentioned in Col. 1:13, and Rev. 1:9.

Now we shall briefly answer some arguments set forth in his summary which have not been given attention again in this negative, and then follow with our final recapitulation and summary of basic facts. He says "regeneration was completed on that day" meaning the first day of the week, "the day of the Lord's resurrection," and he gives 1 Peter 1:3 as proof. This says nothing whatever about the first day of the week. He says Jesus was acknowledged on that day to be the Son of God, and gives Psalms 27, and Acts 13:32, 33, but not one word is said about the first day of the week in either of these passages. Please take them down and read them for yourselves, if you really want the truth. He gives a number of scriptures showing important events occurring on the day of Pentecost, and gives his own word that Pentecost was on the first day of the week, but the scripture to prove it is sadly lacking.

He says the first day of the week began to come into prominence after the resurrection of Christ by the number of meetings with his apostles on that day and gave Mark 16:9, Matt. 29:9, 10, Luke 24:13-15, 33, 36, and John 20: 19-26, but not one of these scriptures speak of a religious gathering being held, of preaching, or even reading the scriptures or praying. These were not religious meetings, but simply appearances of our Saviour to confirm the facts of his having been resurrected from the dead, the evening before, as the Lord has told us. How hard up he has been for scriptures showing meetings on that day. Again he gives John 20:26 where it says "after eight days" beginning on Sunday he met again with the disciples. This he very ridiculously claims was on another first day. How dare him to try to put such an absurd claim before intelligent people. The Lord speaks of the Jews who had a veil over their eyes because they could not look to the end of that which was abolished, and said when they turned to the Lord the veil would be taken away, surely he has a veil over his eyes, and is seeing things that cannot be true. The Jews still held to the old law of pardon through the blood of animals, but when they accepted Jesus this veil was taken away, for then they would be able to see that the old system of pardon by the animal sacrifices was abolished, and that the blood of Jesus which they must accept by faith took its place. Just as Jesus was a stumbling block to the blinded Jews, the Lord says he will be a rock of stumbling and offense to the Gentiles who want to be disobedient, and now we find them stumbling over Jesus, claiming he was resurrected on Sunday, and we are to keep another day, because they want to follow the world in disobedience to the commandments of God, which enjoin rest on Saturday the seventh day.

In Summary No. 3 he gives another series of scriptures, not one of which even mentions the first day of the week except Acts 20:7, where they met to "break bread." He says we never answered this argument, but we kindly ask you to investigate the records of our past arguments and see if this was not repeatedly answered. How dare him to make such a bold statement which the reader can see for himself is not true. Surely he has not forgotten this.

Summary No. 4. In the entire summary number 4 he fails to give further texts or proof of his proposition wherein the first day of the week is mentioned. He repeats Acts 20:7 where it says the apostles came together on that day, and it says plainly the purpose of the meeting. They came together **"to break bread,"** and it says Paul preached to them with many lights in the upper chamber, and he preached until morning. We have clearly and repeatedly shown this to be a farewell meeting of Paul with the church there. Furthermore we have told you the custom of the Jews was to - gather together after the sabbath was passed, which would be on the dark part of the first day of the week and eat a common meal, and Jews will also tell you of this custom. He has failed to show proof that my statement was not true. He says here that it was the custom of the apostles to remain just seven days in one place, and claims this brought them to another 1st day of the week, but in the previous summary he claimed that "after eight days" brought them to another first day. Now I wonder which of these is true. Surely both cannot be right. Where is his evidence in this summary that the first day of the week was their regular day to meet and worship God? We have shown from the scriptures positively that the Lord's supper was a yearly event, and to show forth the Lord's death. We have also referred you to the history of the early church, and to the decree of council of Nice where they fixed Easter on a certain Sunday, and forbid the Christians Judiazing by keeping the passover time with the Jews. Breaking of bread of course in some places refers to the Lord's supper as we have shown, but that event had passed before they came to Troas (Acts 20:6) therefore this breaking of bread was only a common meal.

Summary No. 5. Here he wants me to answer his argument of how the apostles "continued" in breaking bread if it was only practiced once a year. Surely anyone can see that they could continue in this yearly practice of the Lord's supper just as it was introduced by Jesus, the same as they could continue in it, if it were practiced once a month or once a week. Paul says "Christ our passover was sacrificed for us, therefore let us keep the feast" (1 Cor. 5: 7, 8), and we have given numerous other texts in proof that the early church did keep the Lord's supper once a year and on the very day of the month that Jesus died. Furthermore that they could not show forth his death on any other day besides the day it occurred any more than we can celebrate our birthday once a week, or once a month or just any time.

It does not say in Acts 2:42 and 46 that they broke this bread once a week, or that it was broken on the first day of the week as our friend would like to have it say, but it says they broke it daily. It says also they had all things common, and that they "continuing daily in one accord in the temple, and in breaking bread from house to house did eat their meat with gladness and singleness of their hearts" (verse 46). Here too we find that they did go from house to house and met together in breaking bread daily. Therefore in Acts 20:7 when they came together to break bread it was simply a continuation of this very practice. As the argument produced in this summary is all that Elder Porter has given, and it constitutes all he can produce to sustain his proposition, it is needless for me to tell you that he has failed, for you all know he has. We know, however, that it is no fault of his, for the scriptures are silent in teaching any such a doctrine as first day observance.

SUMMARY

1. We wish to call your attention to the fact that not one scripture has been produced by our friend where the

first day of the week commonly called Sunday, was to take the place of the ancient day of worship held sacred by all of God's people. Not one scripture where Christ ever spoke the words first day while he was here on earth, or where the apostles ever told anyone to assemble together on that day: Not one text where it says we are not to labor on that day: Not one text where the first day is called the Lord's day: Not one text where we are commanded to meet together on that day: Not one text where it says the early church sang songs or prayed on that day: Not one text where it says it was the custom of Christ or the apostles to meet on that day: Not one text where it says they ever held preaching services on that day except the one occasion of Paul's preaching all night Saturday night and then walking 19 miles across the cape from Troas to Assos the light part of the first day.

2.   Throughout the discussion we have insisted that our friend show some such scripture, but he has failed to do so. We have repeatedly asked him to tell us why God would be so silent in the introduction of another day of worship, in place of an institution like the sabbath, that those chosen to be saved, both Jew and Gentile, had observed for thousands of years but he has been silent. Does it not look reasonable, dear people, that God would have been very definite and clear about giving another day to take the place of the sabbath institution, and not left the New Testament entirely void of such a command, or of one clear and definite example of first day keeping?

We have shown you that the first day of the week was mentioned but eight times in the New Testament, and that not one of these places speaks of it as a holy day, a sacred day, or even a day of rest or worship, but to the contrary the ancient day of rest which was Saturday, is called the sabbath more than fifty times in the New Testament.

3.   We have shown you that the first day of the week came into general use as a day of worship, through the Roman Catholic church, because they did not want the Christians to hold a day in common with the Jews. We have shown you that the Roman Catholic church ruled the

world for over 1260 years putting to death millions of people who would not follow their decrees, and ecclesiastical dogmas: That the prophecies of Daniel declared that this power of Rome was coming forth and would change the law of God, and set itself up above God, and furthermore that this has taken place thus vindicated God's word and proving it true. Also that they confessed the guilt of having changed the law of God and the sabbath just as Daniel said they would do, and boastfully claim the authority for giving Sunday to the world.

4. We have shown you clearly that the seventh day, and not the first day was the day observed in the New Testament by the early Gentile believers as well as the converted Jews who followed Paul. These scriptures were given in proof. Acts 13:42. 44. also 16:12-14 and 17:2, as well as 18:4-11 where Paul preached a year and six months on the sabbath and made tents during the week, which must also have included the first day.

5. That Jesus made it his custom to preach on the sabbath day (Luke 4:14-16), and that if we follow him we will not walk in darkness but will have the light of life (John 8:12).

6. That Paul taught us clearly on the question by saying that "If Jesus had given them rest, then would he not afterwards have spoken of another day" (Heb. 4:4-9), and in the next verse he tells us that for this reason there remaineth a rest (margin says keeping of sabbath) for the people of God, and that those doing this enter into their rest as God did his. Surely this is plain enough.

7. We have shown that the ten commandments, spoken of in the Old Testament as the law of God, are also mentioned repeatedly in the New Testament, where we are told if we break one of them we are guilty of all (James 2:10, 11). Hence if we break the sabbath by using it for our own work, we are guilty before heaven.

8. That it was the law of Moses, and not the ten commandment law done away by the shedding of the blood of Jesus. Consequently the commandments of God, and the law of God, we are told to keep in the New Testament is the

same law, and it is the only law that points out and defines sin. It is mentioned in the following texts: Matt. 5:17-19, Rom. 2:13, 1 Cor. 7:19, James 2:10, 11, 1 John 2:4, and 3:4, also 5:3, Rev. 12:17, and 14:12 also 22:14.

9. We have shown that the sabbath days and holy days done away by Christ were the yearly sabbaths and feast days included in the Mosaic law of pardon, which was contrary to the apostles. That it did not include the weekly sabbath of the holy ten commandment law, given to govern the lives of all holy men.

10. We have shown that the seventh day sabbath, and not the first day of the week was and still is, God's holy day. That God is unchangeable (Mal. 3:6 and Heb. 13:8), therefore his day remains holy. We have shown that the people in every age who were God's people, kept his day. The seventh day has always been reserved unto God as his holy day, but the first day is the world's holiday, the counterfeit offered by Satan and christened as a day of rest by Rome.

So we leave this important question with our readers, trusting each one will make his choice to obey God, and keep his day, instead of following the decrees of Rome. "Choose ye this day which ye will serve." "If the Lord be God serve him, but if Baal, then serve him."

www.ingramcontent.com/pod-product-compliance
Lightning Source LLC
Chambersburg PA
CBHW031248090426
42742CB00007B/364